# ARAB SPRING

## The New Middle East in the Making

*Essays*

HICHEM KAROUI

# OTHER BOOKS BY THE SAME AUTHOR

THE BUSH II YEARS IN THE MIDDLE EAST (2000-2008) : A CASE STUDY IN THE
SOCIOLOGY OF INTERNATIONAL RELATIONS.
Hichem Karoui ( USA : Middle East Studies/CreateSpace, 2012).


LES MUSULMANS : UN CAUCHEMAR OU UNE FORCE POUR L'EUROPE ?
Hichem Karoui, Arno Tausch ( Paris, L'Harmattan, 2011).

OÙ VA L'ARABIE SAOUDITE ?
Hichem Karoui (Paris, L'Harmattan, 2006).

L'APRÈS-SADDAM EN IRAK
Hichem Karoui - Préface de Burhan Ghalioun (Paris, L'Harmattan, 2005).

# DEDICATION

To the Men and Women of Good Will.

# CONTENTS

*It is dangerous to be right when the government is wrong.*

Voltaire.

*God made Truth with many doors to welcome every believer who knocks on them.*

Gibran Khalil Gibran.

*All progress is precarious, and the solution of one problem brings us face to face with another problem.*

Martin Luther King Jr. *'Strength to Love,' 1963.*

# ACKNOWLEDGMENTS

As much of the material that allowed the production of this book has already been published as essays and articles, on either *The Arab Center for Research and Policy Studies* (ACRPS) website or *The Gulf Today* columns, I am indebted to all those who contributed by their work and their good will in making these essays available to the readers.

First, my thanks go to Miss Aysha Taryam, the brilliant Editor-in-Chief of *The Gulf Today*, for her warm welcome and her indulgence. I am no less grateful to her talented editorial team led by Mr. Shaadaab S. Bakht, Executive Editor; particularly the Chief Sub-Editors, Mr. Shahper Imam Bin Hassan and Mr. Zafar Iqbal, for their kind attention, their patience, and their good work.

Some material has been either presented in symposiums, or published as research papers by ACRPS. As all those essays have been read and reviewed by my colleagues at ACRPS, it is normal that I address them my warmest thanks. Particularly, Dr. Huda Hawa, Dr. Abdulwahhab AL-Qassab, and the anonymous reviewers of my papers. I will not omit my colleague Mirvat Abu Khalil and her team of translators and editors (Amy Hamar and Marc Sirois), for the translation of two research papers about WikiLeaks and the Yemeni Revolution, both initially written in Arabic. Thank you also to Anass Alkhdour, for his help with the Arab Opinion Index raw data, which I used for my research about the Arab spring New Values.

The last essay in this collection is based on a paper I have presented to Georgetown University workshop, and is published here for the first time. I have then to thank Dr. Birol Baskan, Assistant Professor, Georgetown University School of Foreign Service in Qatar, for his kind invitation, as well as all the colleagues from whose discussion I have benefited, with in the first place Dr. Ibrahim Sharqieh, deputy-Director of the Brookings Doha Center and Dr. Tarik Yousif, Chief executive of Silatech.

I cannot omit Mrs. Hala Zeinelabidin Director of Archiving, Documentation, and Library at ACRPS, as well as her assistants Saad Ibrahim and Radwa Zoweil, for their kind support and help during the necessary research time.

To all of them, I express my profound feelings of gratitude.

Finally, I have to emphasize that without the real support of Dr. Azmi Bishara, director of ACRPS, this book will certainly not be available to the reader right now. The process of producing research papers and essays is not an easy one. The material and moral support of a dedicated institution is vital for any author. I therefore acknowledge my debt toward ACRPS and its flamboyant director, Azmi Bishara.

I have chosen to give this collection of essays a special afterwords, which is a piece I have written about A. Bishara's *Revolution and Revolutionary Potential...*

I could not find a better ending for a book on the Arab Spring.

# FOREWORD


# THE NEW MIDDLE EAST IN THE MAKING


When I wrote almost two years ago that for me, 2010 was Turkey's year in the Middle East, I was far from imagining that 2011 and 2012 would also become Turkey's years in the same region ( See: Turkey's Year, *The Gulf Today*, January 1, 2011). Look at what happened.

In 2011, a mounting wave of popular anger has swept away the autocratic regimes established by the military and maintained by force against the will of the people in four countries: Tunisia, Egypt, Libya, and Yemen. They fell down like sand castles, giving way to what has been globally depicted as the "Arab spring" phenomenon. The first free democratic elections that have been organised in these countries after the fall of the dictators showed us another phenomenon, which I hesitate to describe as "new" or "old", for sake of accuracy. It is the Islamist rush to power, and most of all, the Tunisian and Egyptian voluntary identification with the Turkish brand of Islamism led by Prime Minister Recep Tayyip Erdoğan. This is something!

The Turkish Islamist leaders have been much in advance on their counterparts in the Arab world, concerning various issues, in domestic and foreign policies. Because they craved power and have long been rebuked and thwacked by the military, they cleverly and diligently played the card of the European Union to get rid of the military grip. A fake democracy (i.e. supervised or manipulated by the military) would never find its way to join the EU. Thus, their tactics consisted in showing a liberal face of Islamism, which Erdoğan dubbed "Muslim democracy," likening it to the old conservative parties known to Europeans as "Christian democracy." However, the success of the Turkish brand of Islamism is not only the result of an important shift in the political views advocated by the "Justice and Development" Party, but also the result of an economic endeavor encouraged and supported by this party to the benefit of the middle class, the middle and small enterprises, and the holders of investment capitals. That very endeavor was labeled "Islamic Calvinism," as a way to bring it closer to Max Weber's famous thesis on "The Protestant Ethic and the Spirit of Capitalism."

It is never wrong to follow or get inspiration from other people's experiences, wherever and whenever they are successful, provided the conditions are similar or at least reconcilable. Historically, these three countries (Turkey, Tunisia, and Egypt) have played a unique role in advancing the constitutionalist agenda in the Middle East, since the 19th century (maybe even before). They were the first to adopt and enforce a constitution, thus following the Western countries, for whom the elite expressed an admiration conjugated with fear. These facts should also remind the present Islamist leaders in the countries of the Arab spring that those who voted for them, as well as those who voted for their rivals, are just equally right in expecting the fulfillment of the electoral promises. Some of those promises concern the implementation of democratic rules, democratic institutions, and democratic behavior. Some others concern the improvement of the economy. Would they deliver?

In Libya, we have had a surprising phenomenon. The electoral success of the liberals, while everybody was expecting an Islamist landslide.

On July 16, 2011, while the Libyan revolution was raging, I have written in my TGT weekly column about a French intelligence report, which described Libya as "the only country of the 'Arab spring' in which the Islamist risk increases." The report went on saying, "the Western powers have shown an excessive adventurism by engaging in this crisis." (See: Unwise intelligence report, *The Gulf Today*, July 16, 2011). Well, as it happened, this tribal country, plagued, as it was widely reported, by every kind of radical Islamism, is the only that gave rise, in its first free democratic elections, to the Liberal alliance of parties led by Mr. Mahmoud Gibril. The fears of those who saw post-Gaddafi Libya as the hub of militant Islamism - kind of Somali Shebab, or Yemeni Qaeda - revealed to be unfounded, not to say part of Gaddafi propaganda machine.

As for Yemen, nothing really unexpected happened, so far. Because of the Arab-monitored transition of power in this country, the angry revolt of millions of people craving a real change has been reduced to a vulgar reshuffle, as if democracy was already well established in Yemen and only Ali Abdallah Saleh was the offender. Everybody knows, though, that those who took to the streets wanted something else. It is therefore obvious that their revolution has been stolen and their claims completely siphoned. This also is the reason why people continue to die in Yemen, since al-Qaeda and other radicals survived, and with them the threat of destabilization. Moreover, post-Ali Abdallah Saleh's Yemen is so resembling to the previous regime that it would not be odd to see another revolution creeping under the feet of the power elite in the near future.

Lastly, Syria has become the main news, with all the world media focusing on a conflict that grew into an enormous and ugly splash of ill-will, hypocrisy, and criminal behavior. The Syrian revolution, which nobody doubts its final triumph today, revealed to be an opportunity for an exercise of force - as in the old days of the Cold War - between the West, on the one hand, and Russia, Iran and China, on the other hand. These latter are still keeping in "life" a comatose, which without their criminal support, will die instantly. It is a criminal support because the "artificial life" of the Syrian regime costs every day the tragic fall of numerous innocent victims. However, Moscow, Tehran and Beijing still pretend that it is possible to reconcile the victims with their executioners. Such behavior is not amazing, though, coming from those who had bombed Chechnya, crushed the students of Tiananmen, or smothered the Green revolt in Iran.[1]

---

[1] This foreword is based on an Essay published by *The Gulf Today*, September 9, 2012.

# I

# THE SIGNS

This is what happened just a few times before the Tunisian uprising... There were signs... But nobody seemed to understand them... I recorded the following:

*" The point is that many of the attitudes and societal conditions that facilitate political violence may be present and relatively unchanging in a society over a long period; they become relevant to or operative in the genesis of violence only when relative deprivation increases in scope and intensity."*

Ted Robert Gurr: *Why Men Rebel.*

# 1

# SATISFIED WITH YOUR LIFE?

In 2011, according to a recent survey conducted in 12 Arab countries, 73 per cent of the respondents said they were "satisfied" or "very satisfied" with their life; while only 27 per cent expressed dissatisfaction. Based on these findings, how would you explain the anger that burst out in the same year inflaming the whole region and overthrowing long-established dictatorial regimes?

First, let us explain that this is one of the most important and largest opinion surveys of the kind.[1] It is a genuine project of the Arab Center for Research and Policy Studies (ACRPS), covering 12 countries, representing 85 per cent of the population of the Arab world, based on the results of 16,173 face-to-face interviews.

The second observation is that the questionnaire was purposely intended to be varied and detailed, meaning that — as we know the blockages working inside the Arab mind as well as within the society, because of uncontrollable elements like: long oppression, fear, inhibition, etc... The interviewees were asked several times almost the "same" question: then, as soon as the question becomes more precise, the answer would differ. For example, if you link the question about "satisfaction with your life" to "your finances," "the expenses of your family," "your economic condition," "your work," etc... the answer would be more modulated.

---

[1]    The    Arab    Opinion    Project:    The    Arab    Opinion    Index: http://english.dohainstitute.org/release/5083cf8e-38f8-4e4a-8bc5-fc91660608b0

It seems then that this large percentage of "satisfaction" among the citizens of the Arab countries has to be relativized, taken into consideration the religious and traditional mind frame of the average Arab citizen, not to mention the political condition of these countries, and the security-related issues for each individual. Let us put this plainly: in most Arab countries, the citizens are wary of all people intending to "interrogate" them about their opinions and life.

What if they were "spies" of the government? What if they were secret police? So, the interviewer has to surmount the basic mistrust and the first question is just intended to establish the contact smoothly. If you were an Arab citizen and I come to ask you: are you satisfied with your life? What would be your spontaneous answer if not: "Alhamdulillah ala kulli hal" (Praise be to God for everything)? If following you, I insist: Alhamdulillah, but are you satisfied? Most probably, you would invoke the grace of Allah again and reply: yes, I am.

Now, if I go further, and ask you about the financial condition of your family, your satisfaction would be restricted to a precise field, which is: finances. Thereupon, your answer would tell me more about your material condition than your first "spontaneous" assessment of the situation.

Some findings of this survey thus need more explanation.

Examples: We found that 56 per cent of the Saudis are "very satisfied" with their life; along with: 55 per cent of the Mauritanians; and 53 per cent of the Sudanese.

I can understand the Saudi percentage if I link it to the overall economic condition of the country. But how about Mauritania and Sudan?

Actually, in answering the question about "your degree of satisfaction with your economic situation," 26 per cent only of the Saudis said they were "very satisfied," 19 per cent only of the Sudanese, and 12 per cent only of the Mauritanians. Here, we understand with more precision how the first answer about the general question (satisfaction with life) comes to be relativized.

If we come back and explore the degree of dissatisfaction with life, we would find that the largest percentage of "absolute dissatisfaction" is in Iraq: 25 percent; followed by Lebanon: 20 per cent; and Palestine: 16 per cent.

Should we link this "absolute dissatisfaction" to the second question about the economic condition? The answer is: yes, to a large extent.

"Absolutely dissatisfied" with their economic situation are: the Lebanese (32 per cent); the Palestinians and the Yemenites (28 per cent); and the Iraqis (25 per cent).

So yes, the economic condition affects your degree of satisfaction with life.

I should add that if the questionnaire was more detailed, the categories of answers ranged between: very satisfied; satisfied to a certain degree; dissatisfied to a certain degree; absolutely dissatisfied; and no answer.

Concerning the last category, the percentage regarding the question of satisfaction is almost negligible (1 per cent in Saudi Arabia and Morocco, and 2 per cent in Iraq).

Now, those who are satisfied to a certain degree represent the largest part among our sample. Among them: Algeria (58 per cent); Egypt (51 per cent); Palestine (48 per cent); Tunisia (48 per cent)...

If we put Algeria aside (for it is a case in its own right), how would you explain that amazing percentage of satisfaction in countries where popular revolts recently happened?

Let us follow the answers in these three countries (Egypt, Tunisia and Palestine) regarding the economic condition: 47 per cent of the Tunisians said they were "satisfied to a certain degree"; 46 per cent of the Egyptians, and 35 per cent of the Palestinians. This is not bad at all, if you consider the fact that the top level of "satisfaction to a certain degree" with the economic condition is in Saudi Arabia: 49 per cent.

We still have the thorny question: how come that "satisfied" people revolt against their regimes?

This would lead us to formulate a hypothesis about revolutions, which is not necessarily linked to the economic condition, but rather to other social and political issues, like: poor governance, deficiency of public and private freedoms, human rights violations, corruption, and craving for freedom. The hypothesis deserves to be further explored in the light of the data now available thanks to the Arab Opinion Index.

This does not mean that the economic condition does not count; but only that the economic performance, whatever its level, would not guarantee stability and civil peace, if some regions or social groups are excluded from its gains, and the political regime stays unresponsive towards the demands of reform and democratic change.

I would add that I treated here briefly just two little questions (from the first issue) in a large survey that is concerned with six main issues (each with its own series of questions): 1- assessment of the overall situation; 2- the Arab revolutions; 3- Democracy; 4- trust in institutions; 5- religion in public life; 6- perceptions of the exterior environment.

To be sure, we live in a different Arab world. Officials from the international community and the Arab world should be mindful of imperceptible changes occurring in the social segment, without asking for their consent.[1]

---

[1] The Gulf Today, March 10, 2012: http://gulftoday.ae/portal/b1fea713-c447-4935-95d6-ea06361937aa.aspx

2

# DIPLOMACY FACING THE REVOLUTION OF "TRANSPARENT SOCIETY" AND "RISK SOCIETY"

## WikiLeaks: international and regional ramifications

Contrary to the assumption that the leaks of the diplomatic cables represented a heavy and unexpected pressure on American diplomacy – through their exposition of a mode of operation based on hypocrisy and duplicity – I will try to prove that the leaks, in fact, signify greater challenges and pressures to the states of the Middle East and North Africa (MENA), as in all the countries that witnessed a popular revolt, Internet played an informing, mobilizing and organizing role. I will show that the publication of secret documents may have more of an effect on regional relations within the Middle East than on bilateral relations between the countries of this region and the United States, with information contained in the documents likely to prompt some states to reassess their relations with others in the region.

## Methodology

I will examine this hypothesis through a theoretical framework based on the concepts of the "transparent society" and the "risk society" applying them on the diplomatic field, with a focus on certain examples that appear noteworthy in light of recent social and political events in the Middle East. I will thus examine whether a connection exists between the open source of the Internet and the events taking place in some countries, and discuss the American role in the region, as well as the anticipated developments and changes in diplomatic relations in light of these events.

## Introduction and definitions

The WikiLeaks phenomenon could not have happened in a place where "transparency" is not a paramount motto and a code of conduct. The event took place in the democratic countries, and despite that, official reactions warned of the potential threats and suggested a tradeoff between the security of citizens and society on the one hand, and sacrificing transparency on the other.[1] This logic meant that societies were presented with a false dichotomy, forcing them to choose between preserving security and/or maintaining transparency.[2] However, the intensifying events in the Middle East, which have created maelstroms in the face of autocratic regimes, are a refutation of the claim that security could be maintained without transparency. Because these leaks touched on diplomacy, transparency and fear of security threats are not only a concern of local communities, but also of the regional regimes and the world order that dominates the international society. I will begin by defining key concepts in order to avoid misinterpretations. These key terms are: risk society, transparent society, epoch revolution, and diplomacy.

## The risk society

---

[1] The Europeans criticized the official US reaction to Wikileaks revelations, describing it as arrogant and hypocritical, and complaining that the Obama administration took no legal action to attempt to stop the publication of the documents. For an example of this debate, see: Steven Erlanger, "In Europe, sharp criticism of US reaction to WikiLeaks," *New York Time,* December 10, 2010.
http://www.boston.com/business/technology/articles/2010/12/10/in_europe_sharp_criticism_of_us_reaction_to_wikileaks/
[2] Some of the statements of US officials can be read in the following article:
Bridget Johnson, "How Washington Reacted to WikiLeaks" :
http://worldnews.about.com/od/unitedstates/qt/How-Washington-Reacted-To-Wikileaks.htm

I adopt the concept of Ulrich Beck about the transition from an industrial/class society to a risk society, which characterizes our time. For Beck, the risk society, "designates a developmental phase of modern society in which social, political, economic and individual risks tend to escape the institutions for monitoring and protection in society."[1] This transitional period exhibits visible threats, such as the destruction of the environment, with the effects of pollution being perceptible in forests, mountains, and oceans. The same effects can be observed in the degradation of archaeological and artistic monuments, as well as other disasters regularly reported by the media.[2] Add to this a long list of toxic materials and pollutants present in foods and other goods we use daily, as well as the lies and scandals surrounding them, to the point that Beck speaks of a "secret alliance between a rigid scientism and dangers that threaten humanity, which were permitted or favored by this very scientism"[3]. This is due to the fact that the history of sciences is, in Beck's view, "a history of errors ... more so than a history of the progress of knowledge"[4]. Fortunately, however, the risk society is also a society of questioning and self-criticism.

We see the same phenomena in social life, for threats affect the individual as they do the family: unemployment, for instance, is no longer "the fate of a class or the fate of marginal groups, but has become widespread and routine".[5] Relations between males and females even within the same family have turned aggressive and vulnerable due to the pressures of the work market and the needs of the consumerist society, which is evidenced by the increase in the occurrence of divorce. "Due to their dependency upon institutions, individual conditions became vulnerable to crises,"[6]

---

[1] Ulrich Beck, Risk Society: Towards a New Modernity. London: Sage Publications, 1992, p.5
[2] The most recent of which being the "triple whammy" experienced by Japan in March 2011, when an earthquake and a tsunami were followed by explosions in nuclear reactors, exposing local inhabitants to the threat of radiation.
[3] As Beck writes in German, I refer here to the French translation of his Risk Society, Ulrich Beck, La Société du Risque , (Paris, Flammarion, 2001), p113.
[4] Ulrich Beck, op. Cit., p.348
[5] Ulrich Beck, op. Cit., p.200
[6] Ulrich Beck, op. Cit., p.287

Beck argues, and we saw "a generalized lack of job security"[1]; "the educational system has lost its role in distributing social functions: it is no longer sufficient for someone to obtain degrees in order to attain a specific professional position"[2]. This has caused education to lose its authority, which is evidenced by the rise in incidents of violence against teachers. Beck concludes, "The project of rational liberation, which was heralded by modernity, has not been achieved yet."[3] Under such conditions, can diplomacy remain removed from understanding the events taking place, when "threats have become global", with many of the factors, described above being among the motivators of the revolutionary eruption in several parts of the Arab world?

In reality, all governments benefit, to varying extents, from a climate of perpetual threat. Beck warns of "the rise of a regulative policy for the state of exception, which benefits from the presence of a threat situation to grant itself wide interventionist powers and prerogatives. In every place where danger is routinized, this state of exception takes a permanent institutional form".[4]The problem is that the state of exception could become the normal state in the risk society, which Beck also dubs "the catastrophe society".

## The transparent society

In the streets of major cities, in public and private establishments, and in public spaces we live under the watchful eye of video cameras and surveillance satellites. We can no longer limit the number of databases holding information on our lives, habits, tendencies, beliefs, and personal histories. At the same time, attempts to protect the citizen – as well as corporations –

---

[1] Ulrich Beck, op. Cit., p.304
[2] Ulrich Beck, op. Cit., p.326. It is noteworthy that the unintended "fuse" of the revolution in Tunisia, Muhammad al-Bouazizi, is a perfect representative of this social stratum whose members graduated from colleges or universities but found no places in the job market. These were at the front of the protestors in Tunisia and Egypt and other places, where demands began as social ones before they turned political
[3] Ulrich Beck, op. Cit., p.346
[4] Ulrich Beck, op. Cit., p.142. All Arab governmental reactions to the protests demanding social rights and political reforms was to resort to the state of exception ... without exception.

using modern technology abound; these include encoding and protection software designed to preserve online privacy and protect one's identity. If we add to these the regulations that protect privacy and guarantee citizens the opportunity to hold governments and officials accountable, we realize that transparency goes in both directions – or, at least, that is the ideal in democratic societies. Despite the fact that conditions differ in societies that lack democracy, the open source phenomenon is capable of hastening awareness of such necessities while speeding the movement of history. This is what has been taking place in the Arab world since the Tunisian Revolution. This was the opinion expressed by numerous thinkers who believe that "technology is a potentially crucial element in the defense of liberties in the future;"[1] which signifies that there is no escape from transparency.

## The Internet revolution

Truly, any effort to explore the concept of the transparent society must begin with an acknowledgment of the Internet as "the greatest revolution of all ages"[2], and that it has clearly hastened the steps of change in an unprecedented manner, allowing us to face the future right now – instead of waiting for it to happen.[3] The initial issue around which the Internet system was based is

---

[1] David Brin, The Transparent Society, (Addison-Wesley, Reading Massachusetts, 1998) p.21

[2] Brin, op. Cit., p.35

[3] It should be noted in this regard that after the Tunisian and Egyptian revolutions the official position of American diplomacy moved towards the launching of an initiative to support opposition activists, human rights advocates and other civil society forces suffering from the control of despots over the Internet. This could be seen as an acknowledgment of the role of the Internet in democratic transition; more than USD 30 million was devoted to funding technologies that help Internet users in these countries circumvent censorship and detection. See: Mark Landler, "U.S. Policy to Address Internet Freedom," *The New York Times*, February 14, 2011. http://www.nytimes.com/2011/02/15/world/15clinton.html?_r=1&hpw
Hillary Rodham Clinton, Secretary of State, speech at George Washington University, February 15, 2011: "Internet Rights and Wrongs: Choices & Challenges in a Networked World" : http://www.state.gov/secretary/rm/2011/02/156619.htm

"thinking about the unthinkable"; i.e. considering the possibility of a nuclear war and devising a trans-continental communications system that could survive such a war. Planning for the future in order to control it in a scientific manner was inevitably leading to a revolution in communications and information, followed by a revolution in awareness and behavior towards the concepts of the old authority – with the Internet undermining the hierarchical organization of power. The main concept of the Internet is to distribute command over the virtual web rather than concentrate it in one location, which could be damaged in the event of a nuclear disaster, for instance. The basic model also implies that the network cannot be circumscribed or suppressed, for it will always find ways to avoid censorship. What we are currently witnessing is that the Internet has allowed disparate groups of individuals to become closer, coalesce, and form currents, counter-currents, and new balances within communities and across communities. Many of these groups are laboring to institute the concept of transparency in public life while resisting the authority of despotic governments in ways that were unimaginable in the past. It was inevitable that this revolution would affect international relations and its main vessel: diplomacy.

## Diplomacy

Diplomacy is defined as "the process of representation and negotiation due to which states usually deal with each other in times of peace."[1] Effective diplomacy heralds and is based on a set of political, psychological, economic, and military tools in the possession of the state. Technically, diplomacy could be defined as "the act of communication between governments."[2]

If the above were the context of diplomatic action, it would be difficult to find a direct or indirect link between local events and the diplomatic mission; when such an event takes place, it is considered an exception that could lead to a crisis and the rupture of relations. Therefore, we can understand the extent of anger and

---

[1] Norman J. Padelford/George A. Lincoln, The Dynamics of International Politics, (The Macmillan Company- Collier-Macmillan Limited, New York, London, 1967): 314.

[2] Padelford/Lincoln, Ibid., 314.

fear that the publication of the WikiLeaks cables has stirred in diplomatic and official circles. From this perspective as well, talk spread of threats surrounding diplomats and relations between the countries in question, in addition to their relationships with the United States. The problem here was not so much legal as ethical, which comes as no surprise, since many of the codes regulating relations between governments are more related to ethics than to legal texts.

There is no law that can regulate all the happenings in a society, the acquired habits, the polite conversation, and the exchange of ideas between people in different occasions. There is no doubt of the existence of international ethics that are manifested in a number of principles agreed upon by numerous states. "The United Nations Charter, for instance, reflects an international morality in many of its articles"[1], including calls for the respect of human rights and basic freedoms with no discrimination on the basis of race, gender, language, or religion. Moral and ethical rules that have not been codified into laws tend to be more opaque and subject to varying interpretations. In this regard, I note that those who act on behalf of the state are prone to consider it as an objective in and of itself,[2] with "a tendency among governments, as with individuals, to claim the universality of the moral principles that they hold."[3]

Diplomacy, which was allowed this calm demarche for a long period, today finds itself forced to adapt to new necessities, with the communications revolution and the deep changes it has induced in societies and among elites. Diplomacy is forced to assimilate the idea that our age features two elements that did not have the same momentous presence in the past: risk and transparency. It must be stressed that diplomacy and transparency are like fire and water; if diplomatic missions were meant to be transparent, we would not have diplomatic immunity and other laws that protect diplomats, bar the authorities from searching them, and maintain the secrecy of their communications. This in itself makes WikiLeaks' publication of the US diplomatic cables an

---

[1] Vernon Van Dyke, International Politics, (Appleton-Century-Crofts, INC. New York, 1957) 308.
[2] Van Dyke, op. Cit., p.306
[3] Van Dyke, op. Cit., p.309

unprecedented blow whose ramifications could change the nature of diplomacy, or at least some of its tools. However, there is nothing to prove that this blow was directed against American diplomacy in particular, since it is supported domestically and protected in foreign lands by myriad laws and customs; no one believes that the revelation of the names of American diplomats mentioned in the cables will lead to their prosecution over what they wrote. On the other hand, events in Tunisia, Egypt, Libya, Bahrain, Algeria, Yemen, Jordan, etc. show that a time of reckoning has come, which was not incited by WikiLeaks, but WikiLeaks, social media, and the Internet in general had a role in this eruption, as I will demonstrate below.

## American diplomacy in the face of transparency and risk

It is noteworthy that the US government has presented itself, from day one, as the main victim of the diplomatic leaks. While some spoke of a veritable "diplomatic disaster", the US administration, which was aware of WikiLeaks' possession of the large stock of diplomatic documents for some time, did not do more than inform Congress and a few concerned foreign governments of the imminent publication of the documents. The US State Department was content to send a letter to Julian Assange, the founder of the website, warning, "the publication will endanger counter-terrorism operations and will pose a threat to the relations of the United States with its allies".[1] In fact, if the US government wanted to change Arab regimes, or pressure and embarrass them, it would have found no better way than to publish the statements of Arab and Muslim officials to US diplomats, and the American analysis and comments on their statements – which is exactly what WikiLeaks did.

Until very recently, there was a widely held belief among American politicians that, in order to preserve security and stability in the Middle East and North Africa, transparency and democracy must be sacrificed. That remained the state of affairs for many years until the events of September 11, 2001 took place,

---

[1] US warns WikiLeaks against leak," Al-Jazeera, 28 Nov 2010: http://english.aljazeera.net/news/americas/2010/11/20101127171228200116.html

and US Secretary of State Condoleezza Rice admitted, in a 2005 speech in Cairo, that: "for sixty years the United States sought to maintain stability at the expense of democracy in the Middle East, and we achieved neither. Today, we have adopted a new direction, we support the democratic aspirations of all peoples."[1]

It became clear for US diplomacy that real stability can only be built upon democracy. Therefore, transparency, which is the first criterion of any democracy, serves stability when it expresses the will of the people. It was left for the American government to prove the credibility of this new discourse, but the policy of former President George W. Bush failed to do so. The occupations of Afghanistan and Iraq in order to expel the Taliban and Saddam Hussein looked more like fulfillment of American strategic considerations than a response to the demands of the Afghan and Iraqi peoples. Furthermore, foreign military intervention, whose original purpose may have been the deposing of a despotic ruler, ended up reshuffling the cards and producing a new situation in which the political elite collaborating with the Americans was accused of opposing the people and working for its own interests under the umbrella of the United States. As a result, the neo-conservative discourse calling for the democratization of the Middle East – even by force – was received in the region as an expression of new imperialism under the slogan of "democracy for all".

Most noteworthy in this specific case were the neglect of transparency and the stressing of risks to induce fear. The Americans invaded Iraq due to those two factors: they linked Saddam's alleged weapons of mass destruction (WMD) program, which they knew did not exist (lack of transparency) with the potentiality of him striking an alliance with Al-Qaeda to attack America (risk mongering). In other words, the Bush administration excluded transparency while stirring fears of risks.

The new Democratic president, Barack Obama, entered the White House in January 2009, and shortly thereafter, on June 4,

---

[1] Remarks of Secretary of State Condoleezza Rice At the American University of Cairo, Monday, June 20, 2005: http://www.arabist.net/blog/2005/6/20/condoleezza-rices-remarks-from-her-cairo-speech-at-auc.html

he delivered a speech in Cairo in which he attempted to win the Arabs over to his vision, and to stir optimism regarding what this longtime activist would do to US foreign policy, especially in regard to the Palestinian cause. However, in matters relating to the struggle of Arab civil society for human rights and basic freedoms, Obama stuck to generalities, or at least that was the opinion of the Middle East director for Human Rights Watch. [1] In fact, Obama did mention the importance of democracy and the fact that it represents a point of tension between his country and Muslim states, but he did not name specific countries, nor was it expected that he would point to countries like Egypt, Tunisia or Syria or others as human rights violators while he was being hosted by an Arab country.

## Obama and the problem of secrecy

On his first day in the White House, January 21, 2009, President Obama issued two memorandums to "the heads of executive departments and agencies" relating to transparency within the government. The first memorandum focused on the management of the Freedom of Information Act, while the second discussed transparency and open government. On December 6, 2009, the White House's Office of Management and Budget issued a third memorandum (Executive Order 13526) aimed at bestowing a practical meaning on the notions of transparency, public participation, and cooperation. [2] These pre-emptive measures, however, did not prevent what was to take place, or keep the Obama administration from appearing to be in a state of bafflement and nervousness as the WikiLeaks website began publishing thousands of secret documents that were not supposed to be accessed by the public.

In the months following the issuing of the third memorandum, numerous events took place that stirred Congress, public opinion

---

[1] US/Egypt: Obama Dodged Rights Issue Generalities Failed to Send Tough Message on Mideast Repression: http://www.arabist.net/blog/2009/6/6/human-spin-watch.html
[2] (Wendy R. Ginsberg, The Obama Administration's Open Government Initiative: Issues for Congress, CRS Report for Congress, August 17, 2010).

and the media, renewing the debate on the confidentiality of government information.[1]

- *Shamai Leibowitz*, a former contractor for the FBI, was sentenced to prison for leaking classified information to a blog.[2]
- On its website, WikiLeaks published more than 600,000 confidential government and diplomatic documents, some of which related to the Afghanistan and Iraq wars, while others involved various political issues. The Obama administration condemned this unprecedented leak of classified information.[3]
- On August 6, 2010, a memorandum confirmed that the US Department of Defense had purchased the entire first edition of a book with the purpose of destroying all the copies; the book was written by one of its former employees, and it was said to contain secret information relating to military and intelligence operations in Afghanistan.[4]

---

[1] Kevin R. Kosar, Classified Information Policy and Executive Order 13526, CRS Report for Congress, December 10, 2010.

[2] Maria Gold, "Former FBI Employee Sentenced for Leaking Classified Papers," May 25, 2010, at: http://www.washingtonpost.com/wp-dyn/content/article/2010/05/24/AR2010052403795.html

[3] White House Office of the Press Secretary, "Statement by the Press Secretary," November 28, 2010, at: http://www.whitehouse.gov/the-press-office/2010/11/28/statement-press-secretary; and White House Office of the Press Secretary, "Statement of National Security Advisor General James Jones on Wikileaks," July 25, 2010, at: http://www.whitehouse.gov/the-press-office/statement-national-security-advisor-general-james-jones-wikileaks.

[4] Scott Shane, "Secrets in Plain Sight in Censored Book's Reprint," *New York Times*, September 17, 2010, at: http://www.nytimes.com/2010/09/18/us/18book.html; and Ronald L. Burgess, Lieutenant General, Defense Intelligence Agency, "Harm to National Security from Unauthorized Disclosure of Classified Information by U.S. Army Reserve Lieutenant Colonel (LTC) Anthony Shaffer in His Book 'Operation Dark Heart,'" memorandum, August 6, 2010, at: http://www.fas.org/sgp/news/2010/09/dia080610.html. See also Steven Aftergood, "Pentagon Delays Publication of New Book," SecrecyNews.org, September 15, 2010, at http://www.fas.org/blog/secrecy/2010/09/dark_heart.html

- According to John Goldsmith, a former assistant to the attorney general, high-level government officials have leaked highly classified information to journalist Bob Woodward.[1]

Despite all that, the Obama administration stood by as it watched WikiLeaks publish the secret diplomatic cables. After the public condemnation, the publication took place and the administration was somehow embarrassed, but then the moments of discomfort passed and the matter became routine – except in the Middle East, where we saw exceptional happenings.

## The factors affecting US diplomacy in the Middle East

When reading the cables, one can glean the tendencies in American thinking on some major issues – not the official public line, which we receive through the media, but the undisclosed and unpublicized thinking, which is usually the real basis upon which policymakers formulate their positions and decisions. However, in the documents we find nothing that can be considered harmful to US diplomacy and interests, except for some embarrassment and discomfort. The following are some examples found among the cables:

1- The possibility of increasing tensions in Turkey's relations with Israel, Iran and the United States, with the cables presenting a negative assessment of Turkey's regional policy: in a cable from Ankara, dated October 27, 2009,[2] US Ambassador James Jeffrey opines, based on sources within and outside Turkey, that the deterioration in Turkish-Israeli relations is mainly because Prime Minister Recep Tayyip Erdoğan is an Islamic fundamentalist and "simply hates Israel", which also partially explains the shift in the Turkish position vis-à-vis Tehran. In another cable from Ankara,

---

[1] Jack Goldsmith, "Our Nation's Secrets, Stuck in a Broken System," Washington Post, October 22, 2010, at: http://www.washingtonpost.com/wp-dyn/content/article/2010/10/21/AR2010102104848.html
[2] Israeli Ambassador Traces His Problems To Erdoğan: http://213.251.145.96/cable/2009/10/09ANKARA1549.html

dated November 3, 2009,[1] Jeffrey said that Erdoğan's latest statements regarding the Iranian nuclear program represent "a defense of Tehran's defiance of the will of the international community". He added, "We will stress to the senior officials ... as well as to President [Abdullah] Gul that they have an interest in reining in Erdoğan."

2- Evidence emerged of an American inclination to integrate Iraq within the Gulf security framework, as well as the promotion of the image of Iraq as a democracy dominated by the Shia which poses a serious challenge to the regimes in the region: in a two-part cable from Baghdad dated September 24, 2009[2], Ambassador Christopher Hill discusses the relations between Iraq and its neighbors. He writes that the United States must re-engineer the security system of the Gulf Cooperation Council to fully assimilate Iraq as it develops tools to contain Iranian influence in the region. The new place occupied by Iraq will be shaped in a manner that takes into account the interests of the United States as well as its Gulf allies. The biggest challenge, according to Hill, was in convincing the Sunni Arab governments that a strong, stable, democratic Iraq, which would necessarily be led by the Shia, is the best guarantee against Iranian actions, if the future of Iraq is to be linked to its moderate Arab neighbors and the West. These revelations include nothing that would contradict, or negatively affect, American interests.

3- The previous point contradicts the vision of the Iraqi leadership, which believes that some neighbors "are fearful of the success of Iraq in a democratic political process that combines the aspirations of the Sunnis and the Shias in an unprecedented manner". We do not know how such concerns can dovetail with the American efforts to inject Iraq into the Gulf security system.

---

[1] Working Erdoğan Back Into The Fold On Iran :
http://213.251.145.96/cable/2009/11/09ANKARA1583.html
[2] The Great Game, In Mesopotamia: Iraq And Its Neighbors, Part I:
http://213.251.145.96/cable/2009/09/09BAGHDAD2562.htmlhttp://213.251.145.96/cable/2009/09/09BAGHDAD2562.html

4- What Ambassador Hill says in this regard may affect Iraq's relationship with its Gulf neighbors negatively, but it is not clear that it will also affect US interests. In the second part of the same cable,[1] the ambassador expands on his idea, arguing that a Shia-led democratic regime in Iraq could become a model that undermines the legitimacy of autocratic regimes in the region, and that this helps to explain why some neighbors prefer a weak and unstable Iraqi regime. Hill reiterates what he was told by Iraqi Prime Minister Nuri al-Maliki, to the effect that some neighbors "are fearful of the success of Iraq in a democratic political process that combines the aspirations of the Sunnis and the Shias in an unprecedented manner". The ambassador also quotes analyses he heard from Iraqis claiming that, for Sunni Arab neighbors, the success of Iraqi democracy would signify "the end of Sunni political power", which could only be retrieved after a period of violence and instability in Iraq that would undermine the legitimacy of the democratic regime and the Shia as political leaders.

5- These statements are just dangerous concerning their effect on relations between neighbors, and the revelation makes it even graver, for we cannot predict all the reactions that such statements might induce in the short and long terms. The question is: does this opinion really reflect the thinking of Iraqi officials? If the answer is yes, then we can see the amount of mistrust between these officials and their Arab neighbors, as well as the deep impact of sectarian feelings on politics, while the presumption is that the growth of sectarian allegiances goes against national belonging, in addition to its contravention of the notion of democracy. In the democratic world, nobody is elected based on his sectarian belonging rather than his political programs.

6- If we hypothesize that the leaks represent a dangerous turn for diplomatic history in general, and for American diplomacy in particular, we would find that the response to these leaks divided the American political scene into two camps:

---

[1] The Great Game, In Mesopotamia: Iraq And Its Neighbors, Part II:
http://213.251.145.96/cable/2009/09/09BAGHDAD2561.html

- The conservatives considered the WikiLeaks affair to be no less than an attack against the rights of free sovereign nations in managing their foreign policies and directing their diplomacy in a manner serving the interests of a more secure world. That was the opinion of Helle C. Dale,[1] a researcher at the Heritage Foundation, who argued "U.S. national security and ability to be a global leader has suffered as a consequence". The author noted four potential repercussions:

"(1) Foreign governments cooperating with the United States, including several in the <u>Arab</u> world, have been severely compromised, with direct national security implications;

(2) foreign leaders who are treated with less than respect in U.S. cable traffic, such as Italian Prime Minister Silvio <u>Berlusconi</u> or Germany's Angela <u>Merkel</u>, will not be thrilled—and very possibly their publics won't like it either;

(3) Communications between U.S. diplomats will be less candid as public disclosure is a possibility anytime; and

(4) The U.S. will find it harder to act as a world leader."

However, not all those risks mentioned by the author represent evidence that American national security is threatened, unlike the case with Middle East regimes.

- Liberals, on the other hand, are best represented in the United States by the *New York Times* newspaper, which wrote in one of its editorials[2] that even if there are "legitimate reasons for keeping many diplomatic conversations secret ... [t]he claim by Secretary of State Hillary Rodham Clinton that the leaks threaten national security seems exaggerated. The documents are valuable because they illuminate American policy in a way that Americans and others deserve to see." Others within the US State Department believe that the leaks "are

---

[1] Helle Dale, The End of Diplomacy As We Know It, the Heritage Foundation, December 2nd, 2010. http://blog.heritage.org/?p=47561

[2] WikiLeaks and the Diplomats," Editorial, The New York Times, November 29, 2010. http://www.nytimes.com/2010/11/30/opinion/30tue1.html

embarrassing, but not damaging"[1], and that official pronouncements to the contrary aim at supporting the legal efforts to close down the WikiLeaks website and prosecute its owners.

- There is another position that combines the two opinions above, and which was expressed by Steven Aftergood of the Federation of American Scientists.[2] He argues that WikiLeaks, while employing the same practices as other groups working for the spread of transparency, open government, and fighting corruption, was exceptionally treated with contempt. Aftergood finds no good explanation for the refusal of the Knight Foundation[3] to support the project when a request was made, since the Foundation is engaged in funding progressive initiatives related to the First Amendment and freedom of the media. In Aftergood's opinion, "WikiLeaks is a creative response to a real problem afflicting the U.S. and many other countries, namely the over-control of government information to the detriment of public policy."[4]Aftergood adds that while some may view WikiLeaks, which presents itself as fighting censorship, as a traditional liberal organization committed to enlightened democratic values, a closer look reveals this not to be the case. Aftergood believes that "WikiLeaks must be counted among the enemies of open society because it does not respect the rule of law nor does it honor the rights of individuals."

---

[1] Mark Hosenball, "US officials privately say WikiLeaks damage limited," January 18, 2011, Reuters. http://www.reuters.com/article/2011/01/18/wikileaks-damage-idUSN1816319120110118

[2] Steven Aftergood, "Wikileaks Fails "Due Diligence" Review," Secrecy News, June 28, 2010. http://www.fas.org/blog/secrecy/2010/06/wikileaks_review.html

[3] http://www.knightfdn.org/

[4] http://www.fas.org/blog/secrecy/2010/06/wikileaks_review.html

## Regional repercussions

By analyzing many of the cables, it becomes clear that the negative effects touching upon regional relations are more serious than those affecting bilateral relations with the United States. Here are a few examples and comments:

### Iran and the Arabs in the WikiLeaks cables

The most notable instances in this regard were:

1- Some cables implied that the allies of the United States in the Middle East are strongly supportive of action against Iran's nuclear efforts, maybe even military action, and that confidence between the Arabs and the Iranians has completely deteriorated. Also revealed were suspicions on the part of Gulf States over the capacity of the West in reaching an agreement with Iran on the nuclear issue, and expectations of war.

2- Iran's becoming a nuclear power is considered as a red line that cannot be crossed, with doubts even regarding Israel's ability to halt the Iranian nuclear program.

3- The main key for containing Iran is the achievement of advances on the Palestinian-Israeli front.

4- The existence of a veritable cold war between Iran and the Arabs.

5- The acceleration of the arms race in the Gulf in anticipation of what Iran's obduracy might cause.

6- The possibility of the United States' reaching an agreement with Iran "behind the Arabs' back" is not excluded.

7- There are strong evidences of the tensing up of relations between Iran and Iraq.

In the following are some examples:

In a cable from Doha dated December 12, 2009,[1] Ambassador Joseph E. LeBaron describes a meeting he held, along with Assistant Secretary of Energy Daniel Poneman, with a senior Qatari official who described his country's relationship with Iran

---

[1] On Iran: They Lie To Us; We Lie To Them:
http://213.251.145.96/cable/2009/12/09DOHA728.html

thus: "they lie to us and we lie to them". The ambassador adds, quoting the senior official, that Qatar has doubts regarding the West's reaching an agreement with Iran on the nuclear issue, and that he has advised the Iranians to listen to the Western proposal. If no agreement is reached, "war will burst out soon, if not by an American decision, then by an Israeli one."

In a cable from Abu Dhabi,[1] dated July 7, 2009, Ambassador Richard Olson describes a meeting that he attended, in the company of Secretary of the Treasury Timothy Geithner, with officials in the Emirati government. During the meeting, the Emiratis "expressed serious concern over Iran's regional intentions and pleaded for the U.S. to shorten its decision-making timeline and develop a "plan B."" They also encouraged the United States to send Iran a message to the effect that there are red lines concerning the nuclear issue "with direct consequences for transgressions". The Emirati officials "pointed to a nuclear Iran as an existential threat to the UAE" to the point where they viewed "a near term conventional war with Iran as clearly preferable to the long term consequences of a nuclear armed Iran," with all that would involve in terms of Iranian regional hegemony and its exploitation of differences between Sunni and Shia Arabs in order to create further instability. Emirati officials expected Israel to attack Iran if the United States were to delay such an action. And they believed that Iran would respond with a missile counter-attack that could also hit their country, in addition to a series of terrorist operations around the world. Despite that, UAE officials seemed skeptical regarding Israel's ability to stop the Iranian nuclear program. Therefore, there is a need for planning. It is noticeable that the Emiratis were careful to remind the Americans that "the key to containing Iran revolves around progress in the Israel/Palestine issue" and that "it will be essential to bring Arab public opinion on board in any conflict with Iran", which will not happen without the hastening of the "two-state solution over the objections of the Netanyahu government."

---

[1] Alarm On Iran :
http://213.251.145.96/cable/2009/07/09ABUDHABI736.html

In a cable from Cairo[1] dated April 30, 2009, Ambassador Margaret Scobey describes a meeting with Egyptian intelligence Chief Omar Suleiman that was attended by the chairman of the US Joint Chiefs of Staff, Admiral Michael Mullen. During the meeting, Suleiman affirmed that Egypt had begun confronting Hezbollah and Iran and that "it had already begun recruiting agents in Iraq and Syria" in preparation to interfere in Iran if the latter interfered in Egypt. Suleiman expressed his hope that the United States would not follow the European path in negotiating with Iran, warning against focusing on a single issue. He also affirmed that Iran must "pay the price" for its actions, and that it should not remain unleashed in the region. In light of this cable, we may understand why Washington held onto Suleiman as a potential successor to President Hosni Mubarak once the Egyptian people began calling for latter's resignation. Washington needed continuity in Egyptian foreign policy in order to coordinate with it on the regional level.

In a cable from Beirut[2] dated April 16, 2008, Charge d'Affaires Michele Sison quotes a Lebanese minister as saying that "Iran Telecom" has begun expanding its network in order to "control Lebanon", that his ministry has discovered a complete fiber-optic system established by Hezbollah in Lebanon, and that all Arab officials concerned with Lebanese affairs, including the Arab League, have been informed of the matter and supplied with maps showing the extent of the network and its coverage. The Lebanese minister believes that the Christian areas have been targeted, even though Hezbollah was quick to deny that, claiming that the network was established to serve as a defense communications network for Lebanon. However, the main sponsor of this network is Iran, which makes it a "strategic victory", allowing Iran to establish "a bridgehead in Lebanon that bypasses Syria". The Lebanese government informed its allies and friends of the discovery of the network in preparation for its taking counter-measures.

---

[1]   Admiral   Mullen's   Meeting   With   EGIS   Chief   Soliman: http://213.251.145.96/cable/2009/04/09CAIRO746.html
[2] Lebanon: Hizballah Goes Fiber Optic:
http://213.251.145.96/cable/2008/04/08BEIRUT523.html`

In a cable from Jeddah[1] dated  September 11, 2009, Consul General Martin R. Quinn spoke of a meeting grouping President Obama's advisor, John Brennan, with a senior Saudi official, in which the latter affirmed that "over the past two years Iran has hosted Saudis (all Sunnis) ... who had contacts with terrorists and worked against the Kingdom". The Saudi official said this breached the security treaty signed between the two countries in 2001, and emphasized that these events were taking place despite all of the kingdom's efforts to clear the air with Iran, especially after the 1996 Khobar attack.

In another cable from Riyadh, dated December 16, 2006, Ambassador James C. Oberwetter wrote about a meeting between Frances Fragos Townsend[2], Obama's Homeland Security adviser, and some Saudi princes and officials; the discussion included the sanctions imposed on Iran and Iran's reaction. While the US official expressed concern regarding terrorist attacks on oil installations, the Saudis appeared confident of their ability to protect their facilities from terrorist attacks. But they placed a greater importance on the threat of Iran launching Scud missiles against the oil platforms in Ras al-Tannura and al-Jubail, and perhaps also against US bases in Qatar and Bahrain, which would elicit a Saudi reaction. "The more dangerous threat (...) is a SCUD missile launch from Iran (...)The Iranians would target Saudi facilities at Ras Tanura and Jubail, also perhaps the US bases in Qatar and Bahrain, which would cause the Saudis to be involved as well." The Saudis believe that they will be a target for Iran once sanctions against the latter are tightened, they have insinuated that they prefer to be at full military readiness not excluding a "war outbreak through a pre-emptive strike against Iran."

In a cable also from Riyadh[3], dated January 28, 2009, a highly placed Saudi official in the Foreign Ministry told a group of diplomats that the kingdom does not want to see the Americans reaching a deal with Iran at the expense of the region's Arab

---

[1] Presidential Assistant Brennan's Sept 5 Discussion :
http://213.251.145.96/cable/2009/09/09JEDDAH343.html
[2] Meeting between Frances Frangos Townsend with some Saudi princes and officials. http://wikileaks.tetalab.org/mobile/cables/06RIYADH9095.html
[3] Saudi Exchange With Russian Ambassador On Iran's Nuclear Plans:
http://wikileaks.ch/cable/2009/01/09RIYADH181.html

countries, and that "if Iran tries to produce nuclear weapons, other countries in the Gulf region would be compelled to do the same, or to permit the stationing of nuclear weapons in the Gulf to serve as a deterrent to the Iranians". In this regard, we should recall confirmed reports claiming that Arabs are preparing – in coordination with the United States – for a nuclear-armed Iran, and some say that the region is a candidate for dramatic nuclear proliferation. For example, we read in the National Journal[1] that the Obama administration is negotiating with Saudi Arabia over a commercial agreement for the development of nuclear energy, which includes no mention of non-proliferation clauses, meaning that the door could be open for Saudi Arabia to develop nuclear arms.

In a Baghdad cable[2] dated January 11, 2011, a US diplomat detailed a meeting that grouped Iraqi President Jalal Talabani and Vice President Adel Abd al-Mahdi with a delegation from the US Congress. During the meeting, Abd al-Mahdi said that Iraq "cannot risk its future and enter into a new conflict with Iran", and that issues relating to the two countries' long border required a calm resolution. Talabani affirmed that the Iraqis "do not recognize the 1975 treaty between the two countries since it was effectuated under the Saddam regime" and because it has led to many problems. Iran also knows, according to the Iraqi interlocutors, that its influence over Iraq today is not as powerful as it imagines it to be.

In another Baghdad cable[3] dated September 24, 2009, Prime Minister al-Maliki told Ambassador Hill that "Iran was trying to destabilize Iraq" through its constant interventions in the political process in Iraq, with the aim of controlling the Parliament. Maliki also claimed, "Iran has not discarded use of military means to attain its objectives", even though it still focuses on political means. If Iran could not affect the results of the 2010 elections, he

---

[1] Elaine M. Grossman, "Obama Team Eyes Saudi Nuclear Trade Deal Without Nonproliferation Terms" National Journal, January 25, 2011.
http://nationaljournal.com/obama-team-eyes-saudi-nuclear-trade-deal-without-nonproliferation-terms-20110125?page=1
[2] President And Vice President Discuss Iran-Iraq Border Dispute, Elections, And Security:http://213.251.145.96/cable/2010/01/10BAGHDAD70.html
[3] Prime Minister Accuses Iran Of Trying To Destabilize Iraq:
http://213.251.145.96/cable/2009/09/09BAGHDAD2569.html

expected that it would revert to military tools. Maliki believes that what Iran is doing, above all, is an effort to combat Saudi Arabia's efforts to mobilize the Sunnis to its side.

In a cable also originating from Baghdad[1] on September 24, 2010, Ambassador Hill wrote that even though the Iraqi government believes that it can maintain control regarding its relationship with Iran, America's "allies in the region – see the situation in far starker terms and fear that Iraq could fall into Iran's political orbit and be rendered unable to speak or act independently, once U.S. troops draw down."

As we can see, these cables contain no embarrassing revelations about the United States, while they completely de-mask the Arab position.

## Turkey and the Arabs through WikiLeaks

The second example, relating to relations with Turkey, can be summarized as follows:

1- The existence of a gulf between the Turkish and Arab positions regarding the Iranian nuclear issue

2- The presence of doubts regarding Turkish foreign policy under Erdoğan, including what might affect "the continuity of constructive positions towards Iraq", and issues of Turkish rapprochement with Syria and Iran, as well as what is termed "neo-Ottomanism"

3- Linkage between Turkish regional political ambitions and fundamentalist Islam, which might hamper the development of secular Arab democracies.

4- The rise of a belief that the new Turkish role bothers everybody – the Arabs, the Europeans, and the Americans – despite the varying assessments

5- The need of the Arab media to link official Turkish foreign policy positions to the requirements of the political scene in Turkey in order to understand their full significance.

I offer a few examples:

---

[1] The Great Game, In Mesopotamia: Iraq And Its Neighbors, Part I: http://213.251.145.96/cable/2009/09/09BAGHDAD2562.html

In an Ankara cable[1] dated November 3, 2009, US Ambassador to Ankara James Jeffrey spoke of a meeting with the Turkish Foreign Ministry Undersecretary, Feridun Sinirlioglu, in which the American inquired about statements made by Erdoğan in Tehran denying that Iran harbors ambitions of nuclear armament, warning that "Washington was now wondering if it could any longer count on Turkey to help contain Iran's profound challenge to regional peace and stability." The Ambassador stated that Turkish President Gul had a different stance, affirming that Turkey is against nuclear proliferation in the region and that it wants Iran to be transparent in that regard in order to ease suspicions.

In another cable from Ankara[2], dated January 20, 2010, US Ambassador to Ankara James Jeffrey discusses in detail "what lies beneath Turkey's new foreign policy". He claims that "Turkish policy today is a mix of 'traditional Western' orientation, attitudes and interests, and two new elements, linked with new operational philosophies: 'zero conflicts' and 'neo-Ottomanism.' The traditional still represents the core of Turkish foreign policy, and is centered on cooperation and integration with the West." He affirms that Turkey under Erdoğan has attempted to fulfill the "zero conflicts" principle by attempting to resolve all standing issues with neighboring states. However, the instability in Iraq and the lack of willingness among Iraqi Kurds to do more against the PKK "raise questions about the sustainability of Turkey's constructive Iraq policy". Rapprochement with Syria did not result in Damascus moving away from Tehran; and as for "neo-Ottomanism", the ambassador sees it as an accusation made by Turkish politicians of the "traditional Western" persuasion against the ruling Justice and Development Party (AKP), since it insists on having "a unique understanding of the region". But Foreign Minister Ahmet Davutoglu was quick to adopt the accusation, rather than deny it.

Jeffrey discusses a seminal speech delivered by Davutoglu in Sarajevo in late 2009, opining that the speech contained the

---

[1] Working Erdoğan Back Into The Fold On Iran:
http://cablegategame.com/cable/09ANKARA1583
[2] What Lies Beneath Ankara's New Foreign Policy:
http://wikileaks.org/cable/2010/01/10ANKARA87.html

essence of the political philosophy guiding Turkish foreign policy. Davutoglu's proposition was as follows: "the Balkans, Caucasus, and Middle East were all better off when under Ottoman control or influence; peace and progress prevailed. Alas the region has been ravaged by division and war ever since." Jeffrey adds: "While this speech was given in the Balkans, most of its impact is in the Middle East. Davutoglu's theory is that most of the regimes there are both undemocratic and illegitimate. Turkey, building on the alleged admiration among Middle Eastern populations for its economic success and power, and willing to stand up for the interests of the people, reaches over the regimes to the 'Arab street.' Turkey's excoriating the Israelis over Gaza, culminating in the insulting treatment of President [Shimon] Peres by Erdoğan at Davos in 2009, illustrates this trend. To capitalize on its rapport with the people, and supposed diplomatic expertise and Ottoman experience, Turkey has thrown itself into a half-dozen conflicts as a mediator." Those include Iraq, Syria, Israel, Lebanon, and Saudi Arabia. Jeffrey does not see this policy as having produced results, but rather, frictions with US foreign policy, in addition to Europe, which is concerned by Turkish actions. Jeffrey believes this new foreign policy to be useful only for the AKP and the electoral base of its leaders, adding that even if the Arab street responded well to this radical populist discourse, Arab rulers would find little to admire in it.

This cable reveals something not noted by the Arab media that showered unlimited praise on Erdoğan, which is that Turkey now possesses new objectives in the Middle East: it seeks to affect the domestic and regional policies of the region countries, and it also has an organic link to fundamentalist Islam. Even though the American ambassador perceives Arab leaders to be the ones negatively affected by Turkey's maneuver as it attempted to bypass them and communicate with their populations directly, this could also be the position of some democratic, sectarian, leftist, and liberal movements in Arab civil society, which may view Turkey's interferences as unproductive one-upmanship that only serves to strengthen the fundamentalists and religious conservatives in general, at the expense of secular, liberal, and leftist movements. Indeed, it is difficult to find in, for example, Erdogan's support of Ahmadinejad anything more than a blank check presented to the

Iranian nuclear program that could be transformed into an armament program with the support of Turkey. And this is what the Arabs reject in the same manner in which they reject Israel's maintenance of a similar program alongside an arsenal of nuclear weapons. Aside from that, the support for Ahmadinejad is offered to a dictatorial regime, which the Iranian people have revolted against numerous times, especially after the 2009 elections whose transparency was doubted by Iranians as well as foreign observers. This policy is in clear contradiction to many Turkish commitments made to the Americans, especially the claim that Turkey seeks to drive Syria outside the Iranian orbit.

It is strange that Ambassador Jeffrey almost bought into that claim. He wrote: "If Turkey is sincere in its desire to attract Syria away from Iran (...) this will be of interest for us all." However, what is clear is that until now, Syria is the one that brought Turkey and Iran closer; a matter that is not looked upon kindly by Arab countries that reject the militarization of the region and the exacerbation of its problems through nuclear proliferation. Naturally, Syria has its own interests, at the top of which lays the recapturing of its occupied land (the Golan Heights), a matter viewed by Arabs as a legitimate right. The Syrian-Iranian alliance is relatively old and was originally borne out of an ideological conflict: many members of the ruling Baath party in Syria found an Iranian alliance beneficial because the "brothers/enemies" in the Iraqi Baath Party confronted the Iranian Revolution out of fear that it would spread to their country, which hosted a repressed Shia majority. The Iraqi Bath Party fell in 2003, but Syria maintains the same position for strategic reasons relating to its influence in Lebanon and its regional role. Iran may seem a winning card to Damascus, perhaps because it involves key benefits, such as oil, funding, and Hezbollah, at a time when Syria envisions no near-term political solution to its endemic problem with Israel.

Expectedly, Syria wishes to play the role of mediator between the Arabs and Iran, which is also Turkey's objective. But the latter hopes for a bigger role thanks to its NATO membership, its EU candidacy, and its situation in a region linking the Middle East to the Balkans and the Caucasus. Turkish influence bothers all those who cannot perceive it within a limited frame of interests and objectives. The United States finds it suspicious, Europe says that it cannot accept Turkey's claims of being "the voice of the Muslims" in NATO or even within the EU, and Arab rulers are not comfortable with Turkey's leaders one-upping them on Palestine and other matters. Secular Arab elites that are struggling for the establishment of the culture of democracy, law, and human rights are not pleased with Turkey's entering through the window of political Islam and support for Ahmadinejad's dictatorship. In reality, this has weakened Turkey's position after it had been seen by the repressed Arabs as a model for a country that was capable of marrying secularism with Islam.

In sum, I conclude that we do not find in these cables anything that points to real damage to American diplomacy. In fact, some of the revelations endanger regional relations in the Middle East, driving them into further stress and tension. We shall see how the open source influences these societies, where transparency was neglected for decades under the pretext of "threats".

**Effects on regimes and domestic policies**

I will mention just two examples that clearly demonstrate the profound effect of the disclosure of important diplomatic documents on the development of political awareness among large sectors of society, and in support of the opposition and change. These examples are of extreme significance to Egypt and Tunisia, which witnessed popular uprisings against the ruling regimes that soon evolved into two of the most important Arab revolutions of modern times. My comments are as follows:

1. I am not proposing that WikiLeaks is responsible for igniting the revolutions; by disclosing many facts to the Internet audience (the youth in the two countries), it contributed to the impression – which may have been true – that the Tunisian regime's strongest ally, the United States, would abandon it or was ready to abandon it because of its

rampant corruption and the impossibility of reform from within.

2.  Those reading some cables written by former US Ambassador to Tunisia Robert Godec will undoubtedly discern the degree of confusion among the Americans, and even some desperation regarding the possibility of reforming the corrupt dictatorship of Zine El Abidine Ben Ali. Translated into French and Arabic to make them accessible to non-English speakers, these cables contained thorough analyzes, penned by Ambassador Godec, regarding the deteriorating conditions in Tunisia during the last term of Ben Ali, with everyone aware that the deposing of the dictator had become possible – even if nobody knew how that would take place. The answer was provided by a revolution which became synonymous with the youth due to the role played by the new generation, the generation of the Internet, which exchanged this information and others through social networks such as Facebook and Twitter[1], putting modern communication technology in the service of the people in a manner that the former Tunisian and Egyptian governments did not anticipate until it was too late. Mubarak's regime was quick to disconnect Internet services, having been aware that what took place in Tunisia was possible due to the quick exchange of information online. And some spoke of coordination between the revolutionary democratic Arab youth on that level.[2]

3.  Like those sent by its counterparts in Tunis, the diplomatic cables originating at the US Embassy in Egypt contain condemnations of Mubarak's regime. More importantly, they include predictions and perceptions of the succession scenario.

---

[1] We also should not underestimate the role played by satellite television channels, at the forefront of which is Al Jazeera, whose exhibition of courage and efficiency provided the best of service to the democratic movement.

[2] See for example: David D. Kirkpatrick and David E. Sanger, "A Tunisian-Egyptian Link That Shook Arab History," The New York Times, February 13, 2011. http://www.nytimes.com/2011/02/14/world/middleeast/14egypt-tunisia-protests.html?_r=1&hp

Below are some brief excerpts from these cables, which everyone needs to read at length in order to absorb their analyzes, testimonials, conclusions, and predictions.

In a cable from Tunis dated June 23, 2008[1], Ambassador Godec said: "President Ben Ali's extended family is often cited as the nexus of Tunisian corruption. Often referred to as a quasi-mafia, an oblique mention of 'the Family' is enough to indicate which family you mean (...) One Tunisian lamented that Tunisia was no longer a police state, it had become a state run by the mafia. 'Even the police report to the Family!' he exclaimed. With those at the top believed to be the worst offenders, and likely to remain in power, there are no checks in the system."

In a cable from Tunis dated July 17, 2009[2], Godec diagnosed the Tunisian predicament as follows: "Despite Tunisia's economic and social progress, its record on political freedoms is poor. Tunisia is a police state, with little freedom of expression or association, and serious human rights problems (...) Tunisia has been ruled by the same president for 22 years. He has no successor. And, while President Ben Ali deserves credit for continuing many of the progressive policies of President Bourguiba, he and his regime have lost touch with the Tunisian people. They tolerate no advice or criticism, whether domestic or international. Increasingly, they rely on the police for control and focus on preserving power. And, corruption in the inner circle is growing (...) anger is growing (...) As a consequence, the risks to the regime's long-term stability are increasing." Ambassador Godec ended this long analytical cable with the following comments: "Tunisia is not an ally today, but we still share important history and values." He added: "In the end, serious change here will have to await Ben Ali's departure."

These last two sentences contain a true "time bomb". They entail a sharp alteration in the American stance on Ben Ali, who is believed by many to have been placed in his position by the US

[1] Corruption in Tunisia : What's Yours is Mine :
http://213.251.145.96/cable/2008/06/08TUNIS679.html
[2] Troubled Tunisia: What Should We Do?
http://213.251.145.96/cable/2009/07/09TUNIS492.html

Central Intelligence Agency. The statements that his regime "is not an ally" and that the necessary changes (democratic reforms) will not take place unless the president leaves are not mere words – had they not been said under the cloak of diplomatic secrecy, they would have been interpreted as a green light to engineer a military coup in Tunisia. And who knows? Maybe this is what was being planned. But the civil, popular, and democratic revolution surprised everyone, including the United States and France, as it brought about the fall of Ben Ali and his flight from the country, creating a shockwave with long- and short-term effects in the region which we are still unable to fully fathom. I do not wish to turn this paper into an off-topic lecture on the Tunisian Revolution, but there is no escaping the acknowledgment of two factors: first, the role of the Internet in general and of social networks and WikiLeaks in particular in preparing for the revolution, exchanging information, and coordinating mass demonstrations since the middle of December 2010, a matter that still requires further study; second, the disclosure of documents on the WikiLeaks website a few weeks before the outbreak of the revolution in Tunisia makes it difficult to adopt any hypothesis that Internet-savvy youth, who were the vanguard of the revolution, did not read the documents or were unmoved by their content.[1]

In a cable from Cairo dated December 1, 2010[2], Scobey wrote that "since the 1967 war against Israel, Egypt has been almost continuously living in a state of emergency, which allows the implementation of the emergency law of 1958 that grants the government a wide range of power to limit civilian freedoms, outside civil and criminal laws." At the same time, the cable asserts that the emergency law was implemented in situations targeting the Muslim Brotherhood and other extremist Muslim groups; it

---

[1] See in this regard: Hichem Karoui, "Military in Arab politics" The Gulf Today, January 08, 2011.
http://gulftoday.ae/portal/284485f8-a814-4ea1-8344-42e250896bbf.aspx
Hichem Karoui, "Armed governance ," The Gulf Today, January 09, 2011
http://gulftoday.ae/portal/dc8e57d4-7781-46da-b048-826082ca876b.aspx
[2] Egypt's Emergency Law And Its Broad Uses :
http://213.251.145.96/cable/2010/01/10CAIRO64.html

also mentions various instances involving the suppression of Internet and union activists.

The WikiLeaks cables uncovered many issues that had preoccupied the Egyptians, especially the matter of Mubarak's succession. In a cable from Cairo on July 30, 2009, Dr. Ali Al Deen Hilal Al Dasouki, spokesperson for the ruling National Democratic Party, asserts over and over again to American diplomats that the "the real center of power in Egypt is the military," and that despite the fact that military leaders do not intervene directly in the daily flow of governance, they are determined to maintain order, and are committed to a "legal transition" of power. In the same cable, there are reassurances that the military is not against the transition of government to a civilian one, and hints that this civilian will be the son of the president himself. Dasouki admits that violence will inevitably take place during the 2010 parliamentary elections and the 2011 presidential elections. He adds that security forces were prepared for this eventuality, asserting: "Threats to daily survival, not politics, were the only thing to bring Egyptians to the streets en masse."[1]

In a previous cable from Cairo dated April 4, 2007, a member of the Egyptian Parliament asserted to the US Embassy that "the recently approved constitutional amendments package is largely aimed at ensuring Gamal Mubarak's succession of his father." The same cable also includes a conversation about Defense Minister Mohammed Hussein Tantawi and intelligence chief Suleiman, who were viewed as "threats"[2] to Gamal's succession of his father, and about the possible occurrence of a military coup following the departure of Mubarak.

Another cable from Cairo on September 23, 2008 describes the intellectual and social deterioration of the Egyptian military institution according to the analysis of some academics and other observers in the country, as well as their statements to American

---

[1] NDP Insider: Military Will Ensure Transfer Of Power:
http://wikileaks.ch/cable/2009/07/09CAIRO1468.html
[2] MP On Presidential Succession:
http://wikileaks.ch/cable/2007/04/07CAIRO974.html

diplomats. In their analysis, they set the heyday of the military establishment's influence in the 1980s, i.e. before the removal of former Defense Minister Abd al-Halim Abu Ghazaleh due to "his growing political popularity."[1] Since then, the influence of the military has undergone a steady decline; the military profession is no longer what it used to be, and it no longer attracts the ambitious youth, who now see the increasing importance of the business elite. The military institution has grown intolerant of the intellectual freedom in society, and it opposes economic reforms when they contradict its own benefits and economic status. The cable adds that Gamal Mubarak does not enjoy support among the military. From this narrative, we understand that Egypt is witnessing a sharp and escalating competition between the business elite and the military elite over power. The diplomat concludes by saying that in the event of a succession crisis, the military's behavior cannot be predicted.

Many other cables highlight how since 2005[2], American diplomats expected the appointment of Suleiman as vice president, and some cables discuss his role in undermining Hamas in Palestine. The cables also spoke of Arab League Secretary General Amr Moussa as a potential presidential competitor to Gamal Mubarak, of the extension of the emergency law, of the organized attacks on the opposition, and of the intensified oppression of those calling for reconciliation. All this came in the shadow of the succession battle and the attempts by Mubarak to offer his mediation in regional conflicts in exchange for the lessening of Western pressures demanding reforms, which is made evident in a cable dated May 16, 2006.[3]

Another cable dated May 14, 2007 discusses the details of the constitutional amendments that made it impossible for independents to run for the presidency, enshrining Mubarak as

---

[1] Academics See The Military In Decline, But Retaining Strong Influence: http://wikileaks.ch/cable/2008/09/08CAIRO2091.html
[2] Report: Mubarak To Name Vice President: http://wikileaks.ch/cable/2005/06/05CAIRO4534.html
[3] Scenesetter For Deputy Secretary Zoellick's Visit To Egypt: http://wikileaks.ch/cable/2006/05/06CAIRO2933.html

president for life, and limiting the possibilities for succession to Gamal Mubarak, Moussa, and Suleiman by marginalizing other candidates. However, the cable also discusses the possible emergence of then-Trade Minister Rashid Mohammed Rashid as a candidate, unlike the Brotherhood leaders, who do not represent a true threat for the other candidates in a post-Mubarak scenario. The cable ends by saying: "It is inevitable that the next Egyptian president will be politically weaker than Mubarak", and he will need to build his popularity as soon as he is in power. The cable expects that the coming president will attempt to distance himself from Mubarak's methodology, at least in his speeches; he will "appear with an anti-American image in an attempt to highlight his patriotism."[1] He could extend his hand to the Muslim Brotherhood, as Gamal Abdel Nasser did before, in order to maintain control of the opposition. In addition to an analysis of the Egyptian political map, this final cable also offers a vision of a post-Mubarak scenario, with its men and possible policies. Recent events in Egypt have proven that many of the writings and predictions of American diplomats are relatively sound, therefore endowing these documents with historical, social, and political credibility.

## Conclusion and findings

1. It is ostensible that Middle Eastern countries did not benefit from the WikiLeaks revelations, and that all of their governments underwent trials as they were exposed to their peoples in an unprecedented manner. We do not know the extent of the discomfort experienced by the United States, and as for WikiLeaks, it has gained broad international recognition.

2. As far as I know, not one country in the Middle East has even thought of revising its relations with the United States following the WikiLeaks revelations. None of these countries would ever bluntly accuse the United States of being directly or indirectly responsible for the leaks. Bilateral relations do not seem to have been affected much.

---

[1] Presidential Succession In Egypt:
http://213.251.145.96/cable/2007/05/07CAIRO1417.html

3. The events in Tunisia and Egypt have surpassed the traditional political forces as well as the opposition elites. Even if the oppositions in both Egypt and Tunisia observed the WikiLeaks documents, they did not really play large roles in the popular revolutions, which were spontaneous. Hence, one cannot assert that viewing these documents gave any incentive to pressure the government. The reality is that the opposition was in no position to apply any pressure. Only when those parties joined the people, led by the Internet youth, did they gain the ability to negotiate and play visible roles.

4. A US DOD document[1] reveals that the governments of China, Israel, North Korea, Russia, Thailand, Zimbabwe, and many others prevented their citizens from accessing the WikiLeaks website. The presence of Israel on this list of countries practicing such censorship raises the question of what, regarding Israel, is hidden in the documents and remains undisclosed.

5. At the local level, the element of fear will play a major role in the drive towards transparency, especially after the events in Tunisia and Egypt. Although WikiLeaks does not present itself as a political organization of the opposition, with the definition of "opposition" being that it carries an alternative program to the current authority, it continues to inspire opposition groups, while supplying them with additional cards with which to apply pressure and negotiate. In this respect, I anticipate that the disclosure of various documents pertaining to American and Arab diplomacy will play a role in developing political awareness in countries that lack transparency and accountability. At the same time, the interaction between the evolution of political awareness and the reactions of governments based on the element of fear in closed Arab societies will, in turn, drive a new social and political dynamic. This dynamic has indeed begun, as was confirmed by the imagery of revolution and the demands for political participation and reform everywhere in the Arab world.

---

[1] "(U) Wikileaks.org—An Online Reference to Foreign Intelligence Services, Insurgents, or Terrorist Groups?"NGIC-2381-0617-08 ,Information Cutoff Date: 28 February 2008. Publication Date: 18 March 2008. Prepared by: Michael D. Horvath, Cyber Counterintelligence Assessments Branch. Army Counterintelligence Center. [U.S. Intelligence planned to destroy WikiLeaks,WikiLeaks release: March 15, 2010].

6. At the regional level, the element of transparency (releasing the leaks) will interact with the element of risk in order to create a new perception of the challenges at hand. In the near future and under this binary pressure (transparency and risk), we are bound to find either astonishing compromises on regional problems that, up to this point, have been endemic (which would constitute a diplomatic victory, thanks to the exposure of diplomacy), or a resolution of the region's problems by means of war.

7. In any event, I am not convinced that the publication of the WikiLeaks diplomatic cables has exposed US national security to any danger, or that it has resulted in strongly pressuring the US government to revise its policies, as has been the case for Middle Eastern countries. [1]

---

[1] Paper presented at the symposium organized by ACRPS in Beirut (Open Sources and the Leaked American Diplomatic Cables, March 2011), and published on its website as a research paper: http://english.dohainstitute.org/release/df6e333d-c90f-49e0-8081-fedf400140f8#Author

# 3

# TURKEY'S YEAR

I tried to answer the question: who marked the year 2010 in the Middle East? And I did not find better answer than Turkey. As you know, 2010 has revealed a new face of Turkey as a key-actor and Prime Minister Erdoğan as a rising leader in the Muslim world.

Turkey used to be suspect in the Arab world, though for other reasons than its unilateral abolition of the Caliphate institution in 1924. The distrust goes back to the period preceding World War One and the 19th century, and was explained in historiographical accounts by the repressive behavior of the Ottoman rulers and their continual crackdown on Arab nationalists and Arab civil society organizations.

It was not by chance that the Arabs sided with Great Britain against the Ottoman Empire in the great war of 1914-1918. The British betrayal of the Arabs unveiled by the Sykes-Picot agreement and the dislocation of the Ottoman Empire never played as a rapprochement factor between the Arabs and Turkey. The latter took part in Western Cold War arrangements, from Baghdad alliance (1955) to NATO, and incorporated a role as a Western ally and future European candidate, whereas the Arabs went building pipe dreams of Union of all kinds, and never made it.

Yet, despite important changes in the Arab world and regional politics, the relations with Turkey have remained stable in surface and quite opaque and ambiguous in depth.

However, the incident of the "freedom flotilla" in the Mediterranean seemingly marked a new turn in these relations. The tides turned in favor of Turkey throughout the Arab media and Erdoğan was celebrated as the new hero of the "Arabs" and the Muslims as he did not hesitate to tell the Israeli leaders what he had on the mind and condemned Israel's bloody repression against the "freedom flotilla."

The UN Human Rights Council's Fact-Finding Mission Report gave him more support as it stated: The deplorable situation existing in Gaza is totally intolerable and unacceptable in the 21st century. Because a humanitarian crisis exists in Gaza, Israel's blockade is unlawful and cannot be sustained in law... regardless of the grounds used as justification. Israel's blockade is collective punishment, in violation of article 33 of the Fourth Geneva Convention (IV GC) and inflicts civilian damage disproportionate to any military advantage. Since the Freedom Flotilla neither presented an imminent threat to Israel nor was designed to contribute to a war effort against Israel, intercepting the flotilla "was clearly unlawful" and cannot be justified" as self-defense. The report was clear about the circumstances of the Israeli offensive: "The circumstances of the killing of at least six of the passengers were consistent with extra-legal, arbitrary and summary execution."

The Turkish stance vis-à-vis these events have been depicted as "over-reacting" by some observers. However, beyond the enthusiastic welcome the Turkish reaction got in the Arab media and the zeal in describing Prime Minister Erdoğan as the "hero" of the Arabs, may we see in this dramatic development the premises of a change in the Turkish foreign policy?

So far, the most important ally for Turkey was the United States. Any change in Ankara's main political line may affect the privileged relationship with Washington since Turkey is a key-piece in its Middle East strategic device. Any change would also be meaningful to the European Union and the Middle East states as well, whose reactions may in turn affect Turkey.

How about diplomatic assessment?

It may be induced from a confidential cable from the US Embassy in Ankara released by WikiLeaks on November 28, 2010. The cable provides us with its own assessment of these new developments. It was addressed on January 20, 2010 to the Department of State and circulated through other US embassies in the region.

On the one hand, Turkey stays a reliable partner for the US, because the core of Turkish foreign policy has not changed, it said. This core has been described as "a mix of (traditional Western) orientation, attitudes and interests." Cooperation and integration with the West is its basis. It is focused on: "NATO, the customs union with the EU, and most significantly, the EU accession effort." This traditional stance is viewed as solid; its advantages to the elites of all ideologies make sure "Turkey will not abandon it."

On the other hand, the changes are related to what is called the "neo-Ottomanism." This is quite a source of concern to Washington. The AKP's new approach to international affairs contains several elements that appeal to Turkish voters, according to the cable, which cites: "Criticism of Israel post-Gaza, and the relatively soft Turkish position on Iran." The Turkish foreign minister Davutoglu summed up this new approach in a speech in Sarajevo in late 2009. His thesis: "the Balkans, Caucasus, and Middle East were all better off when under Ottoman control or influence; peace and progress prevailed. Alas the region has been ravaged by division and war ever since (...) However, now Turkey is back, ready to lead — or even unite. (Davutoglu: 'We will re-establish this (Ottoman) Balkan')."

For the US diplomats, this approach is baffling. The cable pointed out to the Turkish popularism reaching over the regimes to the Arab street, which may not please the Arab rulers. Even Europe is dissatisfied. "Europeans were furious with Turkey's presenting itself as the 'Islamic' voice or conscience in NATO, having consulted with Middle Eastern States before talking to its NATO allies. Extrapolating that behavior into the even more diversity-intolerant EU is a nightmare," says the cable.

The question however remains: what are the chances of the new Turkish approach to succeed?

The cable gave an answer concerning Europe, which the Turkish leaders should carefully meditate:

"Erdoğan's foreign (and domestic) policy orientation conjures up not just a clash of Christianity and Islam, but the specter of a 'meld' of Europe and the Middle East, and of Europe's secularism with oriental religiosity. Davutoglu and others argue that Turkey's 'success' as a coming Middle East power makes it more attractive to the EU — giving Europe a new foreign policy 'market' through Turkey. While some in Europe appear interested in this idea, ironically including Turkey EU membership skeptic France, this does not seem to carry much weight in most European capitals, let alone populations."

Dixi![1]

---

[1] The Gulf Today, January 01, 2011: http://gulftoday.ae/portal/d47f15cb-176f-4f8c-9068-be73a2e9995f.aspx

4

# THE MILITARY IN ARAB POLITICS

Against all expectations, the military is gaining scope and influence in the Arab world and mostly in North Africa. After over half a century of independence, claims to democracy are retreating while tough military grip is tightening around the neck of the civil society. This is rather a grim picture. In Morocco, Algeria, Tunisia, Mauritania, Libya and Egypt, the military is either in power or watching behind the curtains. The Stockholm International Peace Research Institute (SIPRI) published recent trends in military expenditure showing that its most rapid growth over the 10-year period 2000-2009 was Eastern Europe. However, the bulk of this growth (88 per cent) is accounted for by the Russian federation. The other subregions with the largest increases since 2000 are North Africa (107 per cent), North America (75 per cent), East Asia (71 per cent), and South Asia (57 per cent).

Though the US military spending accounted for 43 per cent of the world total, followed by China (6.6 per cent), France (4.2 per cent) and the UK (3.8 per cent), one cannot but wonder: what on earth North Africa is spending all that money for? None of the Northern African states is presently at war, while all of them have been affected by the global financial crisis and the economic recession. None of them is facing a direct threat from Israel or Iran. So can you believe that they are spending on the military much more than North America, East Asia, or South Asia?

But if you look more closely to the picture, you will come to understand that if these governments are not facing an external threat, all of them are struggling sometimes tragically with an internal one: in all these countries there have been more or less recently troubles with the political process resulting in social upheaval. Recent events point out to Egypt and Tunisia (where two military officers are presidents) as taking a risky turn. However, they are definitely not alone.

In both countries, speculations are going wild about succession and it is believed that a military-monitored change cannot be ruled out.

The legislative elections in Egypt (November 28, 2010) left anger, dissatisfaction and a broad wave of skepticism regarding the future. The 82 years old president Hosni Mubarak who had ruled almost unchallenged for 29 years promised free and fair elections, but the scope of fraud is enormous. Consequently, the presidential elections scheduled for 2011 seem inevitably overshadowed. Moreover, the bomb that killed 21 people on January 1 transferred the social malaise from a clash between the Government and the opposition to a clash between the Copts and the police.

Will Mubarak be candidate in 2011? Nobody knows.

Recently, some WikiLeaks' formerly classified diplomatic cables gave more information about the frame of mind prevailing in Cairo and Washington regarding this issue. Several of these cables repeat what is widely propagated in Egypt and the Arab world about Gamal Mubarak as a possible heir to his father as president.

If Gamal's candidacy in confirmed, it would be the first time ever since 1952 that power escapes the military institution in this country. There is an agreement that unlike his father, the son of President Mubarak, Gamal, has his power base centered in the business community, not with the military. However, Egypt is still a society dominated by its military class although this power is described today as waning.

A cable from the US embassy in Cairo (9/23/2008) portrayed the Egyptian military in which belong all three Egyptian rulers since Nasser, as in intellectual and social decline. The military has been so far considered as a «class apart», at least since the coup of July 1952 that brought Nasser and the Free Officers to power. However, this decline of the military institution does not strip it from its power and influence.

Citing a senior Cairo University political science professor, the diplomat reported that «the military does not support Gamal. So if Mubarak died in office, the military would seize power rather than allow Gamal to succeed his father. » However, it is believed that «the military would allow Gamal to take power through an election if President Mubarak blessed the process and effectively gave Gamal the reins of power. »

Comment of the US diplomat: «The military still remains a potent political and economic force (...) It helps to ensure regime stability and operates a large network of businesses as it becomes a "quasi-commercial" enterprise itself. While there are economic and political tensions between the business elite and the military, the overall relationship between the two still appears to be cooperative, rather than adversarial. »

This comment is not very different from other opinions that have traditionally depicted the military influence in Arab politics as beneficial. The question is: does the military institution still hold the solution for Egypt's problems?

The importance of the armed forces in Arab politics has been noticed by several observers. Some impute a primary reason for this importance to the context of dramatic tension that encompasses the region. Indeed, "a series of episodes in the long struggle for national liberation" seem to emphasize this importance, "as the triple assault of Suez (1956), the Algerian struggle for independence (until 1962) and the departure of the

British from the Gulf."[1] In addition, do not forget the war between Israel and its neighbors, and the catastrophic defeat of June 1967, which helped affirm the role of military in politics.[2]

Yet, the Arab armies are still central to the study of Arab societies and politics, because of their involvement in civil affairs and in the various government processes. The soldiers actually took part in most major political changes in Iraq, Syria, Egypt, Jordan, Algeria, Tunisia, Libya, Mauritania, Sudan, Somalia, Comoros Islands, etc... In Iraq, we can mention the coup of Bakr Sidqi in 1936, the revolt of Rashid Ali al-Kilani in 1941, the Baathist coups of 1963 and 1968. In Syria, there has been a long series of coups in the period directly following the end of World War II, followed in Egypt by the coup of Nasser, etc...

One of the results probably among the most harmful at medium and long term is that military intervention in Arab political affairs is so commonplace that it is almost trivialized. Better: in the Arab countries where coups have succeeded in establishing a new regime, the new military leaders have often been accredited legitimacy that allowed them to settle for long. They not only became the new masters of the country, but they carried also the "laurels of glory," as they were sometimes described as the "Great National Heroes" or the "saviors." How can one fail to notice, in fact, that most Arab leaders, who came to power on the tanks, were also described as "popular"? There is no question that the army is that of the people, but it is also strengthened with such an "armed" support that an ambitious leader is able to forge a "legitimacy" that would never be betrayed by an electoral vote! Nasser had perhaps not had enough time to

---

[1] See Elizabeth Picard: Arab Military in Politics: from Revolutionary Plot to Authoritarian State. In: The Modern Middle East. Edited by Albert Hourani, Philip S. Khoury, & Mary C. Wilson, University of California Press, 1993, p.551.
[2] It is true that some years ago we could read across the Arab magazines (like Dirasat arabiyya, Shu'un falastiniyya, afaq arabiyya, etc...) articles on such topics as "the revolutionary army," "People's Army", or "people's war for national liberation." It should be noted that much of this lexicon has now given way to approaches much less focusing on forcing the change by arms ; and apart from some Palestinian magazines or Islamist websites where "armed militancy" is said to be the child of the "legitimacy of resistance", there are fewer articles calling for the rush to arms as a means for political change. This was not the case in the 1960s and 1970s.

get to this anti-democratic degree, but those who followed him - Sadat and Mubarak - have still a state of emergency declared.

"Armies are also supposed to operate mainly at the level of the national state, and therefore have the ability to strengthen the cohesion of the country."[1] And several observers from varied countries have considered the Armed forces as a solid instrument of modernization, and a major agent for change and renunciation of tradition, especially because the new generation of officers who initialized most of these coups is from a more rural and less privileged origin than their elders."[2]

The armed forces have also been described as "prescribing a new citizenship," "encouraging certain values such as secularism," and to a certain degree "political participation"[3] (so long as it does not run against their own interests). But the backlash against such a positive view of the military in Arab politics was not long to manifest. The limits of these regimes are inscribed in their origin and their horizons.

The "Naksa of 1967 represents a dramatic turning point in Arab history. Going back to the years following the Arab defeat directly (1960-70) one may locate a change in perceptions. Henceforward, Arab leaders turned their nationalist, triumphant, socialist rhetoric that had prevailed over a decade into more pragmatic views to accompany a withdrawal toward more a reduced level of state interests. "A new moderate style had to be found, and the model became Saudi Arabia." [4]   Not only the officers who controlled power in Egypt and Syria had failed to contain Israel or to return even an inch of land to the Palestinians, but even in their own society their authoritarian policy was more than ever exposed. They were facing increasing difficulties in continuing the policies of nationalization, extensive land reforms and industrialization they had entrusted their bureaucracy. The "social development" they   had attempted to establish was brought down by the lead in the wing.

---

[1] E. Picard, op.cit., P.522.

[2] Ibid.

[3] The examples of Nasser's Egypt, Iraq after the Kacem revolution, the Baathist Syria, and Boumedienne Algeria, have been treated as cases of military intervention success ... ibid.

[4] Picard: op.cit., P.552.

At the same time, and from the 1970s onward, studies began to appear in the Western countries on the internal rivalries and the ongoing conflicts between the Arab military elites, their clans, their alliances and misalliances, and the consequences of their rivalry resulting in a series of plots, coups and counter-coups revealed to be quite expensive for the Arab society.

A simple look at the terminology used in these studies and articles describing the regimes of the Arab states where the military has managed to settle in the wake of a coup, is enough to make us realize that they have rarely been appreciated. Terms like "military dictatorship", "government of the army Party," "military oligarchy," "military-civilian coalition"[1] etc... have become commonplace. On this level, the lexicon has changed very little over the years, admittedly, because even if the military was discredited in the Arab world since the 1967 defeat, they are still in power in several countries and they are more increasingly associated with  social, political, economic, and cultural bankruptcy in the societies they govern and in the Arab world in general. In short, the military is no longer the "solution" for the Middle Eastern - North African societies as people naively believed in the late 1950s of the last century. Today they are an integral part of the major problems of these societies. And they remain a problem as long as they cling to power, or seek to intervene in political and civil affairs. We cannot, indeed, imagine a democratic society in reference to the military. The military, by definition, is not a democratically but a hierarchically based-system.

This is true for Egypt as it is for all others countries in the region. The military institution cannot preserve these countries forever from the social and political malaise that is creeping, eroding the regimes, and turning their youth into candidates for Islamic radicalism. [2]

---

[1] Picard: Op. cit., P.557.

[2] A version of this essay adapted to the press has been published in two installments, on the Gulf Today: January 08, 2011 (Military in Arab Politics), and January 09 (Armed governance). See both articles on the following links:
http://gulftoday.ae/portal/284485f8-a814-4ea1-8344-42e250896bbf.aspx
http://gulftoday.ae/portal/dc8e57d4-7781-46da-b048-826082ca876b.aspx

# II

## THE DAYS THAT CHANGED THE ARAB WORLD

*Poverty is the parent of revolution and crime.*

Aristotle (384 BC – 322 BC)

I recorded in the following papers my own testimony on those days, as an observer of this Arab Spring phenomenon...

# 1

# WINDS OF CHANGE

*Those who make peaceful revolution impossible will make violent revolution inevitable.*

John F. Kennedy (*in a speech at the White House, 1962*).

January 14 will go in history as the Day of the Tunisian People. The Day of its Revolution. The Day of its victory on the dictator who usurped power and kept it during 23 years. There will be henceforth a time before and a time after January 14. This revolution has a purpose: freedom. The Tunisians said: they did not want bread, but dignity. Still, this will be the case now until a democratic government is elected. A government representing the people of Tunisia, not imposed on them. Without such a solution, there will be no end to the conflict. The Revolution is in its very beginning. It might change the political and social landscape for the years to come. This Revolution has nothing similar in the region. It is really a genuine making of a suffering people that happens to be one of the most educated, the most modernized in the region.

We know why violence erupted. The government tried to suggest a link with Islamists and terrorists. But this is bogus. The conflict has nothing to do with Islamism. What we see in Tunisia today is traceable to a sociological pattern related to states emerging from the colonialist stage, which after independence have tested some models of economic and political development and were unable to stay the course, thus failing to produce sustained economic growth with stable and representative political institutions.

In predominantly Muslim countries of the MENA region, ideology has several functions including that of the legitimation of power. It may involve Islam or Islamism or be to some degree secular. This is the case of Tunisia since the independence. But the country has never been a democracy. So, the pattern is the same than others in the same case: a conflictual situation remains lurking in the underneath until through accumulation of little and more important events it becomes unbearable and a simple incident may then spark a riot giving way to the open conflict. This is exactly what happened since the immolation of a young man in Sidi Bouzid.

## People's power

True, in some authoritarian states the opposition ideology confronted with all kinds of repressive behavior may easily slide into radicalism and violence. But this did not happen in Tunisia where radical Islamism was really confined in the margin and never grew to become the opposition ideology.

In democratic countries, conflicts are not ruled out; they exist. But they are managed through democratic mechanisms of social and political control. Conspicuous among them is the public debate open to everybody including political and social actors. The themes are often: social unrest, rising prices, inflation, wages, pensions, social insurance, and in some cases, broader issues affecting local economies, such as the dollar and the euro, the recession, etc ... This debate has parameters that meet the expectations of the public. When there is a slide towards violence in the streets (as sometimes happens), it remains isolated and rarely goes beyond its scope to engulf entire cities, as we saw in Tunisia. Furthermore, although Europe has produced some of the greatest revolutions in history, "radical" literature calling for violence and armed rebellion against the system remains marginal and rarely has an effect on social movements, because everybody benefits from democracy, even radical dissidents.

In Tunisia, violence is the result of a discussion of the deaf especially in the absence of the political framework for open debate: democracy. First, the deficiency of democracy excludes the debate. Second and subsequently, it seems that the conflict rather than focusing on the legitimate social and political demands as it happens in Western democracies tends on the contrary to affect the very foundation of the political system: its legitimacy. This is the same pattern that happens everywhere in similar cases.

This is a social revolt that turned political because the regime, unable to reform itself, might well have reached its last stage of survival. No prediction is presently possible; yet, we can see that there are limits to what people can endure. In the Western countries, the recession has made victims among the middle class. But although people protest and demonstrate, they are not gunned down like birds.

## Political game

Nevertheless, the conflict that erupted in Tunisia these days did not oppose the government to political opponents. One may even observe that the opposition has been marginalized, because when people are out, they are out for their lives, not for the opposition purposes. That is what happened. The political game would have now new rules and parameters. No political party is able to claim legitimacy without the people consent. The opposition and the civil society leaders will have to be more courageous and more aggressive in negotiating the new parameters.

So far, it is true, their influence was extremely limited. The reason is that authoritarian regimes allow an opposition to be active only to a certain degree: as long as it does not threaten the interests of the power elite. Once this opposition becomes too troublesome, it is either brought back to order by some repressive measures targeting its symbols and assets, or outright forbidden, almost always with a masquerade referring to the legislation.

This has been well described in the UNDP report on human development in Arab countries since 2004. There is throughout the MENA region a paradox between freedom and democracy, consisting in erecting "democratic" institutions while emptying them of their substance: this goes from legislations violating basic rights and freedoms, through servile parliaments taking their orders from the executive, NGOs directly or indirectly managed by governments, trade unions defending the interests of employers and government instead of employees, media turning into spokespeople for the rulers, not to mention the legacy of power in "republics" from father to son. Unfortunately, most of these features were those of Ben Ali's Tunisia.

In ordering the police and the military snipers to shoot unarmed people, Ben Ali made a choice that would reveal to be fatal to him and his party: 1) He thus expressed clearly that he was at war and the enemy was none other than the people. 2) He gave up his chances to stay credible abroad — his credibility in Tunisia was already eroded — and caused the USA, Europe and the UN to condemn this disproportionate use of force.

The civil society has to be very cautious not to lose the way to democracy. The fight is just beginning.[1]

---

[1] The Gulf Today, January 17, 2011.
http://gulftoday.ae/portal/8d4aeaba-e04a-4b4a-bad1-3c83171c8e59.aspx

## 2

# HIGH SHADOW OF TUNISIA

The second Arab Economic meeting of Sharm El Sheikh could not avoid the high shadow of the Tunisian situation. The Secretary General of the Arab League, Amr Moussa, warned the leaders: "The Arab citizen has entered a stage of anger that is unprecedented. The Tunisian revolution is not far from us." The declaration was on the first page of The New York Times.

This made me wonder: didn't they know? Of course, they knew it. The overall crisis in the Arab world has made the unanimity of the Arab experts who drafted and produced the PNUD Human Development Report in 2004. This unanimity was even made official during the Arab summit of May 2004, which recognized that "the political field, specifically the structure of the Arab state, is the very place of the impairment and its axis, and it is here therefore that reform must begin."

Let us recall some key-points of that important report.

Despite the apparent differences between the regimes (royalist/republican, rich/poor, radical/moderate...) the report recognized some common features that are strong enough to suggest the existence of a regional structure and similarities of methods so that we can reasonably talk of an "Arab type of power." This type was labeled in the report: "the state of the black hole," because of the strong centralization of the executive and the government bureaucracy.

In the "state of the black hole," the enormous powers enjoyed by the Head of State, in addition to specific mechanisms dependent on the executive (such as the party in power when there are parties) mean that everything revolves around one person. In this state "the parliament becomes a quasi-bureaucracy appointed by the executive," having nothing to do with the notion of representing the people.

The system works through what is called "ignored corruption." However, another important feature of those regimes is the central place enjoyed by the security and intelligence apparatus, so that they are also referred to by another label: "police state" (dawlat al Mukhabarat). The report noted a structural similarity between the regimes concerning their submission to the same hegemony: that of the apparatus of police, intelligence and security.

The main particularity of such regimes is therefore their inability to transform and democratize because of a structural deficiency characterized by the ability to "marginalize strategically" all institutions and social forces.

It is normal that in such a situation, we talk of a crisis of legitimacy, and that is what the report just did. In fact, it mentioned several of these crises.

First, there was the crisis of traditional (religious — tribal) or paternalistic legitimacy (emerging from the battle for independence and for the construction of the new State) in front of the elite with radical, Left wing or Pan-Arab tendencies, etc... It lasted at least two decades (the 1960s and 1970s).

Then, with the rise of the hardliners' movement since the 1980s, a new crisis of legitimacy emerged: facing hardliners, some regimes were struggling with slogans praising their "achievements" and even claiming to lead the battle for Democracy and Human Rights, which made people say: the democratic discourse has become another myth for salvation. Maybe is this the worse distortion that can strike democracy: being "supported" by an authoritarian regime that uses and abuses of the discourse on democracy and human rights to better violate them. It is for this reason that the report talked of "legitimacy of usurpation" whenever a regime justifies its own continuity (in tyranny) claiming to be a lesser evil compared to a hardline set-up or anarchy.

Consequently, the crisis is expressed through symptoms that speak volumes about the disease that corrodes the Arab societies, such as the repression and impoverishment of the political parties by means of weakening them and the marginalization of the civil society. The fact that in some countries there is a plethora of political parties is not necessarily a sign of good vitality.

The Report interpreted it rather as a symptom "reflecting the divisions of the political and intellectual elite and the maneuvers of the rulers to divide opposition." Result: no opposition party is enough powerful and convincingly attracting to win elections and take over. Hence, an overall exhaustion and a general apathy related to politics. Moreover, as noted by the report, "the governments are in a hurry to freeze and ban the parties that become popular."

Thus, the barriers to participation in political life are so oppressive that there is a general deficiency of the political process accompanied with a loss of public confidence. The result revealed by the report is expressed in two aspects:

First, the marginalization and neutralization of some parties and a lack of confidence in the whole political process have incited some of them to opt for underground political activity, and even to resort to violence, terrorism and political negativism. On the other hand, the closing of the political space has led some researchers and activists to think that relying on the civil society organizations is more advantageous, particularly the trade unions and professional organizations, considering them more suitable than Arab political parties to conduct the Arab society towards development and democracy.

Nevertheless, the problem is that the civil society's institutions are not in a better situation. Far from it. First, some of these organizations (trade unions or human rights associations, etc...) are handicapped by their allegiance to the ruling party that uses them as a nice shop-window while continuing a policy of containment and repression. Others adopt the discourse of civil society as a strategy to combat rivals, especially if they belong to the hardline opposition. Thus, we see why "despite the existence of tens of thousands of civil society organizations in the Arab world (...) their influence is still very limited."

Other symptoms of the crisis were also identified by the report, including: lack of transparency in business and economics, lack of control and corruption. All this combined with an unhealthy climate in which the security apparatus dominates the society and the state, making the law their servant instead of serving it, shows that there are "bridges" between economic corruption and political decay.[1]

---

[1] The Gulf Today, January 22, 2011: http://gulftoday.ae/portal/b4877ce8-9945-4cab-9395-dcda677200df.aspx

# 3

# NO LONGER BOGGED DOWN

It was something to hear the President of the United States
address a warm encouragement to the people of Tunisia in his
State of the Union speech in unambiguous words: "We saw that
same desire to be free in Tunisia, where the will of the people
proved more powerful than the writ of a dictator. And tonight, let
us be clear: the United States of America stands with the people of
Tunisia, and supports the democratic aspirations of all people."
Similar riots happening in Algeria, Yemen and Egypt suggest that
these may not be just thunderstorms. Anyway, the US policy-
makers might have been aware of these probabilities at least since
the speech of Condoleezza Rice in Cairo (2005), when she
confessed: "For 60 years, the United States pursued stability at the
expense of democracy in the Middle East -- and we achieved
neither. Now, we are taking a different course. We are supporting
the democratic aspirations of all people." Yet, the achievements of
the Bush administration did not level with the expectations
because of the misunderstanding of the real needs of the Arab
people. We know today that a military intervention to "help
democratization" is the last thing they hope for. The US support
for undemocratic governments may obviously generate the
opposite of the expected stability.

Instead, a moral and political support to those rotting in jail
and tortured for their opinion, to those arrested or fired from their
jobs because they demonstrated or wrote an op-ed, and to all those

democratic forces of the civil society that are most feared from the holders of absolute power is what the Arab people need.

The Obama administration is aware of this. The Washington Post said recently: "the administration is openly supporting the anti-government demonstrations shaking the Arab Middle East, a stance that is far less tempered than the one the president has taken during past unrest in the region."

Is there a "Tunisian inspiration" to the Arabs?

For James Zogby, "there is, of course, a difference between being inspired by a performance and repeating that performance." Indeed, what happened in Algeria, Egypt and Yemen so far was not a transfer of the revolution but just the sharing of a "transforming moment" between countries that, despite their differences, have all the same similarities, the top of which is characterized by their being republics and not monarchies.

The question is: why did these huge popular demonstrations happen only in Arab republics?

The answer to this question may be contained in the second characteristic of these demonstrations: all of them mixed up social and political demands axed around legitimacy asking the governments to leave.

The question of the government legitimacy seems to me more acute in Arab republics precisely because republican politics are supposed to be expressing the electoral trends. This is exactly what people blame their governments for: they do not express these trends.

The absence of a true republican spirit in these countries make of them "hereditary" or "monarchical republics" where power politics and money are monopolized by the ruling clique. The corruption plaguing these regimes is also due to the deficiency of a credible multi-partisan parliamentary system accountable to the people, and a free press. In these "monarchical republics", the head of state is endowed with practically absolute power allowing him to introduce whatever constitutional and legislative amendments he deems fit to overstay his mandate.

These are mono-partisan systems where politics is monopolized by a single formation often with the "benediction" of some groups from the opposition in return for a share in the government: a few seats in a parliament overcrowded by the party in power and at best a post or two in the Cabinet.

What about monarchies?

There are two types: the first is represented by Morocco and Jordan, both endowed with a more or less workable electoral system, which exposes the governments not the King during the crises.

The second is represented by the Gulf States. Three main features distinguish them: they are rich and their citizens are not alienated from the profits of the oil rent (which is obviously the case in Algeria); the population benefits from the welfare state at varied degrees (which is not the case in the Arab republics) ; their elite has enormously benefited from the alliance with the West which translates in  liberal tendencies not only on the economic level but also in the media (which is far from being the case in the Arab republics). After all, the two greatest liberal Pan-Arab TV channels (Al-Jazeera and al-Arabiyya) are both Gulf-based and many other influential media assets are either Gulf-based or Gulf-funded.

That does not mean that the Gulf monarchies are immunized against crises. No state in the world is. They too have their social and political problems implying the necessity of continual review of public policies and timely adaptation to the demands of the new generations.

Nonetheless, I note a number of recurring attitudes that dominate Arab politics as a whole:

The absence of free elections.

Elections are sometimes held for a Council that has no real legislative prerogatives if it does not share its meager power with another Council whose members are designated by the ruler.

Elections are also allowed only for the political parties and individuals that are acceptable to the ruling party, insofar as the results are granted for the latter.

To participate in elections, the parties must also be acceptable to the military and the security apparatus, while clearly stating their support for the leading party or presidential candidate.

Limits imposed on the opposition in the Legislative Council, either through a certain distribution of the electoral constituencies to split and reduce the support to opponents, or by adopting an electoral system that can only diminish the chances of the opponents.

Illegal police pressures on the opponents and their supporters with the purpose of reducing their chances to lead a successful electoral campaign.

The pressures on opposition supporters are various and range up from precluding their vote to manipulating and forging the results.

Imposing a single candidate for presidency.

Buying out votes with money or administrative promises.

The real tragedy of the Arab world since so many years is that people feel bogged down. Their demonstrations just showed that there is no other way out of this illegal system settled as the only prospect for politics and entrepreneurship.[1]

---

[1] The Gulf Today, January 29, 2011: http://gulftoday.ae/portal/0de7fa36-89b6-4a5e-87d0-a8f3c455dd75.aspx

# 4

# GAME OVER

There seems to be an agreement between observers that this is the end of the Mubarak era. Revolutions such as the Tunisian and the Egyptian are hard to roll back. These are — theoretically — predictable social movements that should have been long expected if we apply some criteria originating in past revolutionary situations. Social scientists working on the Middle East have been monitoring our societies for years and many of them warned against probable explosions if the ruling elite do not accept to adapt themselves to obligatory social and political changes. But autocratic states seldom listen to the advice of scientists and much less to that of their Western allies who — it must be acknowledged — have for many years insisted on the necessity to introduce democratic reforms in the MENA region while providing their support to the rulers.

Consequently, the message arrived truncated or distorted, for it conveyed a paradoxical meaning: on the one hand, it said, reform, because if you do not accept reform now, you will lose touch with your people over time and you will be forced to accept the worse or give up power. On the other hand, the message said, we are your supporters whatever your decision, for we do not see a reliable alternative to your rule.

This kind of behavior was unlikely to get the expected results (from the Western viewpoint), because of so many reasons some of which are psychological, some sociological, some political, economic, strategic, etc.

— An autocrat by definition is "autistic" in the sense that he lives in a world of his own fancy, supported and helped by his close entourage, "his" media, "his" party, "his" police, "his" state, and even "his" people (e.g. many autocrats believe up to the last moment that the population loves them). Such a person understands your message only if it is supportive and approving; never when it is critique for day in day out he hears praises suggesting he is perfect.

— If we take the previous in consideration, an autocrat would be much inclined to think that his US-Western allies need him and as long as they do he will not have any trouble repressing his opponents with a good deal of violence and compelling his Western allies (advisers included) to accept his rule as the only and unique choice offered to them if they refuse to see the chaos setting up in the country and upsetting their own affairs.

— The previous argument is definitely used as the dissuasive weapon of the autocrat to cling to power during the crises. Generally, it is enough to remind the critiquing allies of the "political desert" around him. Indeed, a "good" autocrat makes sure nobody of his opponents is allowed to grow locally and internationally to the point of matching his political weight in the eyes of the nationals and the Western allies. Thus, he insures that even the Western demands stay leveled to a roof he is the one who defines.

— When a crisis burst out, much of the outcome is determined by the previous context. How the crisis evolves is sometimes a matter of negotiations, at the local level and the international as well. Generally, the forces occupying the social theatre and shaping the social movement cling to their demands and slogans. If they are important in size as we see in the Tunisian and Egyptian uprisings, then it is hard for any political entity, national or international, to put a roof on these demands. The crisis is often resolved (momentarily) through negotiating some kind of transition that may end up in one of two ways:

Yielding to the demands of the social movement, often relayed by political actors working inside or/and outside the transition entity. Then, we can talk of a "happy end" for the social movement, of democratic achievement, etc...

The second case is the counter-revolution. Under the transitional rule, some forces generally encouraged, funded and armed by the former rulers and their allies take advantage of the precarious social condition to spread violence and terror, thus creating a state of total insecurity, where speaking of freedom and democracy would grow frightening for the population incapable of leading a normal life. When the security of the persons and the properties becomes the primary demand, the terrain is ready for the return of the same regime often disguised into a "soft" version, with superficial reforms suggesting that the change has happened all the same.

Whatever your social position, you may agree with me that the context I described above is that of Tunisia, Egypt, and perhaps other countries as well. I would like simply to add a few examples of sayings I have read in varied US Think Tanks. These examples, show that notwithstanding the authors' political background (right or left or liberal), they agree on the main lines I have just described and advise the Obama government to be on the right side, which is the people's on the street:

- "It is past time for Mubarak to go. He has lost the Egyptian people and he has lost legitimacy." [Richard S. Williamson]

- "Today, the US is paying the price for its refusal to cultivate liberal opposition." [Michael Rubin]

- "If Egypt's army — the backbone of all of its governments since Egypt's 1952 coup — takes power, then Washington should encourage it to pledge to return power to a civilian government after a new constitution that is broadly acceptable to Egyptians is devised." [James Phillips]

- "Obama then needs to call Mubarak and tell him gently but firmly that for the good of his country it's time for him to go." [Martin Indyk]

- "There is a fear in the United States that the Muslim Brotherhood could gain power and that a change in leadership will impact Egypt's relations with Israel. Both of these fears are greatly exaggerated." [Marina Ottaway]

- "The gap between Mubarak and the Egyptian people, which has been expanding for a decade, has now grown so wide that it is not possible for the United States to stand on both sides?" [Michele Dunne]

- "I believe essentially that the Mubarak era is over." [Richard N. Haass][1]

---

[1] The Gulf Today, February 5, 2011: http://gulftoday.ae/portal/f24c4930-3364-44a6-a71a-362eb3dcc6d0.aspx

5

# DEMOCRACY NOW

These are great days for Egypt, democracy and the Arab world.

The people determined to come to terms with decades of oppression, corruption and absence of freedoms challenged a crumpling regime that tried everything for its survival. Deaf to the demands of the Liberation (Tahreer) square, unable to rely on its Western supporters to advance its own political propositions that anyway were introduced too late, the regime contemplated the dark horizon of all autocratic regimes when they realize they are doomed: neither able to go ahead nor to go back, jammed in their own contradictions, they would resort to threats and repression.

Addressing an expectant Egypt on Thursday, Mubarak said that he had delegated some powers to his vice president, Omar Suleiman, but would not leave the country.

If we link this speech to previous statements by top-officials, the situation was expected to grow out of control at any time: a senior official was quoted as saying the army would "intervene to control the country" if it fell into chaos (NY Times, February 10, 2011). Mr. Omar Suleiman had already warned that the alternatives facing tens of thousands of demonstrators demanding

Mr. Mubarak's ouster were dialogue with the authorities or "a coup."

Such maneuvers and threats did not work.

Egypt has been ruled by the military since the 1952 coup and all its successive governments have always performed their job under the watchful eye of the military and the state of emergency since 1967. Today, people said enough is enough.

The Egyptian society that gave the Arabs some of their most enlightened minds will not accept a forced choice between the military or the chaos. There is indeed a better option.

However, it is obvious that the military had the upper hand on the situation since January 25, for without their support the Mubarak regime would have already collapsed.

Yet, the civil society forces have now proved how able they are to find allies and supporters among the honest patriotic officers whose loyalty to the people is above blind loyalty to a government that lost touch with the population.

There is no neutrality in this struggle. The military had either to be on their people's side or on the government's if ever the latter gave them the order of blocking people inside Tahreer square or forcing them out.

As the protesters seem determined to continue the struggle, the last days' picture showed that the regime had to account not only for corruption and repression but also for internal terror against the population and manipulation of the truth.

In this context, a question has to be answered related to the former Interior minister Habib el-Adly, recently prosecuted for his role in the New Year's Eve bombing of al-Qiddissin Church in Alexandria in which 24 people were killed. According to British sources quoted in the media reports (al-Arabiyya, February 7, 2011), this is a serious case of a wide plot masterminded by the Minister. Its objective was to blame the attack on Islamists.

Finally, the military made the right choice. They gave reason to their people, and Mubarak was well forced to give up and step down.

Since the first days of the uprising, people seemed confident that the military were on their side.

Since the first days of the uprising, Egyptian officials insisted on making clear the "differences" between their country and Tunisia. More than a self-protection reflex, it was actually a reminder to the protesters as well as to the Western allies that Mr. Mubarak was internationally supported and that his downfall would send a lot of negative messages to the entire region, Israel included.

In his first public reaction to the uprising, Mr. Mubarak emphasized – as I recall – "this is Egypt" (meaning, this is not Tunisia where the president and his family vanish under the pressure of the street!) At the time, not much people among his powerful Western supporters gave credit to the revolt. Worse: they were afraid that if the regime is toppled everything constructed in the region since the signature of the Camp David and the Israeli-Egyptian peace accords might collapse as well. We read surrealist "reports" and "comments" on the "frightening might of the Muslim Brotherhood and their role in this uprising, on the violence promised by radicals to secular Christian Egyptians, and so on, until Western journalists themselves made it clear that all that mumbo-jumbo was rubbish.

Secretary of State Clinton had made a statement saying that she was confident the Egyptian government was stable, just a few days after she warned Arab governments from Doha that if they did not reform and democratize they will face much trouble. Such inconsistency is understandable only to those who, in the USA, wish a smooth controlled transition to a new power that will stay loyal to the international agreements and arrangements (particularly the Peace process) sponsored by Washington and to Egypt's role as a moderator in the Arab world.

Yet, as the days went by, the Obama administration adapted itself to the new situation. But after Thursday's speech, the situation seemed still in the impasse.

The Egyptian government was almost isolated, and the military could not ignore it. They knew that would they have sided with the regime, they will lose their people and the foreign support, included the US. I do not think the Obama administration or the European governments would have condoned a bloody repression against Egyptians yearning to freedom and democracy.

On the other side, the people of Egypt knew that freedom has a price, and if they are willing to pay it, nobody on earth will prevent them from achieving their objectives. Not even the army, unless a bloodbath is allowed. Then, Egypt would perhaps not have got democracy, but civil peace would have been lost for as much time as a dictatorship under the benevolent watch of the military would have been allowed to rule.

Fortunately, wisdom and common sense triumphed.

Less than twenty-four hours after his Thursday speech, Mubarak stepped down.

Egypt is free. Democracy can work now...[1]

---

[1] This is an update slightly changed of the article published in The Gulf Today, February 12, 2011: http://gulftoday.ae/portal/153ad710-b250-469c-af58-be0a278031f5.aspx

# 6

# MAJOR TRANSITION

The Middle East/North Africa region (MENA) is ostensibly going through a process of regeneration, with its procession of hardships, deterioration, re-equilibration or breakdown, installation of new governments and implementation of new policies. These are times of fear and courage, anxiety and hope, reform and change. For some countries, like Tunisia and Egypt, it is already an epic story the happy end of which can only be the disappearance of the authoritarian regime. Yet, as we watch similar social mobilization and protests in neighboring countries (Algeria, Libya, Yemen, Jordan, Iran...) there is a feeling that the trend of protests is unlikely to be momentous. People are encouraged to take to the streets by the success of similar tactics in Tunisia and Egypt. In Yemen, Libya, Algeria ... we hear the same slogans that have been shouted in the Tunisian and Egyptian cities. Obviously, the mobilization across the region is not declining, and the echo-phenomenon has an unexpected impact... It is strengthening the Tunisian and Egyptian movements saying: There is no possible way back.

The MENA region with its peculiar culture, its old traditions and its authoritarian regimes revealed to be quite open to the likeliness of democratic transition without being forced to from outside. This cannot be overemphasized because of the role of the youth in these events. According to "Population Reference

Bureau," MENA experienced the highest rate of population growth of any region in the world over the past century. One third of MENA population is under age 15. Over the next 15 years, these children and adolescents will reach their childbearing years and enter the job market. Authoritarian regimes cannot face the challenges of this generation and the next one with repression. Some will introduce changes from the above (to re-equilibrate); some will disappear. Democracy is the only viable way to development, sustainable growth and stability.

There is empiric evidence that democracies consistently outperform autocracies in the developing world. Democratic leaders have incentives to respond to the needs of their fellow-citizens. Otherwise, they find themselves out of office. Democracies do a better job of fixing mistakes: as power is not monopolized, the scope of disastrous consequences following ill-conceived economic policies is reduced. Democracies are open for investigation: corruption is less important. Democracies are flexible: the political stability is enhanced by clear mechanisms of control and succession.

Although the current trend of protests demanding democratic transition is new to the Middle East, it has been a significant trend in Mediterranean Europe and Latin America during the seventies and eighties, and literature has accumulated since, with comparative analyses of the dynamics of these democratization processes.

Any transition is a complicated process with setbacks, obstructionism (antidemocratic forces) and a certain amount of ambiguity as to the timetable of the transition and the new rules. The anxiety such a process creates is normal considering past experiences where the failure to address the agenda of transition in full has resulted in weak consolidations and incomplete democratizations. Yet, past experiences also reveal a good record of successes. In all cases, obstructionists have to be neutralized so that the logic of transition prevails. This logic, as it has been observed several times, does not necessitate the simple and pure "liquidation" of antidemocratic forces, only that their violence be ceased. It is also worth noting that several governments may come to power between the collapse of a regime and the crystallization of a different one.

Democratic transition may come from above like the Spanish transition (1973-77), which is a successful example showing how despite forty years of dictatorship, the Spanish people was ready for democracy. It is also unique in that it showed a mechanism of transition based on the monarchy with low level of violence and a second role for the military.

Most other cases show a common scenario of military retreat: (Argentina: 1980-83), (Brazil: 1974, 1985), (Uruguay: 1980-85), etc. In Portugal (1973-76), the transition process led by "the movement of the captains" resembled a revolution because they tried to use mass mobilization.

Some people may be inclined to draw a parallel between these processes and those taking place currently in the MENA region, but although it is still normal and useful to think of past experiences, we cannot refer to a unique pattern of successful transition to democracy ready to be applied anywhere, any-time. People have always to find their own way based on their needs, their culture, and secondarily on successful experiences of other countries.

Yet, whatever the country, some features may be associated to similar events and processes.

Because the repressive capacity of any regime is not inexhaustible, the deterioration process and the losses it involves will reach a point at which they become unsustainable, thus necessitating the intervention of the military. That's what just happened in Egypt, while in Tunisia the military were not absent but less involved.

However, in both cases and in others as well, the determinants of the extrication are identifiable, some of which are endogenous to the military, some exogenous:

1- The first factor is related to the military perceptions of the situation and particularly to the military's impression of the

strength and commitment of the opposition.
2- A second is related to the choices available to the military and the actual costs and benefits of these alternatives.
3- A third is the balance between pro-democratic and anti-democratic forces within the military. It should be stated nonetheless that the roles of transition's actors change at different stages of this transition.
4- A fourth is related to the pattern of societal cleavages and to which extent they are represented by different political forces.
5- A fifth concerns the substantive programs of the opposition and their feasibility.
6- A sixth factor would focus on the presence of an actor considered hostile or dangerous by the military.

These six factors represent a causal background to any decision on the part of the military to remove a government (as in Egypt) or stay in the background while it is removed (Tunisia).

The rest is a matter of negotiations between the actors of the transition.

A commitment to an electoral timetable, campaigning and voting safety, an effective restoration of the rule of law including a political amnesty, and several of such measures of appeasement will reassure the democratic forces and prove that the old regime is in the process of being dismantled.[1]

---

[1] The Gulf Today, February 19, 2011: http://gulftoday.ae/portal/9c13e8d0-8a36-4a65-89ce-8f7bef525f3b.aspx

# 7

## LEADER OF MERCENARIES AND SLAVES

For over forty years, Qadhafi claimed he was the unique leader of the Libyan people. He was not. Since February 17, he has the most serious rival any dictator would ever have: the people. It is the people, not any member of the elite that took to the streets to oust him from power. Like similar revolutions in Tunisia and Egypt, politicians would have to rush and join the ranks of the uprising, where the future is happening.

Prior to the February 17th popular revolution, Libya's often contradictory political dynamics were described as a product of competing interest groups seeking to influence policy within the confines of the country's authoritarian political system as the country seemed emerging from international isolation.

Tribal relationships remained important, particularly with regard to the distribution of leadership roles in government ministries and in political-military relations. Tribal loyalties remained strong within and between branches of the armed services, and members of Qadhafi's tribe, the Qadhadfa, have held many high-ranking government positions, reportedly including key positions in the air force. Members of larger, rival tribes, such as the Warfalla, have opposed the regime on grounds of tribal discrimination. Some Libyan military and security officials staged limited, unsuccessful coup attempts against Qadhafi in 1993 and 1996 based in part on tribal and familial rivalries. Qadhafi government has performed periodic reassignments and purges of the officer corps to limit the likelihood of organized opposition re-emerging from within the military.

Political parties and all opposition groups were banned in Libya under Law number 71 of 1972. The government has dealt harshly with opposition leaders and groups over the last four decades, establishing special "people's courts" and "revolutionary committees" to enforce ideological and political discipline and to punish violators and dissidents. Abroad, Libyan intelligence personnel have monitored, harassed, and, in some cases, assassinated expatriate dissidents, some of whom were referred to as "stray dogs."

Libya's myriad opposition movements can be categorized broadly as hardliners, royalist, or democratic in orientation. But like similar organizations in similar countries, their activities and effectiveness have been largely limited by disorganization, rivalry, and ideological differences.

Here is a list of these opposition groups:

1) The Libyan National Group (At-tajamoa Al-watani Al-leebi); Established: September 1976; Newspaper: Saut Ashaab Alleebi.

2) The Libyan Democratic National Movement (Al-haraka Al-wataniya Ad-dimokratia Al-leebiya); Established: April 1979; Magazine: Sawt Libya.

3) The Libyan Democratic National Group (At-tajamoa Al-watani Ad-dimokrati Al-leebi); established: September 1981;

4) The Libyan National Movement (Al-haraka Al-wataniya Al-leebiya); Established: December 1980; Magazine: Sawt Attaleea.

5) The Islamic Group "Libya" (Aj-jamaa Al-Islamiyya "Libya"); Established: 1979; Magazine: Al-Moslim. Newspaper (Ind.): Al-Raed.

6) The Islamic Movement "Libya" (Al-haraka Al-islamiya "Libya"); Established: May 1980; Magazine: Ash-shorouk.

7) The Democratic National Libyan Front (Aj-jabha Al-leebiya Al-wataniya Ad-dimokratiya); Established: August 1980; Magazine: Al-watan.

8) The National Front for The Salvation of Libya (Aj-jabha Al-wataniya Li-inqad Libya); Established: October 1981; Magazine: Al-inqad.

9) The Libyan National Salvation Army (Jaish Al-inqad Al-watani Al-leebi); established: January 1981.

10) The Libyan National Struggle Movement (Harakat Al-kifah Al-watani Al-leebi); Established: July 1985; Newsletter: Al-kifah.

11) The Libyan National Salvation Army Organization (Monathamat Jaish Al-inqad Al-watani Al-leebi); established: August 1988.

12) The Libyan Movement for Change and (Al-haraka Al-leebiya Lil-taghyieer Wal-Islah); Established March 1994; Magazine: Shooun Lib-biya.

13) The Organization for Free Libya (Monathamat Tahreer Libya).

14) The Libyan National Group (Attantheem Alwatani Alleebi).

15) The Libyan Authority for National Salvation (Al-haiaa Al-libiya Lil-kalas Al-watani); Established July 1986.

16) The Libyan Volcano Group (Monathamat Al-burkan Al-leebi); Established January 1984.

17) The Libyan Constitutional Union (Al-ittihad Ad-dostouri Al-leebi); Established October 1981.

18) The Freedom Party (Hizb At-tahreer); Re-established July 1980.

19) The National Libyans Front (Jabhat Al-wataniyeen Al-libi-yeen); Established: August 1980; Magazine: Libya Al-ankaa.

20) The Libyan People's Struggle Movement (Harakat Al-nidal Ash-shaabi Al-leebi).

21) The Libyan Democratic Party (Al-hizb Ad-dimokrati Al-leebi).

22) The Nation's Party (Hizb Al-Umma).

23) The Libyan National Union (Attahalof Al-watani Al-leebi); established: February 1983.

24) The Libyan Democratic Conference (Al-motamar Ad-dimokrati Al-leebi); Established: August 1992; Magazine: Al-motamar.

25) The Libyan Democratic Authority (Hai-at At-tanseeq Ad-dimokratiya Al-leebiya); established: May 1993.

26) The Fighting Islamic Group (Aj-jamaa Al-islamiya Al-mokatila); Established: 1991 (when they wrote their Manhaj); Magazine: Al-fajr.

27) The Libyan Conservatives Party (Hizb Al-mohafi-deen All-leebi); Established: May 1996.

As we see, Qadhafi failed to make of Libya the political desert he wished. In July 2005, Libyan opposition groups in exile including the National Alliance, the Libyan National Movement (LNM), the Libyan Movement for Change and Reform, the Islamist Rally, the National Libyan Salvation Front (NLSF), the Republican Rally for Democracy and Justice, the royalists of Mohammed Al Sanusi (grandson of the former king), and others as well gathered in London and issued a "national accord," calling for the removal of Qadhafi from power and the establishment of a transitional government. A follow-up meeting was held in March 2008. But ostensibly, nothing substantial emerged out of these meetings. Certainly not a strategy to topple the regime that may be described correctly as successful in February 2011.

Qadhafi pretended that the protesters were "drug addict" manipulated by foreign intelligence. He called his people "rats" showing the extent of arrogance and contempt he was capable of. But four decades of dictatorship are enough to turn even a drug addict against his pusher. And in this case, there is no other "pusher" than Qadhafi himself and the state of fear he inflicted on the Libyans forty years long.

Today, the Libyan political elite disseminated all around the globe have to ready themselves to take over and lead their country to democracy and welfare. No people in the world deserve to bear a despot for so many years and when fed up with his womanish whims they shout "enough," he sends the aviation to raid them and buys mercenaries with embezzled money to chase and shoot them down.

Qadhafi who admired Hannibal to the degree of giving his name to his own son has obviously not understood what lost Carthage: mercenaries never won a war against patriots. They will never do. Look at Libya: since its people sought freedom at the price of their lives, the only followers Qadhafi could afford are either mercenaries or slaves. Mercenaries fight for the devil if he pays them. Slaves may be Libyan-born, but assuredly not sovereign citizens. Both could not make a nation.

Foreign legions were used by Hannibal to fight Rome not Carthage.

Has Hannibal turned his weapons against the Carthaginians even when they refused to send him the reinforcement he needed? Never.

But Qadhafi is not Hannibal.

What a sad end![1]

---

[1] The Gulf Today, February 26, 2011: http://gulftoday.ae/portal/0acaaa84-4f64-43ac-bae0-2b454ff955f8.aspx

# 8

# LIBYANS HAVE ALREADY WON

Whatever the contacts the US and the Western allies have with the Libyan opposition, an all-out military intervention by Western powers in Libya is not the best solution. It may even be utterly counter-productive and turn people against the West. Not because they still want Qadhafi, but because it is not right to steal their revolution. It is not the West combat.

They know Qadhafi is isolated and armed indeed. They know he still may harm them. Yet, they also know that regime change and democracy are their own responsibility.

The international community can help with food and medicines, while imposing sanctions on the remains of Qadhafi regime. The lawsuit against the dictator and his cronies in the International Criminal Court is still the best way to confront him with his crimes.

Politically, the man is finished.

He knows the end is close. So, the only political weapon he tries his hands at is now manipulation. If he can sow divide between the Libyan social groups, he gains time. If he can provoke the international community by any means and bring the West in for a military showdown, he wins: the Libyan democratic revolution would become something like the Bush "liberation" of Iraq.

Qadhafi is really crazy, yet not enough to think that he would win a war against NATO. However, he knows that if the West strikes him, all the anti-western radicals and millions of people would forget his massacres and remember only the casualties caused by the Western intervention. Qadhafi, dead or alive would come back as the hero of the day. As there is no clean war, the West would be loathed even more than the dictator. The post-Qadhafi Libyan government that would take over under the protection of the foreign weapons would be insulted. Democracy would be insulted. The population would be hostile, and the real chances to make liberty values progress in the whole region would be undermined.

The wise leaders of the international community should definitely avoid giving a dictator such a chance to survive in reality and in memory as the Arab leader who resisted the attack of foreign powers. Wise leaders know that if war breaks out in Libya, the pacific civil democratic revolution is over. Have not Qadhafi father and son threatened of civil war? Why should the West give them such an opportunity by rushing to war?

To stop the wave of democracy is exactly the scenario Qadhafi was wishing for since the day he insulted publicly the Tunisian people for throwing out his dictator. The Iraq and Afghanistan military mess is still before our eyes. Who wants another Iraq?

They are now speaking of a non-fly zone. Is this without risk of inflammation?

The free Libyan people (the rebels) have their own military, though. To fight and defeat Qadhafi is their job, not that of anybody else, whatever it takes.

If the international community wishes to help, the UN knows exactly what to do in such cases.

Managing a crisis is to a great extent managing perceptions.

Libya is an African country deeply rooted in its Arab-Islamic cultural environment. Do I need to remind anybody of the important differences between Western and non-Western perceptions of interference?

In the West, the post-war response to the Nazi atrocities was the UN charter that included the notion of self-determination as a major principle of international law. Self-determination was balanced against one of the Charter's other major tenets: non-interference in the internal affairs of another country, based on national sovereignty. Non-interference was seen as a way to protect weak states against intervention from powerful states.

Self-determination was perceived as a way to ensure progress in international order, but at the same time, recognize that the humanity needs a "monitoring right" over the relationship between the state and the people. Thus, a state cannot hide behind the shield of sovereignty to oppress its population. That is clearly stipulated in the Universal Declaration of Human Rights the UN General Assembly has adopted in December 1948. At the time, it should be noted, the communist and Muslim states did not vote for the declaration. Yet, in 1948, the majority of Arab and Muslim countries were not yet independent. Since then, they have joined the membership of the UN Human Rights Council.

Nonetheless, interference on behalf the self-determination principle is still a delicate task subject to different interpretations, according to the conditions and the prevailing culture. During decolonization and its aftermath (the 1950s-1970s), self-determination might initially have helped liberate newly independent states, but non-interference was regarded as an important principle protecting the new states from neo-imperialism.

That was the purpose of creating the non-aligned movement in 1961 in Belgrade. This purpose was best served in 1970 and 1974 by two resolutions of the UN General Assembly. The first one — 2625 (XXV) — stated "the inadmissibility of intervention in internal affairs" and the "protection of independence and sovereignty." The second — 3314(XXIX) — stated that "aggression is the use of armed force by a state" against the sovereignty, territorial integrity, or political independence of another state.

Both were considered by developing countries as a "victory" against imperialism and neo-imperialism.

In the present situation, it would be utterly clumsy and irrelevant to help Qadhafi transform the right of self-determination in Libya into a battle against imperialism he is already trying to recuperate.

So far, the only choice he has is dictated by the Libyans: give up and quit or die, they tell him.

Whatever his choice he has already lost.

To allow western forces to go after him is to give him a last chance to throw disgrace upon the values his people is fighting for: why the Libyans or any Arab people need the intervention of the Western military to achieve freedom and democracy?

This is a crazy formula.

What if the Libyans die fighting Qadhafi? The answer is: freedom has a high price. Everybody knows it.

Now if you ask: what if the Libyans die under the "friendly" bombs of NATO or the USA coming to "help?" The answer would change: it would not be about freedom, but about imperialism and oil interests.

Of course, this is sad. Yet, it is the real world.

The West can help with humanitarian and logistical assistance. To go beyond this threshold is too dangerous a game.

The Libyans will never give up to a mad dictator after they revolted. They have already won. Wait and see...[1]

---

[1] The Gulf Today, March 5, 2011: http://gulftoday.ae/portal/8466dcab-1167-4d87-b559-621067789f9f.aspx

9

## ENTHUSIASM FOR DEMOCRACY

As the wave of revolt in the Middle East seems growing and far away from ebbing down, the sprint toward democracy with its wide resonance inevitably reminds us of a similar enthusiasm in East Europe two decades ago with the fall of Berlin wall. Some observers however noted a decline in this mood in Eastern Europe and concluded that the public enthusiasm for democracy is not guaranteed to last.

The point was made lately by James Bell, Director of International Survey Research, at "The Pew Research Center." Based on the results of previous surveys performed by his institution, he stressed that since democratization is a process that may take more or less a long time, we cannot be sure it is an enduring successful process.

Thus, we are reminded that "in the spring of 1991, Eastern European publics were widely enthusiastic about democracy." The change for a multi-party system won approval from large majorities across the region. Bell did not fail to compare this good predisposition of the public to a similar popular mood prevailing in the Middle East, and he recalled a Pew survey in the spring of 2010, resulting in 60% or more among Egyptians, Jordanians and Lebanese saying that democracy was preferable to other forms of government. Better: "Three years earlier, large majorities in these countries said it was important to live in a country characterized by competitive elections, an impartial judiciary, uncensored media and the freedom to openly criticize the government."

Bell argued that the enthusiastic mood for democracy did not last in Eastern Europe. Not that these countries turned over going back to autocracy: they would not have been admitted as members of the European Union if they did. But, as he explained, they became more circumspect about political reform partly because of the destabilizing effects of the adjustments to the market economy and to the multi-party system.

So, if "in 1991, majorities of Russians and Ukrainians clearly favored democracy, rather than a strong leader, as the best way to address their country's problems, by 2002 opinion had reversed." Observe that Bell's remark concerns two countries that are not members of the EU. Consequently, they are not bound by the standard rules that bind all EU members as regards democracy, human rights and all public and private liberties. However, when he came to speak about these new EU members, he said: "In Poland and Bulgaria views were mixed on the issue, while public in the Czech Republic and Slovakia continued to strongly support democracy."

The fall 2009 Global attitudes Survey found Russians and Ukrainians believing that a strong leader was still needed to solve their problems. According to Bell, this is "now the attitude of the Bulgarians." And while the shift to a multi-party system is approved in all these countries by half the population or more, "the level of support declined between 1991 and 2009 in all but Poland, the Czech republic, and Slovakia."

The conclusion Bell drew from this situation is that East Europeans did not abandon democracy, although these results pointed to the gap between what they hoped for and what they reached. The unfinished transition to democracy suggests that the process in the Arab world may be even longer.

This opinion of the Director of the Pew International Survey Research is indubitably well argued. Yet, while I join Mr. Bell on his analysis regarding Europe, I disagree with him concerning the process in the Arab world.

The enthusiasm for democracy we see today is not a new phenomenon in the Arab region. It was less visible simply because it was repressed by the autocratic regimes for so many years. But all those who know the Arab world and have connections with the populations and particularly the young generation, know that there is a true hunger for democracy that cannot be satisfied without introducing real changes in these societies.

We cannot just talk of a mood (of enthusiasm) as we see everyday people hanging around the streets in several Arab cities, protesting against the regimes. Moods change, ideals do not. Thus we can say that any euphoria will be followed by more a down-to-earth attitude. Yet, democracy as a philosophic notion and a political system has been at the core of the Arab intellectual and political movements since at least the seventies, if not many years before.

Actually, we observe a persistent inclination toward democracy since the struggles of the seventies of the last century, expressed by the emergence of several organizations of democratic opposition in the countries that are today leading the movement: Tunisia and Egypt. From that time on, the civil society institutions kept growing in importance. In the eighties, a new political Lexis gradually appeared on the social stage, carried up by some independent or partisan liberal media. In Tunisia for example, independent magazines like: Le Maghreb, Réalités, al-Ray... played a key-role in linking the activists of the Human Rights League and the newly born political parties to the large public.

But the main difference between the Arab world democratic movement and the East-European is, on the one hand, that the Arab democrats do not fight against a single despotic system (with several copies) whose values were imposed and supported by an Empire, as did the USSR in East Europe. Their struggle was — still is — against their own rulers, who — despite their open alliance with the West — were the keepers of a system completely at odds with the values of the West. That explains how they fall easily under the pressure of the masses as soon as the West withdraws its support.

In East Europe, the USSR never withdrew its support to the regimes facing trouble. Nevertheless, as the leading state was itself undergoing important changes with the Perestroika and the Glasnost, it had not had enough time to react or even to understand what was going on inside the USSR and inside the Eastern bloc.

On the second hand, the Arab countries are newcomers neither to the market economy nor to the multi-party system. In Tunisia and Egypt, the former rulers have not excluded the free market from their countries business as did the former communist regimes. So, on the economic level, these countries are much more prepared to build a liberal democracy on past acquirements than East Europe. Nor are they deprived of a multi-party political experience. Many parties were already there and active prior to the revolution.

Therefore, I am rather inclined to think that Arab democratization has all chances of success, which does not mean that it will be achieved without trouble and sacrifices.[1]

---

[1] Gulf Today, March 12, 2011: http://gulftoday.ae/portal/89f87776-01b6-48b2-8ac1-27653fc50f8d.aspx

# 10

# FREEDOM AND SECURITY

There seems to be an irreducible paradox in the increasing demands for liberty, political participation, equality, and justice and the responses given to them; a paradox between: freedom and security. But it is only appearance. For if one uses reason, it becomes clear there is no possible security without the free adherence of people. The recent uprisings happened in countries where security was the chief-concern of the government. Yet, despite the power of the Mukhabarat in Tunisia and Egypt, the regimes were incapacitated and bypassed.

It is also clear that the Arab governments confronted to democratic demands have either to enhance their own capacity to satisfy them and adapt their constitutional and legislative structure to embody them, or repress them, which is just a painkiller, not a remedy.

Nevertheless, the democratic movement in the Arab world cannot be stopped, at least because it is genuinely emanating from society not imposed or imported from outside, and because what we see today has not started in January with people victory in Tunisia, but decades ago.

During the 1980s, popular dissatisfaction with authoritarian leaders and regimes grew steadily, with Morocco, Algeria, Tunisia, Libya, Sudan, Egypt, Jordan, and Syria all experiencing major public riots or other disturbances expressing opposition to the established order.

Partially in response to these domestic pressures, a number of Arab countries began experimenting political liberalization and democratization.

Few among the Arab rulers do not recognize today the need for continuing democratization and perhaps its inevitability. We can give several examples of official statements and actions abounding in this sense since the 1990s. The late King Hussein told the people of Jordan in a November 1992 address, "We perceive Jordanian democracy as a model and an example... from which there will be no turning back."

In an insightful article published in 1995, about "Arab and Western conceptions of democracy," Dr Jamal Al Suwaidi, head of the Emirates Centre for Strategic Studies and Research (ECSSR) reminds us that "demands for political participation in the Gulf States began as early as the 1930s." Suwaidi recalls how Kuwait was the first to respond to these demands since it established its National Assembly in 1963. And he was right. Kuwait was then a pioneer for all Arabs, not just the Gulf, despite its Assembly has been dissolved several times. How can we forget that some of the best products of modern literature and social sciences in the world (not just the Arab region) have been published by the famous "National Council for Culture, arts and literature" in Kuwait? That would not be possible without respect for culture and freedom of thought, which is impossible in autocracies.

We feel as if several Arab regimes today are caught into a dilemma: freedom or security? What to do?

Let us neither dramatize nor minimize the current developments in the Arab world. The process of evolutionary change has been set up in the Gulf, for example, since a while, and it is quite normal to see a tension between governments and society over speeding the pace of reform.

In Bahrain, in Jordan, in Yemen, in Syria and elsewhere there is a situation. No country in the Maghreb or the Mashriq is spared.

Bahrain was one of the first countries that have followed Kuwait by establishing its first National Assembly since 1973. Dr Al Suwaidi mentioned it in his afore-cited paper, along with other cases in the Gulf: Qatar established its Consultative Council in 1972; the National Federation Council of the United Arab Emirates was established in 1971; the Consultative Council of Saudi Arabia was announced in 1992; and Oman replaced its appointed Consultative Council with a new elected in 1991.

The question is: was it enough?

The Gulf is not excluded from the social changes; it might even have spearheaded them through its liberal media.

Several of today's Arab Think Tanks are founded or supported by the Gulf countries.

To mention only a few examples: "The Foundation of Arab Thought" (born in Beirut: 2000, with the support of Prince Khalid Al Faysal, Prince Khalid ibn Sultan ibn Abdel Aziz, and several other Saudi princes and sheikhs whose names we find on the Board of trustees; the "Arab Democracy Foundation," Born in 2007 in Doha, whose chair of the Board is none other than Her Highness Sheikha Mozah Bint Nasser Al Missned; "The Gulf Research Centre" (2007, Dubai); or the most recent "Arab Centre for Research and Policy Studies" (Doha)... The multiplication of such centers for research and reflection is in itself a significant indication that the Arab world is changing, and it is changing rapidly from a receptacle of ideas to a producer of knowledge. Such intellectual activity cannot be fully productive in terms of qualitative output and excellence without financial, political and moral support. So, one may reasonably assume that the political will exists to give these institutions the scope they need to produce qualitative knowledge about the Arab region in this particularly delicate phase of its history.

Yet, without a liberal orientation, the funders and supporters of such institutions would be throwing their money away, whereas the output of these Think Tanks is supposed to serve the progress of society and to make evident that security should serve freedom.

While change is the inevitable destiny of all societies, it is important to stress the differences, because they exist. Some years ago, two social scientists (Almond and Powell) investigated the conditions for a trade-off between liberty and security by constructing a three-part typology of societies.

Their findings went as follows:

Society (A) is usually culturally homogeneous and lacks divisive ethnic or religious cleavages. Here, the citizens enjoy substantial amounts of both liberty and security as long as the pendulum-like movements emphasizing now liberty, now security, goes on. The examples they give concern: Israel, Algeria (tilting more toward security); Turkey, Tunisia and Egypt somewhat more sensitive to liberty.

In society (B) the pendulum swings away from security, back through liberty, and ultimately into anarchy. The cause: ethnic and class tensions are deeply embedded in the social body. The prototype is Lebanon. But Sudan and Afghanistan are also concerned.

In Society (C) coercion and repression are dominant. The mechanisms of control destroy liberty, yet provide little security. Syria and Iraq were given as examples.

What should we conclude from this picture?

The push and pull between the demands of society and the government are in constant change. Societies are in continual move from one type to another. The governments that refuse to lead the changes their societies demand may become their first victims when anger explodes.[1]

---

[1] The Gulf Today, March 19, 2011: http://gulftoday.ae/portal/11d37998-8d44-405d-8ea8-0d63f997c3ff.aspx

# 11

# DEMOCRACY UNDER DICTATORSHIP

Jennifer Gandhi who studied "the Political institutions under dictatorship" raised an interesting question. "Why, she asked, do non-democratic rulers govern with democratic institutions such as legislatures and political parties?"

Of course, these institutions are emptied of their substance under dictatorship; they are mere form. Still, we find that a ruthless dictator like Saddam managed to project a "democratic" image, like the nonsensical and impossible 99, 99% landslide.

Qadhafi, who is no dictator, since he is not even president, has no power. The power is in the hands of people. And the people after 40 years of this rubbish want him out and make him look much like a mad man.

Even when nobody was really threatening his power, Qadhafi needed to convince himself and all those who were willing to lend him an ear, that he was an innovator of democracy. The Green Book assumed to create a "third way" to "pure democracy" led Libya towards errancy. The "leader" is so convinced he detains The Truth that, if we let him do, he would even rival with Muhammad (PBUH) himself. While the Libyan people fight him, he still pretends they love him.

A few hours before he flew away, Ben Ali too claimed he was still legitimate in people's eyes, just after ordering his police to shoot down two hundreds of them. The terms he used to appease the raging Tunisians were: "I understood you. Wallah! I understood everyone." For those who know a little bit about North Africa's history, these words were exactly those used by General de Gaulle in a famous speech in Algeria before the French settlers. In history books, these words passed as the perfect example of total (perhaps intended) misunderstanding. De Gaulle said he understood them and did exactly the contrary of what they were expecting. It follows that those who advised Ben Ali in using the same words were either ignorant of their historical semantics or pushing a blind man towards the precipice. Naturally, those words infuriated people and marked the end of the regime. Nonetheless, during twenty-three years, Ben Ali tried to seem democrat whereas he was crushing people under his boots. For those who did not know, there used to be a parliament in Tunisia with representatives from different parties... under Ben Ali.

In Egypt, same thing. Mubarak was not leading a police state, but a "democracy" with "elected" representatives of the people. After 32 years of uninterrupted presidency, Yemen's Ali Abdallah Saleh has not had enough. To the people pressing him to leave, he too gave evidence of democracy ordering his police to shoot them down. Thereafter, he asked them to negotiate. How can you kill and still pretend to be legitimate? And who would negotiate with killers and mass-murderers even if they were in power? Saleh too – like Ben Ali, Mubarak, and Qadhafi – would never acknowledge he is mistaken about almost everything he thought right. Mistaken about his allies in power: family, tribes, and military. Mistaken about government: how did he convince himself he was leading a young democracy? Come again: are democracies those regimes where people are shot down when they protest against government? And most of all, he was mistaken about power: whoever the ruler, he cannot rule without even a simulacrum of consent. Such a simulacrum works for a time and comes to an end at another. And today, it is his turn to leave.

Syria has recently joined the parade of the angry republics where the rulers believe they are uncrowned kings of Divine Right.

President Bashar Al Assad may walk in the footsteps of his father and be tempted to reduce the Syrian protesters to silence using heavy weapons and helicopters. But we are no longer in the eighteens. The entire world would know about any butchery in few minutes. Al Assad would have trouble convincing the world opinion and his own people that nothing happened in Syria.

Let me now come back to the question of the beginning. Gandhi reported that the proportions of non-democratic regimes with legislatures in the period following World War Two varies from 60 to 88 per cent. The majority of non-democracies (58%) have allowed for multiple political parties to exist. So why autocrats need democratic institutions?

Simply, because democracy has changed of meaning over time. Remember that the first who talked of it ever was the early Greek philosophers (see A. Taryam: Democracy alive and unwell, Oct. 24, 2010). In their texts, it was just a system of governance, to be distinguished from oligarchy, aristocracy, etc... and it was not even the "best" by the criteria of that period. But since then, democracy developed as a system as did the thought about it, so that today, it is not just a system, for it has acquired a new quality – that of: moral force.

In our time's criteria, democracy is certainly the best system of governance, although it is not perfect. Consequently, the moral force it acquired has become compelling for rulers and polities. That is why all governments need to be perceived as democratic or at least working to implement democracy, autocrats included.

Yet, this is only a part of the answer. The second part is that in order to thwart challenges to their rule, autocrats need some co-operation and compliance from the people. If we look at the Arab world, we will realize that the problem the rulers face is not the same, depending on the resources they have access to and the degree of strength and mobilization of the opposition.

In short, the degree to which autocrats may solicit co-operation is different. If they have huge sums of cash and other hidden assets, they may be less willing to negotiate compliance with domestic groups. That is the scenario of Libya. Can we compare Tunisia, Egypt, Yemen, and Syria to Libya? And Libya to a rich country of the Gulf? That is the point.

In some autocratic countries, democratic institutions are instruments of co-optation. They become forums of negotiations for organizing policy compromises. "Legislatures and parties serve as a forum in which the regime and opposition can announce their policy preferences and forge government" (J. Gandhi).

That is to answer the question we raised above.

Now, it is sure that using void democratic forms may work for a time but not every time as it is increasingly obvious. Wherever the rulers emptied democratic institutions of their substance and used them to support their power, societies grew more resisting and more demanding.[1]

---

[1] The Gulf Today, March 26, 2011: http://gulftoday.ae/portal/f1a547ae-fa8d-448e-8b5b-a70330dfdcd1.aspx

# 12

# YEMEN: OPEN SUCCESSION

Unlike Tunisia and Egypt, Yemen's uprising was triggered by the opposition parties. A March 2011's report to the US Congress emphasizes that well before unrest in these two countries, Yemen's opposition parties had been angry over President Saleh's plans to amend the electoral law, form a new Supreme Commission for Elections and Referenda (SCER), and amend the constitution to allow himself to stand for re-election—all without opposition agreement.

However, though opposition protests started in Yemen on Jan.16, 2011, it has acquired weight and popularity with key-elements of the elite and the tribes joining the protesters and more and more defections from the party of the president, included prominent members of his own family, particularly after the brutal reaction against the demonstrators.

Today, the urgent question is about succession. But it is not new. On Sept.17, 2005, a cable from the US embassy in Sana'a (released by WikiLeaks) addressed the succession issue.

1- It admitted that "true power still derives from the military and the tribes, and the next president would have to meet with their approval." This may be still the case in 2011.

2- It reported the belief that the next president will come from the inner circle of family and military allies. In 2011, several members of the president's family and clan defected, and as such, the future candidate for succession may be one of them.

3- It explained the long rule of A.A. Saleh by its dependency upon a cornerstone called "tripartite alliance": two powerful men were mentioned in this context as part of a tribal-military "power sharing" arrangement written in 1978, following the assassination of President Al Ghashmi: Brigadier General Ali Mohsen Al Ahmar, and the late Sheikh Abdullah Al Ahmar, then in his three qualities as head of the Hashid Tribal Confederation, Speaker of Parliament and head of Yemen's largest opposition party, Islah. Today, in 2011, this very alliance is no longer available: A) Sadiq and Hamid, the sons of Sheikh Abdullah have both joined the opposition.

Hamid was a major supporter of the primary opposition candidate in the 2006 presidential election. In the summer of 2009, He appeared on Al Jazeera television and called on President Saleh to step down from his office. B) Brigadier General Ali Mohsen Al Ahmar has recently defected and joined the opposition.

4- The cable estimated that Mohsen "controls over 50 per cent" of Yemen's military resources and assets, which makes him "the second most powerful man in Yemen." However, what are the chances of Mohsen in the race for succession today? True, the opposition welcomed Mohsen support, but many among Northern Shi'ite rebels see him as a ruthless military leader who led the military campaign against them in a bloody civil war. Leftists and southerners worry that their goals for democracy will be overtaken in a military power struggle, while the Islamist opposition is thought to view Mohsen more favorably.

5- In 2005 the US diplomat did not see a potential rival matching Saleh. Today, it is no longer the case if we consider the fact that Ali Abdallah Saleh cannot deliver any more on the issue of stability viewed by the Americans as essential in the fight against Al Qaeda.

But most interesting is the scenario the 2005 cable imagined for 2013.

Given that many Western observers (US included) expressed their worries about the future of this country, whose population is often armed, with some regions believed to be offering Al Qaeda a "safe haven," the placidity of the US diplomats in 2005 is just amazing. We read for instance: "Despite weak institutions and submissive political parties, democracy has permeated Yemen enough that the public will expect to choose its next President in open elections."

Similarly, we find the 2006 EU Election Observation Mission Report pretty positive, describing Yemen "as the only country in the Arabian Peninsula to have representative democracy enshrined in its Constitution, Yemen has been widely regarded as an important potential model for the development of democracy in the region."

For the report, the elections were successful. Yet, does it make sense to say Yemen is a democracy relying on tribal-military power sharing? These positive assessments of Yemen's democracy are all the most amazing that one can hardly ignore that the country's history is troublesome and violent; and that Saleh himself played a major role since 1977 in the events which led to Ibrahim Al Hamdi's assassination (president since the coup of 1974), and Al Ghasmi's subsequent assumption of presidency. Eight months later, Al Ghashmi would be killed by a bomb and Saleh would take over.

Nonetheless, in the present situation, the country needs confidence in its institutions shaken by the brutal reactions of the regime, and without a democratic behavior, Yemen cannot progress. But who is more likely to influence the events?

The Congress party might choose another candidate in case Saleh is ousted. Would it be Ahmed Ali, the son of A.A. Saleh? Another eventual candidate is Brigadier General Ali Mohsen Al Ahmar, Commander of the Northeastern region, cited as the most powerful of the military elites. Is he still the man of the Congress party?

There is also a question about whether the opposition would unify and choose another personality, as it happened in 2006. The Joint Meeting Parties (JMP) covered the spectrum of opposition politics in Yemen including: the traditionalist Congregation for Reform Party ('Islah'), which is composed of various Islamic and tribal interest groups; the Yemeni Socialist Party (YSP), which formerly ruled South Yemen; and the Nasserite Unionist Party (NUP).

For the 2006 elections, the JMP announced common policies on political and economic reform and jointly selected Faisal Ben Shamlan as its presidential candidate.

Today, potential candidates of the opposition may include the second generation of Al Ahmars: Sadiq, the eldest of Sheikh Abdullah's ten sons, is the head of the family and may prove to be a key figure in the weeks and months ahead; and Hamid, who as head of the Al Ahmar group runs the family's considerable business empire.

Finally, although the ongoing revolutionary process may change the whole picture, we should all the same mention President Saleh's three nephews who hold senior positions in the military and intelligence services: Colonel Amar Saleh, Yahya Mohammed Abdullah Saleh, and Tariq Saleh. And let us not forget the president's half-brother, Ali Saleh Al Ahmar, commander of the Air Force.

And before and beyond all those people there are the youth who form the core of this revolution, and who, like in Egypt and Tunisia, would like to have a say about the future of their country.[1]

---

[1] The Gulf Today, April 2, 2011: http://gulftoday.ae/portal/963c1689-c08e-49ae-9c2a-416cf1c7c47f.aspx

13

# THE DILEMMA OVER LIBYA

Libya's events since the uprising put the international community on the rift and unveiled a dilemma: for the US and the West the question is: who would we be supporting in this internal conflict? That is not an issue of choosing between Qadhafi and his opponents, but rather between opponent and opponent, if it is possible to choose one's allies.

The lessons of Afghanistan and Iraq are still reminded. They say: Arm rebels without a clue about their doctrines and real objectives, and you will end up with them fighting you. Example: The Mujahidin that the USA trained and armed to fight the Soviet army later formed the core of Al Qaeda.

On the other hand, in Iraq, the Western allies who controlled the northern and southern no-fly zones did not move a finger when Saddam massacred the Kurds and the Shiites. The Iraqis did not forget it and they showed it when the US troops invaded in 2003 to finish the job with Saddam.

The situation in Libya created a movement towards military humanitarian intervention initiated by France, which was joined by the Western allies as well as by two Arab countries (Qatar and the UAE). The Arab League was first on their side, but its Secretary General shifted position since and showed dissatisfaction, for a good reason: Mr. Amru Moussa is preparing to run for President in Egypt and needs to be labeled "pro-foreign military interventions" almost as much as a monkey needs to be lectured on eating bananas.

However, all the Libyan opposition leaders who were interviewed on TV recently criticized the reluctance of NATO's countries either to intervene more powerfully or to arm them. They also held Erdogan's Turkey as responsible for NATO's difficulties.

Yet, the dilemma is still there: what are the limits of NATO's intervention? Should it take sides and be part of the conflict?

If NATO's leaders did not intend to take sides, it is anyway too late. Since the first day, it was understood that the military intervention was not in favor of Qadhafi, and thus it did take sides.

It is pointless and almost impossible to disguise the fact that NATO's intervention in Libya (the UN actually) may make the difference and force Qadhafi to give up. Although it is UN backed, in internal conflicts – as Stratfor's G. Freedman made the point – "the challenge of the intervention is to protect human rights without undermining national sovereignty or the right of national self-determination."

Nonetheless, "those intervening can claim to be carrying out a neutral humanitarian action, but in reality, they are intervening on one side's behalf. If the intervention is successful — as it likely will be given that interventions are invariably by powerful countries against weaker ones — the practical result is to turn the victims into victors. By doing that, the humanitarian warriors are doing more than simply protecting the weak. They are also defining a nation's history."

The modern international system is founded on the premise that external involvement in the internal affairs of sovereign states is not accepted. Yet, this idea is increasingly opposed by the right of civilians to be protected from harm.

Military responses to politically induced humanitarian crises in northern Iraq in 1991, in Bosnia and Herzegovina, Somalia, Rwanda and Kosovo, and in East Timor in 1999 expressed the concern of many governments and the United Nations, although responses to mass killing were often inadequate to provide full and timely protection.

Despite the mistrust from some countries and organizations, human security as a justification for military intervention is gaining widespread acceptance.

At the September 2005 World Summit, the General Assembly of the UN endorsed the concept of "the sovereign responsibility to protect civilians, including by using force as a last resort against states that do not live up to that responsibility" (Resolution 59/314, 26 Oct. 2005).

Today, we have moved beyond the question of whether military intervention is morally justified; the questions remaining unanswered relate to the "tactical" forms and "timing" of interventions.

In Libya, the problem is obvious: on the one hand, there is a blood-thirsty dictator  who, having nothing to lose any more, seems ready to take the country to the most dreadful civil war, which may last long years and profit only to the weapons merchants. On the other, we see the opposition that grew into armed rebellion and seems also ready to fight to the last man for freedom and dignity.

In this conflict, the Libyan opposition forced to lead an armed struggle against a super-armed tyrant has the absolute right to ask for aid and assistance. Objections of some Arab and Muslim leaders and organizations against the intervention of "foreign countries" in Libya is blurring the limits between the justified fear of imperialist hold and the unreasonable backing of a tyrannical rule against the will of the people for the sake of "anti-imperialism."

The point is military humanitarian intervention is a "short-term activity with limited political objectives. It is intended only to stop the worst suffering. It is not intended to establish a lasting peace or to put a new, or renewed, political system in place, although it can establish a basis for peace-building by creating an environment in which people can think about more than mere survival."

The question those who oppose the military humanitarian intervention should answer is: "would we like to see a quarter or more of the Libyan population murdered and Qadhafi and his sons triumphant and justifying their crimes with our own arguments: i.e. national security of the sovereign state?" For this is exactly what will happen in case the humanitarian intervention is stopped.

Lastly, as military operations of this kind may involve collateral damages, a reasonable prospect of success should then be assessed: if an intervention is not likely to do more good than harm from a humanitarian point of view, it cannot be justified in humanitarian terms.[1]

---

[1] The Gulf Today, April 9, 2011: http://gulftoday.ae/portal/9116c0cb-d373-4a42-88df-891335ed7d08.aspx

14

# INDEPENDENTLY OF THE WESTERN WILL

The yearly report of the Centre for Security Studies (CSS- ETH Zurich) titled "Strategic Trends 2011" made some remarks about the ongoing situation in the Middle East and the global and regional power shifts. The overall picture emerging from this analysis is that a "new multi-polar international order is gradually emerging that is marked by diversity, a lack of leadership, and potentially growing instability."

In this new order, emerging economies will not be dependent on the West. The US and the EU still suffering from economic hardships are already lacking the resources and the political will to provide global stability. The divergences about the Libyan issue are a symptom of a crisis, which stays largely unscrutinized. The domestic problems may hinder Europe from playing a major political role abroad. In France, we already see people going live with questions like: how are we going to pay the costs of our intervention in Libya? Or, why are we "obliged" to interfere in the Côte d'Ivoire, in Libya, and in Afghanistan? The distrust that these military interventions arise is also related to doubts about the ability of the legislature to keep these expenditures in check, for unlike the USA, where the Congress can block any budget, the French system accords more prerogatives to the President.

But money apart, the issue is also about the changing dynamics in a region upon which the Western economies are still dependent. In this regard, three observations should be made:

1- These are not anti-American, anti-Western revolutions:

The above-mentioned report acknowledged that the 2011 "surprising" upheavals emphasized the profound cleavages between the rulers and the ruled. But the point underlined concerns the USA whose influence as "the regional hegemon of past decades" is seen in decline, and the reason explaining such a decline is: "these domestically-driven secular revolts."

Yet, the CSS report failed to give evidence of such a decline or of how to link the two phenomena. Actually, I did not observe the least anti-American slogan in these uprisings, contrarily to the Mullahs in Iran who, since the first day, pretended that the Arab revolutions were following their model, since they were "Islamic" revolutions "against the great Satan." Obviously, they did not understand the Youth in Iran; how could they understand the Arabs? In Tunisia, the demonstrators raised Obama's slogan: "Yes, we can." The Egyptians, the Yemeni, the Syrians, and the Libyans who continue their fight for freedom, are aware they are not fighting the US but their own oppressive regimes.

2- These are not remote-control revolutions:
I read some amazingly naive or completely vicious pieces alleging that the Arab revolutions have been planned long ago by the CIA with the complicity of Julian Assange and WikiLeaks. In Beirut last month, I had had an argument with Dr. Azmi Bishara who thought I was defending this "conspiratorial" point of view, according to which all the new technology of social networks enjoyed by the youth and everybody would fall under the category: "agit-prop instruments" controlled by the CIA to foment trouble in the Arab world. But I was not actually. How could I? I even find these speculations complete nonsense. I mean, come on: did the CIA program Mohamed Bouazizi to set himself afire? Has the CIA ever heard about Sidi Bouzid, or Kasserine, or all the obscure Tunisian villages that even the petit bourgeois of Tunis do not know where or how they are, or what their people do, because they just made no news before the uprising? And so may be said about the events in Egypt or Yemen. What is the American interest in toppling a good "friend" like Mubarak or making trouble to Ali Abdallah Saleh who was handling the Al Qaeda issue with the American military? Even the Libyan crazy colonel was already "aligned" and cash was flowing from Tripoli to the US and Britain and the relations were back and prospering. Who is enough mad in

Washington DC to topple such rulers with whom business is "safe"?

The point is that if the Americans could not even handle properly the transition to democracy in Afghanistan and Iraq while they were – maybe still – in charge and supported with thousands of troops, how could they remotely control Arab streets? If this is what the CSS report intended by "waning influence," then yes, but in these specific limits: the USA has nothing to do with the Arab uprisings. That does not mean they are not anxious now about where the region is heading and who would be the people in charge?

3- The Gulf region is not immune. Yet, the changes do not depend on the West.

If the West is unable to control what happened in Egypt, considering its role in the Arab-Israeli relations, how about controlling the Gulf?

The CSS report pointed to "the most vulnerable authoritarian Arab regimes" as "the old Arab Nationalist republics." Most of them are situated in North Africa, but the Near East is included: Yemen and Syria are outstanding examples. This is indeed a point of agreement between the observers. These republics are bungled and plagued with a wide array of flaws. Yet, is the Arab Gulf region immune against upheavals? Certainly not. And the report asserts that "the Gulf monarchies will likely be able to weather this storm." When we ask: how? The only answer the report could provide is: "offer tactical concessions along the way to quell the Arab street." What does that mean in practice? No answer. The issue is left to the judgment of the local elite.

However, the point is made when the report emphasizes that "unless you are willing to put democracy above interests in the most critical oil-producing region in the world," changing the guard in the Arab Gulf by "inviting further unrest is a risk that few regional or external players would want."

"Inviting further unrest" is not the correct expression we should use in the present situation, though. Nobody invited people to demonstrate in those countries, because nobody controls the streets, unless it is the rulers, and their own policies and police.

Anyway, it is definitely obvious that the Arabs cannot expect to have the right answers to their problems from the West. The West can give advice based on its experience (and it is worthwhile) and necessarily linked to its interests. But today, the Arabs are maybe on their own for the first time in modern history, independently of the Western will.[1]

---

[1] The Gulf Today, April 16, 2011: http://gulftoday.ae/portal/128aa18b-3ea9-4d91-8a34-1c47c8922722.aspx

15

# SECTARIAN DIVIDE

It seems that Iran has enormously profited from the upheaval in the Arab countries at least in one aspect: it has eased the international pressure regarding its nuclear program and maybe removed the shadow of war.

In his memoirs (Decision Points), former US President G.W. Bush said that in dealing with Iran he faced three options:

1- Negotiate directly with Mr Ahmadinejad, which he believes "would legitimize him and his views and dispirit Iran's freedom movement."

2- "Multilateral diplomacy conducted with both carrots and sticks."

3- A "military strike on Iran's nuclear facilities."

Apparently, Bush was leaning toward the third option, as he acknowledged, but was thwarted when a "National Intelligence Estimate" produced in 2007 reported that there was no active nuclear weapons program. He did not hide his disappointment and cast doubts on the report.

WikiLeaks diplomatic cables have made public what was intended to remain in the secret vaults of diplomacy, as they showed the tension preceding the wave of protests in the Arab world that caught the attention of the whole globe, and the signs interpretable either as conducive to a war against Iran, or to a proliferation of nuclear programs in the region. Comment from pundits and observers about an "Arab-American conspiracy" against Iran and an Iranian conspiracy against the Arabs filled up the TV shows and the press columns. As the Obama administration was still reluctant to make another presidential doctrine out of another war, Israel seemed well designated and even happy to strike Iran, betting on the rising fear of the Arab leaders regarding Iran's intentions.

At such a time, a series of uprisings burst out and Mr Ahmadinejad was just too happy to welcome those who - involuntarily - relieved him from his greatest worries: to give up the nuclear ambitions or to face war.

That was not for the time being the least advantage, though frail, to be added to some previous. Over the past three decades, the Islamic Republic of Iran has shown remarkable endurance. It has survived an eight-year war with Iraq, mounting economic sanctions, and serious domestic unrest. It has benefited from the missteps of adversaries, which have created opportunities for Iran to expand ties to militant movements in Iraq, Lebanon, and the Palestinian territories, and to increase its influence in Afghanistan. Then came the Arab uprisings, and the pressure on Iran started to fall until it almost vanished.

The last developments concern the Gulf region itself, where Iran is accused of pulling the strings, behind the curtains, on a background of espionage (Kuwait), street protests (Bahrain), and politics (Iraq).

Prime Minister Nouri al-Maliki has reportedly made statements considered hostile to GCC on March 19, in Baghdad, and on March 26 iterated that "Bahrain is different from both Libya and Egypt. Now the issue has become a Sunnite-Shiite (conflict). The intervention of Arab troops qualified as Sunnites to support the Sunnite Bahraini government made the Shiites feel they are besieged by Sunnites" (al-Sharq al-Awsat, April 13, 2011.)

Whereas one cannot condone violent repression for any reason, it is also fair to observe that the statement of the Iraqi prime minister was irresponsible insofar as he has no means to know and assert that the "Dir' Al-Jazeera" forces were Sunnites or Shiites or both. Assumedly, these forces were Sunnites, as it is indeed the case in many Arab countries with a Sunnite majority, how can we be sure that the conflict is between Shiites and

Sunnites in Bahrain? Why should we stress the sectarian divide every time we have to analyze politics in the Middle East?

That such a discourse might have been introduced by Western powers in the imperialist period seeking a way to share the spoils of the Ottoman Empire between them, and finding their "happy opportunity" in the ethnical and religious mosaic of the region, would not even brush the mind of the Iraqi prime minister. (I advise him to read T.E. Lawrence again).

To assert that the conflict in Bahrain was about Shiism and Sunnism, while it is actually a political issue concerning participation and power representation for citizens, whatsoever their religious creeds, expressed plainly a sectarian view of the political world, good for medieval politics and Western imperialism, not modern national statehood.

This attitude led to the GCC demand for cancelling the Arab summit expected to meet in Baghdad in May 10-11, 2011.

The justification is: the GCC countries and several others refuse to make of an Arab summit a sectarian Sunni-Shiite confrontation.

Unfortunately, Iraq has not bypassed the sectarian views of politics and policy-making. Here too, one may speak of the Iranian influence deeply felt. Barbara Slavin pointed to Iran playing "a pivotal role in the formation of Iraqi governments since 2005" and recently helping to keep "Prime Minister Nouri al-Maliki in power despite the better showing of Iyad Allawi's secular Iraqiya party in the March 2010 elections."

However, although aware of the misgivings about him and his Da'wa party, Mr Al-Maliki had shown his own mistrust toward Iran in talks with US diplomats, unveiled by WikiLeaks, as well as in his behaviour toward other pro-Iranian Shiite organizations, he failed to keep a cogent attitude.

As more and more analyses show, the Bush administration since the first years of Iraq occupation has empowered the pro-Iranian Shiite parties and played on the sectarian divide lines to have the upper hand in the country. Creating havoc by dismantling the Iraqi army, and destroying the structures of the centralised state, was made possible through "debaathification" and the replacement of modern notions of polity and citizenship by medieval sectarian alignment (Sunnites, Shiites, Christians, etc...)

To be sure, Iranians and Arabs have a lot to reproach to each other. But the dichotomy Shiite/Sunnite, Muslim/Christian, Arab/Kurd, has been largely artificially created to keep the peoples of the Middle East under domination.

Modern politics as well as the needs of their own peoples advise them to minimise these antagonisms and consider that their differences are exactly what make their human wealth. Iran has to be more reassuring toward its neighbours and explain its policies.

To move forward, Iranians and Arabs should accept each other's differences and open a large debate that may only enrich them and keep their region away from absurd conflicts and war.[1]

---

[1] The Gulf Today, April 23, 2011: http://gulftoday.ae/portal/d01ef90b-e678-481f-893f-95f10728941e.aspx

# 16

# RELIGION AND POLITICS

There seems to be an assumption that the recent uprisings shaking the Middle East region might bypass the "Islamist" wave called "Neo-Fundamentalism" in the eighties and the nineties of the last century, whose backbone was a resuscitation of the old views of Ibn Taymiyya and a new mix with ideas from Rashid Rida, Hasan al-Banna, Seyyed Qutb, Abu al-Ala al Mawdudi, and other thinkers.

*Foreign Affairs magazine* published on April 26, 2011, an article by Asef Bayat titled "the Post-Islamist Revolutions," suggesting that what happened in the Arab world might bypass the "Islamism" of the eighties and the nineties. It is an interesting point of view.

But how can we know that the Islamist wave is over?

If the Arab protests so far do not concern the enforcement of religious laws, but positive laws and respect of Human Rights and construction of transparent democracies, who can guarantee that the secular democratic views will not be deviated in the future?

True, the protesters did not demand the application of the Shari'a or the establishment of a theocratic state, but to live in a modern democracy, with equal rights and duties to all citizens, and nobody above the law.

Therefore, we may call them "Post-Islamist revolutions," but not in the sense given to the expression by Asef Bayat.

The latter argues that "Post-Islamism is not anti-Islamic or secular; a Post-Islamist movement dearly upholds religion but also highlights citizens' rights. It aspires to a pious society within a democratic state."

We may retort that this is not an encompassing definition, able to explain the phenomenon of Arab revolts to which Bayat linked it. These revolts may be Post-Islamist, in our view, insofar that they bring a different solution to the Arab crisis than the one proposed by Islamism, and represented by the slogan of the Egyptian Muslim Brotherhood (and several others in Arab countries): "Islam is The Solution."

For Seyyed Qutb and other Islamist theorists, the motto means: Neither capitalism, nor socialism. Neither liberal democracy, nor communism. Islam can (in his view) solve all our political, social, cultural, and economic problems.

So far, the Arab revolutions have distanced themselves from this discourse. Thus, if they are not deviated from their course (on the assumption that all revolutions have been betrayed) they may bring about a new democratic, pluralistic, and liberal project of society, thus encompassing a wide range of political movements from the right to the left. This is what I call: Post-Islamist revolutions. With such a concept, we may then further scrutinize and analyze these movements and eventually figure out their problems and assess their future.

However, the examples Bayat gave underline the Islamist orientation of the movements more than their post-Islamism. Actually, he included "the reform movement in Iran in the late 1990s and the country's Green Movement today, Indonesia's Prosperous Justice Party, Egypt's Hizb al-Wasat, Morocco's Justice and Development Party (PJD), and Turkey's ruling Justice and Development Party (AKP)." Bayat thinks that each of these movements was initially fundamentalist, but over time, it changed and came to criticize the excess of its theses, "its violation of democratic rights, and its use of religion as a tool to sanctify political power," with eventually the acceptance to "work within the democratic state."

Though interesting, this opinion is flawed, maybe even tricky, for several reasons:

1- Bayat wanted to explain the meaning of the Arab world revolutions, but none of these movements has had any weight in them.

2 - The Islamist parties that took part to the revolutions, joined them after they started, like all other opposition parties. They did not trigger them, but tried to recuperate them. The

absence of Islamist slogans during the protests is evidence that Islamists were bypassed.

3- The argument of Bayat is paradoxical. For the movements he called Post-Islamist are still Islamist. We hardly need to explain the difference between "Islamist" and "Islamic." Yet, let's remind people that while all political movements in the Muslim world (included the secular) claim to be Islamic, since they are inheritors of this cultural patrimony, only the "Islamists" present a project of society based on the return to a strict appliance of "Shari'a" in our life, coupled with a world-view largely based on medieval clerical politics.

4- Though it is acknowledged that some of them criticized their former stances, they did that only under an immense pressure from their opponents or to avoid being forbidden. Yet, they came back under different denominations. But did they really change out of conviction or out of tactics...just to be in the game and reach power?

5- Did these movements really criticize the "use of religion as a tool to sanctify political power," as Bayat suggests? I very much doubt it. For if they did, that would be the very definition of hypocrisy, as they are still using religion to sanctify or condemn political power.

Finally, I think that even with the collapse of police-regimes in North Africa and the looming fateful defeat of others in the Near East, the Islamist militant movements that were victims of those regimes, just as secular opposition parties were as well, have no guarantee that they would be tomorrow's winners. All their thought, their strategy and tactics, were shaped in the autocratic period, with the clear objective of toppling the dictatorial regimes and taking over. In an open society, they miss everything future statesmen should have: a rational project of society and a rational program of government, able to win the minds and the hearts of the voters.

Yet, if rationality gave its sense of orientation to modern politics, we would not have had in the self-proclaimed first democracy of the world the kind of coalition that brought to power George W. Bush, half of which were Christian fundamentalists.[1]

---

[1] The Gulf Today, April 30, 2011: http://gulftoday.ae/portal/1d7fb436-1205-4054-921f-022ef1f1d60e.aspx

# 17

# LEGITIMACY

Osama bin Laden has been killed between two deadly suicide bombings: the first, on April 28, at a café in Marrakesh (15 dead); and the second, at a paramilitary force academy in northwest Pakistan on May 13 (69 dead). Whatever the reason behind both operations, the terrorists find it "legitimate" to assassinate people, unknown to them, because so is their belief!

Identifying the sources of radicalism has always been a problematic issue.

I make an assumption: so far, most European and American researchers have lingered at the description of radical groups without linking their analysis to the institutional channelling of legitimacy in authoritarian states. Some have explained the cause of Islamist violence, for example, by such things as injustice, poverty, lack of democracy, even hatred of the West. All this may be true. Yet, I think the most important factor relates to another issue: legitimacy.

Indeed, ruling elites and Islamist opposition have been passing the buck by making higher bids on the Koran as a source of legitimacy- an issue upon which most «secular-leaning » powers in the region do not intend to be second to anybody, especially their opposition. All claim an unwavering loyalty to Islam, which they take as a basis of the constitution if they do not proclaim the Koran itself as the constitution...

Violence is the result of a discussion of the deaf especially in the absence of the political framework for open debate: i.e.democracy.

From Afghanistan to Morocco, via Pakistan, Iraq, Saudi Arabia, Iran, Yemen, Egypt, Algeria, Tunisia, etc … the leaders and the theorists of modern Islamism have always raised the question: who is best able to govern Muslims and in what consists his legitimacy?

To this question, the authorities have always made up roughly the same answer: we are legitimate because we are Muslims (meaning no less Muslims than them). In fact, apart from Lebanon (where power is shared between a Christian, a Sunni and a Shiite), all other countries define Islam as the religion of the state. However, in the history of the Muslim world, the question of legitimacy has been raised before or during any conflict for power. This problem arose immediately after the death of Prophet Muhammad and has led to violent conflicts and certainly millions of deaths throughout history. This is the source of the first ideological division between Shiites and Sunnites.Today; we still find the issue of legitimacy behind all conflicts for power in the MENA region, with different ideological and political cleavages.

Ideology is a system of shared beliefs that intervenes in the action, integration and social stability, although not necessarily based on truth. In predominantly Muslim countries of the MENA region, ideology has several functions including that of the legitimation of power. But since these are mostly authoritarian states, a conflictual situation remains lurking in the underneath until, through accumulation of little and more important events, it becomes unbearable and the most banal incident may spark riots giving way to the open break out of the conflict. Meanwhile, confronted with all kinds of repressive behavior the ideology of the opposition may easily slide into radicalism and violence becomes then an answer to the state violence.

In democratic countries, conflicts are not ruled out; they exist. But they are managed through democratic mechanisms of social and political control. Conspicuous among them is the public debate open to everybody including political and social actors. The themes are often: social unrest, rising prices, inflation, wages, pensions, social insurance, and in some cases, broader issues affecting local economies, such as the Dollar and the Euro, the recession, etc ... This debate has parameters that meet the expectations of the public in democratic countries. When there is a slide towards violence in the street (as sometimes happens), they remain isolated and rarely go beyond their scope to encompass the entire society. Furthermore, although Europe has produced some of the greatest revolutions in history, « radical »literature calling for violence and armed rebellion against the system remains marginal and rarely has an effect on social movements.

This is not the case in the authoritarian states of the MENA.

First, the deficiency of democracy excludes the debate. Then it seems that the conflict rather than focusing on the legitimate social and political demands, as it happens in Western democracies, tends on the contrary to affect the very foundation of the political system : its legitimacy.

Indeed, in countries with Muslim majority, the hardline fundamentalist opposition often seeks to undermine the legitimacy doctrine of the regime by comparing it with its own ideological benchmarks considered as sources of recognized authority : Specific interpretation of Islamic law (Sharia) in first position ; and sovereignty (as measured by the degree of independence vis-à-vis the Western powers).These two themes are quasi-linked. In any case, they are so in Islamist literature.

Of course, there are other trends of opposition apart from the Islamists. But their influence has been limited, so far. The reason is that authoritarian regimes allow an opposition to be active only to a certain degree: as long as it does not threaten the interests of the power elite. Once this opposition becomes too troublesome, it is either brought back to order by some repressive measures targeting its symbols and its assets, or outright forbidden, almost always with a masquerade referring to the legislation.

There is throughout the MENA region a paradox between freedom and democracy, consisting in erecting « democratic » institutions while emptying them of their substance : this goes from legislations violating basic rights and freedoms, through servile parliaments taking their orders from the executive, NGOs directly or indirectly managed by governments, trade unions defending the interests of employers and government instead of employees, media turning into spokespeople for the rulers, not to mention the legacy of power in « republics » from father to son.

The absence of mass political movements able to be in charge of the struggle for freedom is significant. It is noteworthy that neither Pan-Arabism (Nasserite and Baathist) nor the Islamist movements that have succeeded it have made freedom a priority.

Today, freedom is the song chanted by everybody on the Arab streets, from Tunis to Sana'a, and from Cairo to Damascus...

This hope of freedom seems like a light in a dark and long tunnel for the Arab people. Should it go off, we will spend another half-century (or more) in darkness, wondering about our own legitimacy to exist in history.[1]

---

[1] The Gulf Today, May 21, 2011: http://gulftoday.ae/portal/1f53dfda-d50a-446f-95b6-a737132dfb78.aspx

18

# THE YEMENI REVOLUTION:
# REPLACING ALI ABDULLAH SALEH
# OR REPLACING OBSOLETE INSTITUTIONS?

When the Yemeni uprising broke out, it appeared to follow the same model that had begun in Tunisia: a series of social protests that became a political movement once the opposition parties joined the spontaneous youth revolt, followed by the emergence of a program for democratic reform. But the situation in Yemen has become slightly different.

President Ali Abdullah Saleh, despite very few qualms about his electoral majority in 2006, decided to follow the dictator's handbook and interfere in the country's laws, and perhaps in its constitution, introducing changes that would enable him to retain power - despite the fact that this would upset established balances - and then pass it on to his son. This is what led the opposition parties to confront him and ally themselves with Yemeni youths, forming a movement that has been demanding the resignation of the president since day one of the protests.

This paper examines the effects of the crisis that led to the revolt, and interrogates possible alternatives: will the replacement be democratic, military, tribal, a mixture of all three, or something else altogether? In other words, are the protesters seeking to replace individuals, or institutions? [1]

- <u>Introduction</u>
- <u>The role of the opposition parties in the Yemeni revolution</u>
- <u>The US Embassy in Yemen and corruption</u>
- <u>The US Embassy in Yemen and the succession</u>
- <u>The West and democracy in Yemen</u>
- <u>The goals of the revolution</u>
- <u>Tribalism or citizenship?</u>
- <u>To what should we pay attention?</u>
- <u>Conclusion and results</u>

## Introduction

Yemen is a unique case in the ongoing Arab revolutions. For example, the Yemeni regime is facing demands for its fall raised by many of those who until recently were some of its closest allies. However, this is not even the main difference: the main difference is that, in this case, we are dealing with a "tribal democracy," a form of government not quite related to either modern democracy or traditional tribalism. The Yemeni president is elected and has represented the majority since 2006, unlike former presidents Zine al-Abidine Ben Ali (Tunisia) and Hosni Mubarak (Egypt), both of whom were accused of widespread vote rigging. If Saleh's removal from power would end the struggle and place Yemen on the path to democracy, this would suggest that the solution were simple. Yet democracy is more than just replacing the ruler; above all, it is a system based on respect for certain basic premises, one

---

[1] I am indebted to Dr. Azmi Bishara, who read this paper and provided a number of criticisms and questions that drove me to re-examine my perspective. In truth, these comments were absolutely timely, because had the paper been published in its initial version, it would have missed out on the issue of the developing role of the Taghyir Square youth, and the subsequent development of the opposition demands from abstract stances that seemed to be negotiating for a power transfer, to deeper positions demanding democratic change and a modern state.

of which is that no one is above the law. The Yemeni system that Saleh has headed since 1990 is based on a power-sharing agreement among the president, the tribes allied to him, and the army. This is not really a rational understanding of modern democracy. If the aims of the current revolution were simply to remove a person and replace him with another while the regime continued on the same bases, then not much would change once that individual was gone.

Let us begin by specifying some issues that should receive the attention of the relevant political forces during the revolution and after the prospective end of Saleh's rule. In my opinion, Yemen faces two kinds of problems: those that are socio-political and those that are socio-economic. The second variety seems more pressing and is more interesting, since it relates to a number of worrisome and mutually exacerbating factors. Unemployment is growing, at least 42% of the population already lives on less than USD 2 a day, and many sectors of society suffer from unfair distribution of water resources, all of which contributes to vast amounts of social suffering, particularly among children - and now an explosive demographic situation is making matters even worse.[1] All of these are factors that lead to explosive anger and tension.

The first set of problems is more complicated, principally due to Yemen's social makeup. This matter is related to the following issues: overlapping and/or conflicting loyalties (to the tribe, the clan, or the state); a lack of transparency in appointments and positions, which leads to the marginalization of certain social groups; and paucities of transparency and accountability, both of which lead to corruption. Perhaps even more dangerously, the country suffers from a pronounced lack of modernization, which is essential to the creation of a modern, democratic society; consequently, this has led to an increased military and tribal presence.

---

[1] The opposition's initial demands in February 2011 included some social and economic issues, which the state authorities truly need to address. However, the opposition's demands in March and the beginning of April focused on political aspects and revolutionary reforms. For a discussion of the social and economic issues, see the United Nations Development Fund's report for 2010 "Yemen Report, 2010," *Millennium Development Goals,* UNDP, http://www.undp.org.ye.

In this paper, I will focus on the first problem (i.e., on Yemen's socio-political issues, which are related to issues of modernization in the Middle East with which some scholars have already dealt).

Theoretically, this paper places itself within the same critical discourse as Burhan Ghalioun,[1] Azmi Bishara,[2] Halim Barakat,[3] Khaldoun Hassan al-Naqib,[4] Hisham Sharabi, and Saadeddine Ibrahim, as well as others who have studied the problems of modernity and the modernization of society in the Arab world. This paper is also indebted to the work of David Apter,[5] Freeman,[6] Dale Eickelman,[7] Carl Brown,[8] and the "school of action theory" in the social sciences.[9]

This paper emerges from the idea that a limited understanding of the role of the tribe in Arab societies has led to unbelievable and unacceptable conclusions, such as the belief that, "in situations where the tribe (which was divided into branches and divisions) represented an independent unit, then the tribal Arab region must

---

[1]Some of Burhan Ghalioun's publications include, Al-Mihna al-Arabiyya:al-Dawla dudd al-Umma [The Arab Challenge: The Nation vs. The Umma], (Beirut: Markaz Dirasat al-Wihda al-'Arabiyya, 1993); al-Hadatha al-Maghdura [Wasted Modernity], (Paris: La Découverte, 1993); al-Wa'i al-Dhati [Self Awareness], (Beirut: al-Mu'assassa al-'Arabiyya li-l-Dirasat wa-l-Nashr, 1992).

[2] See, for example, Azmi Bishara, Turuhat 'an an-Nahda al-Mu'aqa [Propositions about the Stunted Renaissance], (Beirut: Riad al-Rayyis li-l-Kutub wa-l-Nashr, 2003).

[3] See, for example, Halim Barakat, al-Mujtama' al-'Arabi al-Mu'asir [Contemporary Arab Society], (Beirut: Markaz Dirasat al-Wihda al-'Arabiyya, 2008).

[4] See Khaldun Hassan al-Naqib, al-Mujtama' wa-l-Dawla fi al-Khalij wa-l-Jazeera al-'Arabiyya [Society and the State in the Gulf and the Arab Peninsula], (Beirut: Markaz Dirasat al-Wihda al-'Arabiyya, 1989).

[5] David E. Apter, The Politics of Modernization, (Chicago: University of Chicago Press, 1967).

[6] L.C. Freeman, Patterns of Local Community Leadership, (Indianapolis: Bobbs-Merrill, 1968).

[7] Eickelman Dale F., *The Middle East, an Anthropological Approach,* (Prentice-Hall, Inc. 1981).

[8] Carl L. Brown, International Politics and the Middle East, (Princeton University Press, 1984).

[9] In particular, Talcott Parsons, Edward Shills, and Jesse Pitts,*Theories of Society*, (The Free Press, 1961); see also, Talcott Parsons, *The Structure of Social System*, (Routledge & Kegan Paul, 1951).

be imagined as a place of chaos.[1] In a more contemporary period, we note that anthropologists and ethnographers discuss the tribal issue either as a "state institution," or as a "force that opposes the state," or as "groups that contribute to the formation of social and political cohesion on the local levels."[2] In short, as Khaldun Naqib points out, the result is that "tribal organizations are portrayed as established and powerful, and anyone who opposes them appears to be ineffectual, creating social and economic structures that lack any clear historical roots."[3]

It is clear that "systems do not rely on abstract social phenomena when facing sensitive issues such as controlling the military."[4] Each regime develops its own ways of achieving control, in which the leader tries to protect himself from officers with political ambitions, and "these methods differ depending on the level of political maturity that the particular regime has reached, so some of them resort to tribes, or sects, or even to mercenaries, while others use manipulative strategies that reach into patrimonial roots and histories; yet, others seek to rely on institutions, and we, sometimes, find governments that resort to more than one method," depending on their needs.[5]

Undoubtedly, the success of democracy in a country like Yemen will require an extreme effort on the part of the elite in order to move beyond the tribal era and old tensions. It also needs to proceed intelligently in order to acquire popular support through mechanisms that do not limit opportunities for anyone. The elite, which lead the change, must remain attentive to the difference between agents and objects in politics and society.

---

[1] R.B. Serjeant, "The Interplay Between Tribal Affinities and Religious (Zaydi) Authority in the Yemen,, *Al-Abhath: Journal of the Center for Arab and Middle East Studies*, Faculty of Arts and Sciences, American University of Beirut, 1982.
[2] Nelida Fuccaro, *Histories of City and State in the Persian Gulf: Manama since 1800,* (Cambridge University Press, 2009):20.
[3] Khaldun Naqib, *op. Cit.* p. 22.
[4] James A. Bill and Robert Springborg, *Middle East Politics*, (Harper Collins Publishers, 1990, 260-261).
[5] Ibid.

## The role of the opposition parties in the Yemeni revolution

Unlike in Tunisia and Egypt, where the events that led to the revolution and the fall of the ruler were spontaneous, and where the protesters' demands were social at the beginning, the revolution in Yemen was motivated by political factors.[1] Several analyses have indicated this,[2] such as a recent report presented to the US Congress.[3] It is worth noting that the Yemeni opposition parties, even before the revolts in Egypt and Tunisia had started, had already expressed strong disapproval over President Saleh's plans to modify the electoral law, to create a new Higher Commission for Elections and Referendums, and perhaps to modify the constitution to allow himself another chance to run; the opposition's anger was inflamed, too, by his apparent ambition to pass power onto his son.[4] The Yemeni opposition protests began on January 16 (i.e., two days after Ben Ali's fall in Tunisia) and gained more weight and popularity with the passing of time, especially after important elements of the political and military elites joined the protesters, and more schisms and resignations occurred within the regime, including members of the president's

---

[1] This matter becomes clear when we recall the arrests of Yemeni opposition protesters as early as the first days of the protests, which did not happen in Tunisia, where the opposition seemed to be as shocked by the breakout of protests as the government was. We know that human rights activist Tukal Karman, a leadership figure in the Islah party, was arrested for her role in organizing the student protests that broke out on January 16. We find that the Joint Meeting group led a protest in Sanaa on January 24, in response to a speech by Saleh. See, "Student Protests Continue for a Second Week," http://www.al-tagheer.com/news26185.html.

[2] See, for example, this passage from *The New York Times*: "unlike Egypt, peaceful protesters in Yemen were not led by young people, but by opposition parties, particularly Islamist ones." Anthony Shadid, Nada Bakri, Kareem Fahim and Liam Stack, "Waves of Unrest Spread to Yemen, Shaking a Region,"*The New York Times,* January 27, 2011, http://www.nytimes.com/2011/01/28/world/middleeast/28unrest.html.

[3] Jeremy Sharp, "Yemen: Background and U.S.Relations," March 3, 2011, CRS Report to Congress: http://www.fas.org/sgp/crs/mideast/RL34170.pdf.

[4] Indeed, one only needs to recall some of the slogans raised in those days, such as "No bringing the clock back to zero, no to passing on to your children"; "Revolution, revolution, oh young people", "Jobs for your friends"; "Oh Yemeni people, learn a lesson from Tunisia"; "I swear, I swear, you leader, that your rule will end"; "Ali, your time has come, we will throw you off the throne."

family and some of his allies, especially after the regime brutally cracked down on peaceful protests.

The question that now needs to be answered is about succession. This is not a new subject in any case, since it is easy to find examples in Yemeni political discourse and in leaked American assessments of the situation that discuss what would happen if the president suddenly died, resigned or was forced from power. These assessments were contained in diplomatic cables issued by the US Embassy in Sana'a in 2005, (and later published by the WikiLeaks website) at a time when Saleh - like Mubarak and Ben Ali - was considered an ally of Washington.

## The US Embassy in Yemen and corruption

According to one of the aforementioned cables, in 2005 officials close to Saleh confessed to the US ambassador in Sana'a that the regime was facing one of two options: "Either resignation, or collaborating together to force the government to fight corruption and bring in reforms."[1] The cable reveals how Saleh's coterie assessed the president: "[He] is more interested in enriching his family than in making the strategic choices necessary to lead Yemen into the future." From the confidences of Yemeni officials with direct contacts with the US Embassy, it appears that President Saleh was "more and more isolated, and less and less responsive to advice" offered to him by members of his close personal circle whom the cable describes as "practical progressives". Saleh "listens to no-one," and is "unrealistically and stupidly confident"; he always makes the correct decisions, the ambassador's source was quoted as saying. The cable's language and tone recalls similar communications from the US Embassy in Tunis, which went into considerable detail about the corruption of Ben Ali, his family and his cronies.

The same cable reports accusations of corruption against Saleh, his family and his inner circle, including allegations against Brigadier General Ali Mohsen al-Ahmar, commander of the

---

[1] Cable sent on February 23, 2005, http://213.251.145.96/cable/2005/05/05SANAA1352.html.

Yemeni Army in the crucial Northern sector, and the tribe of late Sheikh Abdullah bin Hussein al-Ahmar, who had been speaker of Parliament and head of the Islah ("Reform") party, as well as leader of the Hashid tribe, prior to his death in 2007. All of this was said - and recorded - prior to the 2006 elections, during which Ali Saleh announced he would not run - before later changing his mind.

## The US Embassy in Yemen and the succession

A second cable from the US Embassy in Sana'a[1] is more specific and detailed about the issue of Saleh's successor. First, it confirms, "true power still derives from the military and the tribes, and the next [p]resident would have to meet with their approval." This reality does not appear to have changed since that time. As we continue to hear news about more tribes joining the revolution, this suggests that either this is a "tribal" revolt against the state, or that tribalism in Yemen is more influential than modern institutions and organizations.

Secondly, the cable transmits a widely held belief that the next Yemeni president will come from the inner circles of Saleh's family, or from his allies within the military. And in 2011, prominent members of the president's family and tribe have broken with him, announcing that they have joined the protesters in the streets. A presidential candidate could very well be among them.

In addition, the cable indicates that "there is no clear chain of command should the [p]resident step down, die or become incapacitated while in office," which is complicated for the diplomats. However, just as in other countries where such changes have recently taken place (Tunisia and Egypt), the Yemeni elite knows that the guidebook for the transfer of power during the transitional period figures to be the current constitution, despite

---

[1] Cable on September 17, 2005, http://213.251.145.96/cable/2005/09/05SANAA2766.html.

reservations they may have about it. In this view, any modifications or re-writing of the constitution would be one of the missions of the next regime, and should be subject to popular referendum.

The cable also explains that Saleh's long tenure (32 years) has been due to his reliance on what is known as "the triumvirate". The cable also identifies the two other sides who, in 1978, formed this tribal and military alliance with Saleh based on a "power-sharing" agreement following the assassination of President Ahmad Hussein al-Ghashmi on June 24, 1978. They are Brigadier General Ali Mohsen al-Ahmar and Sheikh Abdullah al-Ahmar. Today, this alliance is no longer in place since Abdullah al-Ahmar's two sons, Sheikh al-Sadiq and Sheikh Hamid, now support the protesters in Taghyir Square calling for Saleh's resignation. In fact, Sheikh Hamid was one of the main supporters of the late opposition candidate Faisal bin Shamlan in the 2006 elections. In the summer of 2009, Sheikh Hamid appeared on Al-Jazeera, calling on Saleh to step down.[1]

General Ali Ahmar has also split from the regime and joined the protesters. However, it is important to note that the collapse of the old tribal-military alliance does not mean that this alliance will not search for another way to return to power after Saleh's removal from office.

According to the same cable, sources estimate that Ahmar controls at least 50% of the military's forces and resources, which makes him "the second most powerful man in Yemen". Given this, we must ask: what are the general's chances of succeeding Saleh? It is true that protesters welcomed his split from Saleh and his alliance with the opposition, but Shiite rebels in the north consider him to be a harsh military ruler who led the armed forces' campaign against them during the bloody civil war. As for the leftists and southerners, they fear that the goals of the current revolution will be obliterated by a struggle over military power, while the Islamist opposition seems to be more accommodating

---

[1] See, "Ahmar is supporting Saleh for Yemeni president, while his son predicts that the ruling Congress will fail," *al-Watan*, September 9, 2006, http://www.alwatan.com/graphics/2006/09sep/9.9/dailyhtml/politic.html.

and welcoming of him. Moreover, he poses a problem for the Americans due to his former ties to Osama Bin Laden.[1]

Finally, according the cable, in 2005 the US diplomat who wrote it could not see a single competitor who could be a true counterweight to Saleh. Until recently, top-level US officials made similar statements, in which they expressed their fears that change in Yemen would happen suddenly, without time for preparations.[2] Frankly, what concerns America is the stability of a regime that guarantees continued cooperation on various fronts against Al-Qaeda. However, recent events have altered the facts on the ground, and it is no longer possible to describe Saleh as a guarantor of stability. What is even more interesting is the scenario that the cable's author imagines occurring in the year 2013. Having correctly predicted that the president would prevail in the 2006 election despite widespread disillusion about corruption in his regime, the cable anticipates a transfer of power within the same circles of influence - raising serious questions about the nature of "democracy" under Saleh.

## The West and democracy in Yemen

Several definitions of democracy circulate in the West. Some focus on its institutional and procedural elements, while others give priority to the principle of equality. To quote a simplistic definition from American political science attributed to the late Samuel Huntington, "a system is democratic if the most-powerful

---

[1] Some of these reports indicate that General Mohsen was mobilizing Islamists to work with bin Laden. See, for example, Sudarsan Raghavan, "Yemen's future hinges on its two most powerful men," *The Washington Post,* March 31, 2011, http://www.washingtonpost.com/world/yemens-future-hinges-on-its-two-most-powerfulmen/2011/03/29/AFLxOnCC_story.html?hpid=z2. See also, Jane Novak, "Yemen: Al Qaeda in Broad Daylight," May 28, 2005, *World Press,* http://www.worldpress.org/Mideast/2089.cf.

[2] US Secretary of State Robert Gates real concern was that al-Qaeda in the Arabian Peninsula could find in the removal of Ali Abdullah Saleh from power the opportunity to develop its own activity. Gates apprehended a "weak power" in Yemen. See his remarks to ABC: http://blogs.abcnews.com/politicalpunch/2011/03/defense-secretary-yemen-govt-collapse-a-real-problem.html

collective decision-makers are chosen in fair, honest and periodic elections in which candidates freely compete for votes, and all adults are capable of voting."[1] The main feature of this definition is its capacity to resolve disputes through peaceful channels, which are enabled by the rule of law and the protection of civil and political rights. In such systems, the constant tension between the government's need to assert its authority and its need to remain responsive to its citizenry is mitigated through various measures and institutions, including elections, political parties, strong legislative bodies, free press, etc. These are all more prevalent in what Karl Popper describes as an "open society," as opposed to a "closed society," in which one of the main differences between the two is related to the transfer of power.[2] This can be clearly seen in the following table:

| Open society | Closed society |
| --- | --- |
| Democracy | Oppression |
| Personal decision-making | Tribalism |
| Individualism | Ethnic, national, or class primacy |
| Social fractiousness | Social cohesion |
| Bloodless transfer of government power | Blood accompanies government changes |
| Political ethics | Politicization of morality |
| Humanist fraternalism | Totalitarian nationalism |

Given the strength of such intellectual currents in the West, and since many Western observers (including American ones) have expressed anxiety over the future of this country where weapons are widespread, and where some regions are thought to be safe havens for Al-Qaeda, the attitude of some American diplomats as expressed by the 2005 cables is astonishing. For example, we read that "[d]espite weak institutions and submissive political parties, democracy has permeated Yemen enough that the

---

[1] David Garnham and Mark Tessler (eds.), *Democracy, War and Peace in the Middle East*, (Indiana University Press, 1995):67.
[2] Dominique Colas, *Sociologie politique* [Political Sociology], (Paris, PUF, 1994):217-218.

public will expect to choose its next [p]resident in open elections".[1] In a report by a European Union delegation sent to monitor the 2006 elections, there is similarly optimistic language: "As the only country in the Arabian [P]eninsula with a constitution that explicitly describes it as a representative democracy, Yemen can be considered to be an important and possible model for the development of democracy in the region." The report even affirms that the elections were successful "since they offered an open space for political competition in which all the major political parties participated, and in which voters were able to pick freely between candidates."[2]

In reality, this kind of flattery - despite its partially factual content - is inconsistent with the fact that democracies cannot be tied to the approval of tribes or armies. And while one cannot question the results of an election in which no proof has been found of widespread irregularities, the question is: how can Yemen be described as a true democracy when we know, according to these same Western experts, that the regime is based upon tribal alliances and military might?

Nonetheless, it is worth noting that these words were written more than six years ago. Since that time, Yemen's democracy has been interrogated by its own people, who took to the streets chanting for the fall of the regime, demanding the resignation of a president who officially won 72% of the vote. If such things can take place in a democracy, then what would be the case had Saleh been as bereft of popular endorsement as Ben Ali, Mubarak, Libya's Moammar Gaddafi, or others like them for all those years? And how can we speak of a democratic system when we know that Yemen's history - both recent and older - has been drenched with blood? Indeed, going back to the 1970s, Saleh himself played a significant role in the events that led to the assassination of then-president Ibrahim Mohammad al-Hamdi and the ensuing rise to power of Ahmad Hussein al-Ghashmi, who was his direct

---

[1] See the previous cable, above.
[2] EU Election Observation Mission, Yemen, *Final Report on the Presidential and Local Council Elections*, 2006:
http://eeas.europa.eu/_human_rights/election_observation/yemen/final_rep ort_en.pdf.

commander and to whom he owes a great deal. Not even eight months went by before Ghashmi met his own end in a bombing - and was succeeded by Saleh.

There is no doubt that Yemen currently needs its people to gain confidence in state institutions, especially since that confidence has been undermined a great deal by the regime's brutal repression. What might save Yemen from an internecine conflict, whose consequences can only be guessed at, is neither flattery, nor claims that democracy has deep roots. Had such narratives been accurate, Yemen's democracy would not have been shaken by one protest - or 20 - on the street. For these reasons, I argue that the basic political issue on the table in Yemen today is this: rather than a simple power transition, what is needed is a correction of the democratic pathway through the creation of institutions which guarantee that everyone is equal before the law, and which can block the way to any power center attempting to compete with the state.

## The goals of the revolution

Democracy cannot arise and develop in the shadow of a state whose structure and support rely on forces that run contrary to modern understandings of the state. There are several definitions of the nation-state, but also common factors on which all agree. The major characteristic in a nation-state, according to Black, is the support provided to "the political decision or its equivalent, a centralized political power."[1] This takes advantage of the modern information revolution and emerges, according to Black, from "modernizing leaders" [both the business and political elites] desire to mobilize social resources and rationalize them through a vision that aims to achieve the greatest amount of control, effectiveness and production". The second quality of the nation-state, according to Black, lies in the expansion of its functions vis-à-vis earlier forms of political organization. Therefore, it is impossible, according to this theory, for tribes or any other primordial political groups to take on the role of the state. The

---

[1] C.E. Black, *The Dynamics of Modernization*, (New York, Harper and Row Publishers, Inc., 1966): 13-18.

third quality is the rule of law, which generally leads to increased bureaucracy. The fourth quality is the development of the role of the citizen in the modern nation-state, and his or her increased role in public life.[1]

If we now turn to the demands of the Yemeni opposition, we can observe that there is a movement within it that is pushing towards reforming institutions, and not just replacing individuals. The opposition is itself the field for a struggle between two visions: one of them is focused on the smoothest and quickest route to getting rid of Saleh, replacing the sources of his power and achieving necessary reforms; the other insists that modern, democratic change demands modern, democratic institutions, and not just the transfer of power from one leader to another.

Much if this has been reflected by the development of the protesters' demands: the goals announced in February 2011 were quite different from those, which emerged over the couple of months. The statement issued by the main opposition alliance on February 14, 2011 consisted of six demands to which the ruling party, the General People's Congress (GPC), was expected to respond.[2] Three of these were: 1) the construction of a non-centralized state for all Yemeni citizens in which justice and equality would reign supreme; 2) admitting that there was an issue in the South and reaching a just resolution to the conflict; and 3) bringing a complete stop to the wars in the Northern Suda region. The protesters also demanded an equitable distribution of resources and the resolution of Yemen's economic problems in order to achieve fairness and equality in distributing public sector jobs, among other things, to put an end to corruption, and to create meritocratic national institutions on national grounds, and not on alliances or cronyism. The sixth demand was "the necessity to make the war against terror a national issue, and remove it from circles of opportunism, because this plague threatens national

[1] Anthony M. Orum, *Introduction to Political Sociology,* (Prentice-Hall, Inc.1978): 307-308.
[2] See, "The Yemeni Opposition Rejects President Saleh's Proposal and Raises Six Demands," *ArabNet 5*, February 14, 2011, http://www.arabnet5.com/news.asp?c=2&id=78590.

security, and all possible national resources must be used to combat it, in a manner differently from that being done today." These goals can be slewed, not only because they target the ruling party - the party responsible for the crisis - but because they do not assume a structural change in the power institutions, or in traditional alliances.

Then, on March 30, 2011, the following list of demands emerged, none of which were mentioned in the first:[1]

- That Saleh step down;
- That his family be banned from participating in civil and military affairs;
- That the current constitution be declared obsolete;
- That an interim national council be formed consisting of five members with no connections to the Saleh regime, one of whom would represent the country's youth; and that a transition period of six months be announced, during which the parliament and Shura Council would be dissolved;
- That the interim council would appoint a technocrat to form an interim government;
- That purloined public and private funds and property be re-distributed, and all political prisoners be released;
- That the Ministry of Communications be dissolved and journalists be allowed to operate freely;
- That the security apparatus, the intelligence agencies, and the Defense Council be dismantled, and a national security council be established instead. This body would fall under the purview of the Interior Ministry, and its mandate would be limited to investigations and to guarding against external threats to internal stability;
- That town councils and the Higher Judicial Council be dissolved, the solicitor-general removed, and a supreme constitutional court established.

---

[1] Mohammad Hatem, "Yemen's Opposition Lists Key Demands as Demonstrations Continue," *Bloomberg,* March 30, 2011, http://www.bloomberg.com/news/2011-03-30/yemen-s-opposition-lists-key-demands-as-demonstrations-continue.html

Finally, on April 2, 2011, the opposition parties taking part in the Joint Meeting caucus announced that they had decided upon a shared vision for the period of power transfer. The statement was as follows:

**First**: The president should announce his resignation, and his powers and privileges should be transferred to his deputy.

**Second**: The deputy, upon assuming power, must work towards restricting the roles of the national security and central security forces, and the presidential guard. This includes defining their duties according to the constitution and the law, and finding able leaders with high nationalist and professional standards who have attained their posts through merit rather than blood or cronyism. All of this should take place under the purview of the Interior and Defense ministries.

**Third**: That an agreement would be reached with the interim leader (the former deputy) over distribution of power during the transition period, based on the foundations of national unity, in which the following would happen:

1. The formation of a transitional national council that represents all the elements of political and social life, including youth, businessmen, civil society members, and women from across Yemeni society. This council would take on the following:

a. The creation of a national dialogue in which all the political actors participate, both internally and externally, without exception, and in which all issues are brought forth. This dialogue should propose solutions for all major issues affecting Yemen, including the Southern issue, and formulate a vision for constitutional reform that would guarantee political and cultural freedoms, and the construction of a modern civil state, which would be a civic state with a decentralized system. The dialogue would also develop a political regime on the basis of a parliamentary system and popular consensus.

b. The formation of a council of experts and specialists to formulate a program of constitutional reforms in light of the results of the comprehensive national dialogue.

2. The creation of an interim national unity government chaired by the opposition in which all political actors are represented, including businesspeople and youthful protesters. In addition to its constitutional duties, it would also take on executive matters, stabilize the country's economic and financial affairs, and ensure that the social situation does not continue to deteriorate.

3. The formation of an interim military council whose members would be military leadership figures known for their competence and honesty, and who would be respected and appreciated by the rank-and-file military. All the armed forces must be represented in the council, and those officers who were forced to resign after the 1994 war would be able to participate, which would increase this institution's national unity role, since it would be fulfilling its constitutional role as "the property of all its people whose role it is to protect the republic, secure its territory and safety," in addition to its temporary role in safeguarding the popular peaceful revolution, maintaining security and calm, and preserving the state.

4. The formation of a Higher Council for Elections and Referendums that would undertake:

a. A referendum on constitutional reforms; and
b. Parliamentary and presidential elections based on the new constitution's guidelines.

5. The public affirmation of peaceful expression, the right to peaceful protest, and other civil rights for all Yemeni citizens. The launching of an investigation into the hostile actions taken against protesters across Yemen, but especially the massacres in Aden, Sana'a and Ibin, and other situations in which live ammunition and tear gas were used; those responsible must be brought to court, and those injured and disabled, as well as the families of the martyrs, must be compensated.

This manifesto, for the first time, explicitly laid out the issue of constitutional reforms that would guarantee political and cultural freedoms, and build a modern civil state within a decentralized government where the political model would develop based on a parliamentary system, and be based on a popular consensus. This would place the Yemeni revolution on the same footing as the Tunisian and Egyptian revolutions. Of course, the creation of the modern nation-state in both these countries entailed bureaucratic challenges, more than tribal ones. In Tunisia, the army managed to remain completely neutral.

What is clear from the development of opposition demands is that the Yemeni revolution has now entered a new, possibly more radical, phase. The protesters know that the transfer of power is not an end in itself, but a means to lay down new political foundations. At the beginning, this revolution was rather nebulous, due to the absence of a coherent leadership, and the heavy presence of traditional leaderships; this led to the belief that what the protesters wanted was the removal of Saleh from power while retaining the same existing institutions and procedures, with only partial changes and reforms. This could have been possible by negotiating the succession in a peaceful manner, and then putting into place steps that would preserve everyone's dignity in order to preserve Yemen's unity and to prevent the return of civil war. In the second phase, presidential elections would be held, making possible a smooth transfer of power.

However, the youth in Taghyir Square now seem intent on imposing a different kind of agenda, one that brings forth a democratic civil revolution like those in Tunisia and Egypt, in order to establish a new political system. In this case, the results would be very different from what the Saleh-led GPC envisioned, namely the continued consolidation of power by getting the protesters to accept his reform proposals after he stepped down from office.

If the revolution is to succeed in imposing its democratic agenda, which was laid out in the aforementioned statements, it also will be necessary to break with undemocratic traditions, such as allowing tribes and the military to intervene in the priorities of the new government. At this point, whether the latter breaks will take place or not remains uncertain.

## Tribalism or citizenship?

For many years, Yemen has been on the brink of becoming a "failed state" due to its own civilian and tribal struggles, foreign interventions, low education rates, dilapidated infrastructure and poor governance. All these problems have become both more critical and more complex in recent years.[1] Since 2009, Yemen has witnessed alliances between radical Islamist fundamentalist groups, such as Al-Qaeda, and certain tribes, which has worried both its Gulf neighbors and Western states.

Despite official attempts to limit the movements of Al-Qaeda members, powerful groups have been ensuring their and their allies' interests in a manner that tramples Yemeni law and exposes the state to considerable harm.[2] It is no secret that Al-Qaeda aims to transform Yemen into a new Afghanistan, which would completely contradict the demands of the democratic nationalist revolution.

The accommodation of tribal belonging was part of the unity agreement of 1990, in which the Presidential Council was made subject to "consideration for regional concerns and members' tribal belonging".[3] This needs to be revised. A better method must be found to guarantee maximum representation of Yemeni citizens in state institutions, and this in a manner that reduces the extent to which tribal and family tensions undermine democracy and national unity. This requires new standards for political representation in which parties, unions and civil society organizations must play a role similar to the one they play in more

---

[1] Sarah Phillips and Rodger Shanahan, "Al-Qaida, Tribes and Instability in Yemen," *Lowy Institute for International Policy*(Sydney), November 2009.

[2] See : Hichem Karoui, "Yemen: The Law of the Tribesmen...Is There a 'Pilot' in the Cabin?," *Journal of Alternative Perspectives in the Social Sciences*, *Vol.* 2(2), December 2010, http://www.middle-east-studies.net/?p=8799.

[3] On the subject, see, "Potential for the Continuation of Unity and Separation in Yemen," the Arab Center for Research and Policy Studies, http://www.dohainstitute.org/Home/Details?entityID=5d045bf3-2df9-46cf-90a0-d92cbb5dd3e4&resourceId=5ccd2a6c-199f-4560-ae62-33eaf9c5418b.

advanced societies, instead of the army and the tribes. If Yemenis succeed in overcoming this hurdle, they will be better situated to form laws that preserve the gains of the national, civil democratic revolution and its base: the power of the people through representative institutions. The choice here is clear: either citizens and understandings of citizenship and the rule of law will prevail, or the tribes and old methods will.

## To what should we pay attention?

Today, Yemenis have before them a democratic civil solution that matches the aforementioned demands. It will not be easy to implement this solution, but it is the best guarantee of their stability and civil peace in the long run. Leaders must strive to achieve this, and it will not happen without a clear plan with well-defined steps that can be executed with the support of the new majority to which the first phase of the revolution will lead. However, those in power will not give up their privileges and wealth without resistance. It is possible that some influential powerbrokers will play a role in the current and future period, due to their resources in terms of allies and wealth. There are five groups that could have an effect on this situation: 1) the opposition parties; 2) the GPC; 3) the youth; 4) the tribes; and 5) the army.

### 1. The opposition parties:

The question here is whether the opposition is capable of consolidating its ranks and choosing representatives who can transcend their tribal and clan belongings within a new conception of the democratic state. The group known as the Joint Meeting, which since 2003 has brought together the Yemeni Congregation for Reform (Islah), the Yemeni Socialist Party, the Nasserite Unionist People's Organization, the Arab Socialist Rebirth Party, the Haq Party, the September Alliance and the Popular Forces Union Party,[1] is now in the opposition ranks against Saleh and his

---

[1]     See     "'The     Joint     Meeting'     parties," http://www.aljazeera.net/NR/exeres/EF7EC359-9FBB-4B11-A7DE-AB5214C1A988.htm.

GPC. But opposition is one thing, and foundations are something else. If Saleh resigns, perhaps the perceived need for a Joint Meeting will dissipate, and each side will pick a representative in new foundational organizations.

## 2. **The GPC:**

The GPC will not necessarily disappear upon Saleh's departure, and could instead - maybe for the best - continue if it accepts the new rules of the game, the most important of which are overcoming tribalism and alliances against democracy and the modern state. The Joint Meeting headed in this direction when it suggested that it would agree to Saleh's transferring power to his deputy, who would take over during the interim period.

## 3. **The youth:**

Some of those who began the revolt in Sana'a's Taghyir Square played a similar role to that of the young revolutionaries in Tunisia and Egypt. Some, of course, are active in Yemeni political parties, and one way or another, these are the people who represent Yemen's future. It is necessary for them to have their say, and they have truly begun to make their voices heard through the announcement of their movement's manifesto.[1] We must envisage a situation in which the leaders of the youth movement can be at the helm of new institutions.

## 4. **The tribes:**

The Yemeni system was built on the cornerstones of the tribe and the military. Despite the fact that a modern, and especially a democratic, state does not rest on such understandings, the situation in Yemen and in some other Arab countries depends more heavily on the tribe and the army than on any other social institution in order to achieve some sort of stability based on balances that are today uneasy, because they were based for a long time on serving autocratic rulers, and opportunistic sheikhs, and

---

[1]See, "Peaceful Youth Protesters in Sana'a Insist on their Demands for Regime Change," http://www.al-tagheer.com/news27384.html.

not "the people" in the modern sense of the term. At the moment, it is unclear whether the Yemeni opposition is genuinely interrogating this situation. Consequently, I expect, at least in the short term that the tribes will continue to have a strong influence on the political scene; I also would not be surprised if some sheikhs refrained from participating in discussions about the country's future. This would not be in the interest of the democratic civilian revolution, but rather in the continuity of the old regime through new institutions. If, at this stage, it is impossible to avoid this kind of non-participation, or to mitigate its effects, one must nonetheless remain acutely aware of it. If this new Yemeni generation believes in democracy, the next step in building a modern state necessitates the breakdown of all tribal structures and everything else that could place the word of the tribe or clan above the rule of law.

## 5. **The army:**

What has been said about the power of the tribes can also be said about the military. There is not a single modern and truly democratic state in the world that allows the military to intervene in politics, but the construction of the modern state in Yemen, as in other Arab countries, fell upon the military. However, since the Yemeni street does not seem to currently be examining the role of the army, apart from criticizing its actions in the Suda war, it is possible that some attempts will be made to co-opt the democratic uprising and to bring the military to power. Here, we must insist that the place of the military during peacetime is in the barracks.

## Conclusion and findings

The demands made by the protesters at Taghyir Square have brought Yemen into a new situation that no one could have anticipated. It is no longer possible to act as if traditional parties, or tribes, are the only ones on the field. It is no longer possible to say that this revolution was a "political maneuver" by the opposition in order to break Saleh's hold on power, as some reports have suggested. Even if the opposition was the one that motivated people at the beginning, under the influence of events in

Tunisia and Egypt, something extremely dangerous happened at that time: Yemeni society was split vertically and horizontally. The youth were joined by members of the civilian and military elites, and by some of the tribes. This did not take place in a vacuum, but in the context of objective social and political conditions that could change in the future if the revolution succeeds, but which must be taken into consideration.

The problem now cannot be posed in the old manner (i.e., by simply asking "what is the alternative to Ali Abdullah Saleh?"). There are thousands of alternatives. In modern states, people come and go, but institutions remain. Instead, the real question is: what kinds of institutions do Yemenis want to build to replace the system against which they have revolted? We know that "Yemeni democracy" during Saleh's regime did not produce leaders as much as it consolidated the leadership of a single man for 32 years. This would not have been possible had the structures and institutions on which the Yemeni state was officially founded held sway over traditional loyalties and belongings. This largely places Yemeni governance among the group of patrimonial systems, which are less drastic than the outright dictatorships of a Ben Ali, Gaddafi, or the late Saddam Hussein in Iraq. Despite its similarities with other patrimonial systems, however, Saleh's regime is a different system by many standards. One should not be misled by the common refrain that Yemen is "the one democracy in the Arabian Peninsula". What is the alternative to Saleh? The protesters in Taghyir Square have comprehensively answered that question with their numerous and cogent demands.

The current period is somewhat uncertain - largely due to the so-called "special nature" of Yemeni society which Saleh and other power-brokers have been trying to take exploit in order to secure their own "solutions" to the crisis - but these "solutions" have been known for years. It is clear that the Americans (and recently, the Europeans) had their own ideas of the post-Saleh landscape, as well as their fears. The most likely candidates to succeed the embattled president are:

1.  General Ahmar, described in leaked US Embassy cables as among America's most powerful allies within the Yemeni

establishment. Interestingly, the cables also painted him as the most likely to lead a military coup. There are indications that if Saleh were suddenly removed from power, "the five leaders of [Yemen's] military region[s] will be potential candidates for the tribal elders to select a president from within them". Today, the leaders have changed. Saleh made a habit of rotating these commanders - except for Mohsen. But who would want the general? Do Yemenis need a "strong man" - military or otherwise - or do they need strong civil institutions?

2. Also among the potential candidates are the brothers described above. Sheikh Sadiq al-Ahmar, who has inherited his father's position as head of the family, could become the central figure in the coming weeks and months. Sheikh Hamid al-Ahmar, who runs the family's extensive business empire, also wields considerable influence. Regardless of how crucial these men are to their tribes, however, they should undergo a test of democracy in which the tribal leader is equal to more modest individuals, and the rich landowner to the poor citizen, or the middle-class one.

3. Some other names are being talked about, such as Ahmad Ali Saleh, the president's son (a general in the Yemeni Army and head of both the Special Forces and the Presidential Guard), whose father has groomed him as a successor. However, in a recent attempt to placate the opposition, President Saleh announced that he had no intention of running for another term, or of passing power on to his son. This seems reasonable in a situation that is boiling over and uncertain; in any case, one of the demands of the opposition today is the removal of President Saleh's family from the regime. They also might be held accountable for abuses committed over the past 32 years, making it difficult to see how Ahmed Ali Saleh could gain widespread support for his candidacy.[1]

---

[1] It is worth noting that President Saleh's son is reportedly willing to burn Sana'a down if his father accepts to step down after EU-mediated negotiations with the opposition, "and for this reason, Saleh reneged on his deal with the

Lastly, notwithstanding the clear demand to purge Saleh's family from state institutions, a democracy must guarantee equality to all its citizens and cannot punish those who had no hand in corruption or violence. It would therefore be unfair to represent all members of Saleh's family as enemies of the revolution, especially since some of them have announced their support for the protests in Taghyir Square. The only appropriate course will be to investigate and prove any accusations, since some of them may stem from nothing more than a desire for revenge, and this would only perpetuate tribal mentalities. This particular aspect demonstrates once again the pressing need for an independent judiciary. Revolutions have their own logic, one that often transcends the past and establishes the future. In this dialectic (transcendence and establishment), the page is turned. It is as if history begins again.[1]

---

mediators about his resignation and his handover of power" See, *al-Hadath*, March 30, 2011, http://alhadath-yemen.net/news12239.html.
[1]　　　Published　　by　　ACRPS,　　May　　29,　　2011: http://english.dohainstitute.org/release/a81c810b-9b30-4cbc-bede-c03b5bf69eac

19

# HAMAS, HEZBOLLAH, IRAN AND OTHERS...

Could Hamas influence Arab uprisings?

On March 10, 2011, U.S. Secretary of State Hilary Clinton expressed concern that Iran is using its relationship with Hamas to influence the uprisings in the Middle East. She stated, "We know from our intelligence reporting, from anecdotal reporting, our embassies, our political officers that everywhere Iran can take advantage, they're going to, either directly or indirectly through proxies like Hezbollah and Hamas... You've got Hamas right on the border of Egypt. You have absolutely every reason to believe that with Iran now supporting Hamas that they're going to be in there trying to figure out what they can do to influence the outcome."[1]

Some days before (March 2), Hillary Clinton testified in a Senate Appropriations Committee hearing that Iran is using its relationship with Hamas to influence the uprisings in the Middle East. She stated, "[the Iranians] are using Hezbollah, which is a political party with an armed wing, to communicate with counterparts in Egypt, in Hamas, who then in turn communicate

---

[1] "Hearing of the House Appropriations Committee on Foreign Operations: 2012 State and USAID Budget Request," CQ Transcriptions, March 10, 2011. Available at Lexis Nexis (accessed March 16, 2011). Iran-Hamas Relationship Tracker 2011, By Katherine Faley, Gisue Mehdi, March 10, 2011: http://www.irantracker.org/military-activities/iran-hamas-relationship-tracker-2011#_edn1

with counterparts in Egypt. We know that they are reaching out to the opposition in Bahrain."[1]

It is not clear what Clinton means by "influencing the uprisings in the Middle East." The connection between Hezbollah and Iran is acknowledged as based on confessional solidarity (i.e. between Shiites). But the connection between both of them and Hamas is of a different kind, since Hamas is a Sunnite Islamist organization. So far, unlike Iran and Hezbollah, Hamas has not interfered in Arab and Muslim countries, nor did it lead military operations outside Israel and the occupied territories. Therefore, why should this basic stance change today? Will Hamas act as a "proxy" for Iran in Egypt, whereas the new Egyptian regime is trying to make a different approach of the relations with Iran, with the risk of undermining these efforts to the disappointment of Iran? It does not make sense. Nor Hamas is known to maintain a solid connection with the Shiite Bahraini opposition that may induce the assumption that it is able to intervene on behalf of Iran and influence the events out there. As for Libya, the situation does not need more meddling either from Hamas or other parties to be tragically chaotic. In Tunisia, Hamas has never had the least influence. This country has always been popularly and politically acquired to the PLO. The only people that may today be tempted to support Hamas are the Islamists of Rashid Ghannouchi's Nahdha. Still, Hamas is more in need of external support than the Islamists of Egypt and Tunisia and elsewhere. And one just cannot see what kind of "influence" Hamas could exert on them "on behalf of Iran"! The only country that was open to Hamas is Syria, since its political bureau was officially based there. Here too, it seems absurd to assert, without the least evidence, that Hamas could – with the help and support from Iran – try to "influence the outcome" of the uprising. For which side?

Historically speaking, it is quite the opposite that has always happened, insofar as it concerned the Palestinian national

---

[1] "Hearing of the Senate Committee on Appropriations: FY 2012 State Department Budget," CQ Transcriptions, March 2, 2011. Available at Lexis Nexis (accessed March 16, 2011)

resistance movement. All the Palestinian organizations that have been, at one moment or another, hosted by an Arab state, have been actually under its influence. This fact may be deduced and evidenced from a simple comparison between the stances of any given Palestinian organization and the official stances of the hosting state over a determined period of time. For instance, if we recall the policy led by Ahmed Shuqayri under the regime of Abdel-Nasser in the fifties of the previous century, we would easily understand why Fatah emerged in Kuwait in the sixties and why it opposed Shuqayri-Nasser's policy concerning the Palestinians and claimed a new autonomous representation. If we compare the stances of Fatah (Arafat) with those of the PFLP (George Habash) and the DFLP (Nayef Hawatmeh), and Fatah (Abu Nidal), we would find evidence that much of their controversy was caused and nurtured by the controversy between the Arab capitals that support each of them. Just look at what happened since the ousting of the PLO from Beirut in 1982. Arafat and his lieutenants were hosted in Tunis, where the regime has always claimed never to interfere into their affairs. Maybe it did not; yet, why did Arafat wait until he was in Tunis to start peace talks with the USA (helped then by the US ambassador to Tunis, R.H. Pelletreau Jr.) and subsequently with Israel? Why was he "unable" to do so during decades in Beirut? Pay attention: I do not say, the Tunisians have pushed him, just as I don't say the Iraqis "pushed" Abu Nidal, or the Syrians "Hamas" and others. However, it seems odd enough and too big a coincidence that each time, a Palestinian organization had to fall under the "spell" of its host and behaves exactly as he wishes. No, they don't receive orders. But they receive friendly support whenever they act as theirs hosts wish them to act.

Therefore, in my view, Hamas cannot influence ongoing uprisings and current politics in the concerned Arab countries, and much less if it tried to do so "on behalf of Iran."

Actually, why Iran? On what grounds Secretary of State Clinton has founded its declaration?

Maybe because on January 4, "Tehran Times" reported a statement by the Speaker of the Iranian Parliament Ali Larijani saying, "it is Iran's policy to fight against the global arrogance and support the oppressed, so we say openly that we back Hezbollah and Hamas."[1]

Some days later, on January 24, Iranian Student News Agency (ISNA) reported that Iran's acting foreign minister Ali Akbar Salehi met with Hamas Politburo Chief Khaled Meshaal, Head of the Popular Front for the Liberation of Palestine-General Command Ahmad Jibril and Deputy Secretary General of the Islamic Jihad Movement Ziyad Nahala. Salehi said, "Resistance is rooted in the region."[2]

Yet, even if these news reports were accurate, it is really hard to imply that Hamas is henceforth acting on the orders of Tehran to influence events in the Arab world the way Iran wishes them. To do this, Hamas should have, first, an acknowledged weight in the domestic politics of these countries, which is far from being proved, so far.[3]

---

[1] http://old.tehrantimes.com/index_View.asp?code=233569
[2] http://old.isna.ir/ISNA/NewsView.aspx?ID=News-1702033&Lang=E
[3] Press version for The Gulf Today, June 11, 2011: http://gulftoday.ae/portal/80cdd94c-f806-4269-8ee2-cea0984963c6.aspx

20

# THE UNEASY RELATIONSHIP BETWEEN FRANCE AND SYRIA

In March 2011, the public anger witnessed in other Arab countries surfaced in Syria, putting the regime of President Bashar al Assad on the defensive for the first time in his 11-year presidency.

As the Syrian security forces continue to fire on unarmed civilians, while the United Nations Organization now talks of more than 1200 dead, recalls countless cases of torture and violations of human rights, and thousands of refugees fleeing Syria, a statement of the Quai d'Orsay on June 14, 2011, notes that "this is an abysmal record.

France hopes that the UN Security Council (UNSC) takes a decision on the intolerable situation prevailing in Syria and the headlong rush of the Damascus regime. Each member of the UNSC must take responsibility. We regret the lack of consensus within the Council."

The same day, answering a question before the National Assembly, Mr. Juppé said: "What can we do? France cannot and will not act but within the framework of international legality (...) At the Security Council, despite all our efforts, especially with the British and the Americans, we have not yet reached our goal. Indeed, China and Russia (...) threat to use the veto. We will not take the risk of a vote on a draft resolution condemning the Syrian regime if we cannot reach a sufficient majority. Today, we have probably nine votes in the Security Council. We still have to convince South Africa, India and Brazil (...) I think if things evolve so that we could have eleven votes, we would put the draft resolution to the vote and everyone would then face its responsibility: we will see whether China and Russia would even veto."

France's relationship with Syria has never been easy and was even further complicated by the ongoing revolt as it was surely by the unresolved assassination case of former Lebanese Prime Minister, Rafik Hariri.

Received at Brookings Institute on June 6, 2011, French Foreign Minister Alain Juppé explained to his audience the position of his country regarding the "Arab Spring." He emphasized that either for Libya or for Syria, the rejection of the reforms and the vicious circle of violence are just intolerable. "We don't have two different policies in these two different countries," he said and clearly denounced the current repression linking it to the previous massacre of Hama population in 1982. At least 20 000 people were killed in Hama (February 2008). However, President François Mitterrand, then newly elected, did not condemn this brutal repression. On the one hand, France felt it was better to ignore the massacre rather than support the Muslim Brotherhood. On the other, France's Syrian policy, has always been commanded by its interests in Lebanon.

On the morning of October 23, 1983, in Beirut, fifty-eight French peacekeepers died in an explosion at their headquarters: "Drakkar". A few minutes earlier, another bomb destroyed the US headquarters, killing 239 soldiers.

The period of the eighties was particularly stressing for the French-Syrian relations. Terrorist actions orchestrated by Syria killed French soldiers in Lebanon. There is a resulting legacy of distrust of Syria among many French officials.

One of the principal reasons for improvement in French-Israeli relations has been the Jospin government's strong criticism of Syria. In February 2000, Prime Minister Lionel Jospin told the Knesset that Hezbollah militants operating in southern Lebanon were guilty of "terrorist actions," and condemned Syria for supporting them. France praised Israel's decision to remove its forces from southern Lebanon in May 2000, and expressed a willingness to send a force of 1,600 peacekeepers if UNIFIL is reinforced to number 4,500 men.

Members of the Jospin government were reportedly critical of President Chirac for attending the funeral of Syrian President Hafiz Al-Assad in June 2000; he was the only western head of state to do so. Foreign Minister Védrine, according to media reports, told the French cabinet that Assad's son and successor, Bashar, might not be able to exercise power in Syria in the long run, and was unlikely to liberalize the country.

These remarks were interpreted as critical of Chirac's decision to go to the funeral and thereby implicitly endorse Bashar's succession. The French President had received at the Elysée Palace (November 7, 1999) the young man who will take over as President of Syria.

During the first mandate of the Bush presidency, France has been critical of the US Administration's desire to promote democracy in the Middle East, but that did not hinder them from coordinating some policies. Thus, following the 60th anniversary of the Normandy landings, Jacques Chirac launched with George W. Bush, a diplomatic initiative leading to the 1559 UN resolution directed against Syria. Adopted September 2, 2004, the text demands the withdrawal of 15,000 Syrian troops from Lebanon and an end to the interference of Damascus in the country. A turning point in the French diplomacy.

When Rafik Hariri was murdered in Beirut (February 2005), some people in France, saw it as the "Syrian answer" to the US-French humiliating initiative.

Being a close friend of Rafik Hariri, Jacques Chirac did everything until the end of his second term, to isolate Syria diplomatically. Even today, the former president is housed in an apartment owned by the Hariri family, on the banks of the Seine in Paris.

The period 2005 to 2008 saw the isolation of Syria as a result of its association with Hezbollah, Hamas and Iran. This was the policy of the Bush administration and France, which instigated the same stance in the EU.

Nevertheless, once elected, President Nicolas Sarkozy made a clear change in favor of a diplomatic rehabilitation of Syria. He proposed Syria to join the Union for the Mediterranean (UfM), claiming that engaging Syria would be more productive than the apparently failed policy of ostracism. Most EU members acted in agreement. Twenty-five years after the operation that killed fifty-eight French soldiers in Beirut, the Syrian head of state was present at the summit of July 13, 2008 and the next day, despite the controversy, he attended the July 14 parade among the "guests of honor." As the victims' families felt offended by the presence of Bashar al-Assad in Paris, an article appeared in Le Monde penned by one of the staff of the Elysée, saying: "This is a historic mistake! The Drakkar was Iran's operation! Syria was only behind the murder of ambassador Delamare. "The representative of France in Lebanon was murdered, September 4, 1981 in Beirut.

In 2009, France was even well disposed toward the Syrian regime and probably had instigated the proposal of an association agreement offered by the EU to Bashar, who, oddly enough turned it down.

On February 2010, at a press conference in Damascus, French Prime Minister Mr. Fillon wished to move up a gear and step up an economic partnership "currently well below its potential." But as he warned shortly before, "the condition of a continued economic development in Syria is peace and security." In his view, "Syria has a key role in establishing peace in the Middle East." He then asked for Syria's help on the Iranian nuclear issue.

But his Syrian counterpart Muhammad Naji Otri, refused categorically and definitively. "We have always supported the right to the peaceful use of nuclear energy," said Otri, who then called for a "denuclearization of the region" because "the threat comes from Israel."

Mr. Fillon also reiterated that France was "disposed to help resuming the dialogue between Syria and Israel with the participation of Turkey." "There is no time to lose," he said, saying that France would begin discussions with the three parties "without delay" for a resumption of peace negotiations also interrupted during the war on Gaza.

The visit resulted in the signature of a 27 million Euro contract for the sale of two regional jets, and a protocol for the sale of 14 Airbus to the Syrian Arab Airlines Company blocked by an extended U.S. embargo. Fillon referred to the project of a new metro in Damascus and a new airport terminal, which "could be emblematic of a fruitful cooperation between our two countries."

However, all these efforts came to a nought, when Bashar refused the calls pressing serious reforms, preferring the policy of confrontation with his people.

Since last Wednesday, the Security Council is examining the draft of a UN resolution submitted by France and the United Kingdom with the aim of condemning the repression in Syria. To obtain the necessary majority, the text must reach eleven votes of the fifteen in the Security Council. The most reluctant are: Brazil, South Africa and especially India, whose position is very close to that of Russia. Lebanon would also be unfavorable to vote against its powerful neighbor and former occupier.

The French still hope to convince Brazil and South Africa.[1]

---

[1] Published on al-Arabiya, June 18, 2011: http://english.alarabiya.net/articles/2011/06/18/153800.html

21

# IMBROGLIO OVER SYRIA

Despite the continuing killings in Syria of the protesters demanding the removal of President Bashar al-Assad, the conspicuous fact is: the Arabs have not weighed in behind the call for a condemnation of the Syrian regime in the UN Security Council (UNSC). There is no noticeable diplomatic or political movement in the Arab League, favorable to a course of action similar to what was decided for Libya.

This might be due to the fear that Israel would be the first beneficiary from a military intervention against the Syrian regime. Moreover, as with Iraq, the Arabs do not want to run the risk that foreign powers sustain groups that have no credibility on the ground.

However, the Syrian government is not alone to talk about a worldwide conspiracy against the regime. In Global Research, a Canadian think tank, there are assumptions about the ongoing Syrian uprising described as "an armed insurrection" pushed by foreign powers including the US, Turkey, Israel, and even Saudi Arabia. Referring to The Voice of Russia (June 17, 2011) reporting that "armed insurgents belonging to Islamist organizations have crossed the border from Turkey, Lebanon and Jordan," and to the US State Department's public support of the protests, the Russians, the Chinese, and some left-wing naive propagate that a conspiracy has been concocted against Syria. It is not the Syrian population which is on the streets, but a "bunch of conspirators"!

Michel Chossudovsky (director of Global Research) is a renowned scholar and a respected anti-globalist militant. But the article he recently published about "the destabilization of Syria" is full of half-truths. He cites for example, the statement by US State Department official Victoria Nuland: "We started to expand contacts with the Syrians, those who are calling for change, both inside and outside the country," as evidence of an Iraq-like plan for intervention ready to go.

But the relations between the US Department of State and some Syrian activists is hardly a scoop. The Bush administration has preceded Obama years ago, in encouraging and supporting the Syrian opposition, and the Americans did the same for the Libyan opposition since at least the Reagan era. Does this imply that the popular revolt that burst out in Syria or in Libya in the wake of a general Arab uprising has been cooked in Washington and Tel-Aviv?

How could we overlook the consequences of long years of dictatorship?
The point here is that combining authoritarianism with radical rhetoric is no longer a winning equation. It may work for a time, mainly because of the stupid rigidity of Israel and the US sheepish followism, but it will not work forever, as the Arab uprising in these countries showed.
Radical rhetoric may earn the regimes using it Washington's wrath and the disgrace with its Western allies, but it cannot be the remedy for domestic and social problems. Nor is the "resistance" against Israel a license to kill your own people.

However, Michel Chossudovsky thinks, "action against Syria is part of a military roadmap, a sequencing of military operations." He cites former NATO Commander General Wesley Clark, asserting that the Pentagon  had clearly identified Iraq, Libya, Syria and Lebanon as target countries of a US-NATO intervention: "[The] Five-year campaign plan [included]... a total of seven countries, beginning with Iraq, then Syria, Lebanon, Libya, Iran, Somalia and Sudan."

That might be true at a time. But you know, each new US administration comes up with a new blueprint called "National Security Strategy," and believe it or not, it is never the same, from an administration to another. Ask them why each US president has his own "doctrine."

The simplest answer is: the world we live in is fast changing, and the US strategy has to adapt itself permanently to these changes, and so do the presidents. Therefore, citing Wesley Clark as evidence that the US has a plan ready to go for an intervention in Syria, could be in the present conditions quite misleading and inaccurate.

Furthermore, such a discourse may reinforce the overall paranoia of the Arab governments and serve to hindering a condemnation of the atrocities happening in Syria every day.

And because Turkey is the most influential neighbor with US-NATO and EU connections, "conspiracy theorists" assume it to play a central role in Syria, although many indices point out to the contrary. What we see actually, is an enormous strain on the Turkish borders, and self-control in the Turkish reactions.

Admittedly, there were plans for destabilizing Syria, in Israel and the USA. It is obvious that the "Arab uprising" made them just obsolete. Why should the US-NATO carry out military intervention plans, while there is no certainty as to the regime's ability to survive after the protests spread out to engulf the whole country? In Libya, the UN resolution was only meant to protect the civilian population and certainly not to change the regime, although its effects would come to the same result. A course of political and diplomatic action is still wished through the UNSC. But would it include necessarily a military action?

Chossudovsky may think that because Turkey is a member of NATO "with a powerful military force" and because it had signed with Israel a "long-standing joint military-intelligence agreement," this would compel Mr. Erdoğan to arm the Syrian insurgents without more referring to anybody (no UN, no EU, and no NATO). His conclusion is:

"Israel and NATO signed a far-reaching military cooperation agreement in 2005. Under this agreement, Israel is considered a de facto member of NATO. If a military operation were to be launched against Syria, Israel would in all likelihood be involved in military undertakings alongside NATO forces (under the NATO-Israel bilateral agreement). Turkey would also play an active military role."

However, not many Turks would agree on such talk. "How do you do it? Do you send troops and face the Syrian army? I don't think the Turks are really interested in doing that," stated Political scientist Soli Ozel of Istanbul's Kadir Has University.

Sinan Ulgen of the think tank Edam, said Turkey is haunted by past experiences. "In 1991, when Saddam had started to massacre his Kurdish population, Turkey ended being host to 550,000 Kurds in a few days. That still remains on the consciousness of Turkish policy-makers."

Yet, there is still another reason why the West is reluctant to take a decision implying military action in Syria, despite the Assad regime's sustained brutality against its opponents, and the burgeoning refugee crisis along the Turkish border: who wants to see a sectarian civil war (another one) developing and threatening to draw in partisans in Lebanon and Iraq?[1]

---

[1] The Gulf Today, July 2, 2011: http://gulftoday.ae/portal/7658b083-74cf-4b56-8062-c9f998196e37.aspx

22

# UNWISE INTELLIGENCE REPORT

An intelligence report may be behind the change in the French official position concerning Libya.

The hypothesis that the Libyan conflict might extend beyond what was initially figured out in France made many people nervous. The statement of Mr. Gerard Longuet, the French defense minister, that bombing has produced a stalemate in Libya and should be abandoned, preceded the debate that started on July 12 in the French parliament about the military engagement. The suggestion by Mr. Longuet that talks should start even if it means Colonel Qadhafi remains in Libya and shares power, caused consternation in London and understandably in Libya among the insurgents. Prime Minister Alain Juppé considered that there was an "underestimation regarding the despot's capacity of resistance." Some think that president Sarkozy is growing impatient, although on July 14, speaking to the reporters, he did not regret France's engagement.

Recently, a report was published on the Libyan conflict. The only I heard of. The point is: it was definitely negative; and some of its findings were, in my opinion, biased.

At the initiative of the International Centre for Research and Studies on Terrorism and Victims of Terrorism (CIRET-AVT) and the French Centre for Research on Intelligence (CF2R2) and with the support of The Forum for Peace in the Mediterranean, an international delegation of experts visited Tripoli and Tripolitania (March 31-April 6), and Benghazi in Cyrenaica (from April 19 to 25), to assess the Libyan situation on an "independent and neutral ground" and to meet representatives of both parties. The delegation included:

- Mrs. Sayda Ben Habyles (Algeria), former Minister of Solidarity, former Senator, founding member of CIRET-AVT, United Nations Award for civil society;
- Mrs. Roumiana Ougartchinska (France / Bulgaria), essayist and investigative journalist;
- The Prefect Yves Bonnet (France), Prefect Emeritus, former MP, former Director of Territorial Surveillance (DST), chairman of CIRET-AVT;
- Mr. Dirk Borgers (Belgium), independent expert;
- Mr. Eric Denécé (France), director of the French Centre for Research on Intelligence (CF2R);
- Mr. André Le Meignen (France), independent expert, vice president of CIRET-AVT.

The report released in May 2011, asserts that the Libyan revolution "is neither democratic nor spontaneous. This is an armed uprising in the eastern part of the country in a spirit of revenge and dissent, which attempts to fit into the dynamics of the 'Arab spring', to which it has no connection, though. The Libyan movement cannot be compared with the Tunisian and Egyptian popular revolts. More worryingly, the National Transition Council (CNT) appears to be a coalition of disparate elements with different interests, whose only common feature is their determined opposition to the regime. The true democrats are a minority there, and must live with those formerly close to Qadhafi, and with supporters of a return to the monarchy and sympathizers of radical Islam. Consequently, the CNT offers, therefore, no guarantee for the future, despite the determination of the Democrats, because the other factions fully intend to steer the board in the direction of their goals."

"Above all," the report went on, "Libya is the only country of the 'Arab spring' in which the Islamist risk increases, Cyrenaica being the region of the Arab world that sent the highest number of jihadists to fight against the Americans in Iraq. It seems then that the Western powers have shown an excessive adventurism by engaging in this crisis. What should have been an easy victory became a semi-failure due to the inconsistency of the rebel forces. Stalled insurgent operations leave them only with two possibilities: either an inglorious retreat or more involvement in the conflict, including sending ground units."

The report asserted, "The Western intervention is creating more problems than it solved. It is likely to destabilize the whole region of North Africa, the Sahel, the Near East, and encourage the emergence of a new hub for radical Islam or terrorism, in Cyrenaica. The coalition might be able to eliminate the Libyan leader. But the West must be careful not to replace him by a more radical and similar undemocratic regime."

Is there a basis in the reality for such a dramatic assessment? What is the method adopted in this investigation? These questions are not answered. Actually, the report sounds more like a series of impressions revealing the anxiety of its authors than an objective blueprint based on data gathering from varied sources. The narrative of this assessment is similar to the accounts of the 19th century's travelers in North Africa, full of biases about almost everything. Curiously, the report embodies the same thinking once shown by Sayf al-Islam Qadhafi in a famous speech, when he referred to Libya threateningly, as: "this is not Tunisia, not Egypt. Libya is different. Libya is divided in tribes, each with its affiliates, each with its power..." Meaning "we" will use everything within our reach to destroy the country that "we" cannot rule.

From the first sentence, the report defines Libya as "a state with a tribal structure..." A little further, it states that "Cyrenaica has always been reluctant to accepting the dominance of Tripoli and Qadhafi's authority."

Reluctant? To 40 years of dictatorship? Is this only the case of Cyrenaica? What about Tunisia, Algeria, Yemen, Iraq, Egypt, Syria... Etc..?

As to tribalism, is it really particular to Libya?

In Tunisia, there is a kind of tribalism linked to entire regions, known as: "jihawiyya." It has been weighing in politics for more than half a century, as well under Bourguiba than Ben Ali. Apparently, it did not hamper the civil democratic revolution. It has even boosted it, since Sidi Bouzid, Kasserine, and the whole south-western "jiha" (region) was actually the launching-pad of the protests.

Further, the report asserts: "the Libyan protest - despite its popular character initially - does not represent the whole population..." How did they reach such a finding? The report is full of similar biases. Nowhere, could we find an explanation as to the method adopted to reach these conclusions. Subsequently, it cannot be creditable of any knowledge useful to cast a new light on the situation or make it progress.

In an oil-rich country like Libya, the revolution against the dictator is logically expected to be more rewarding for the people. Unfortunately, the report failed to see that, so undermined it was by its paranoid focus on Islamism and royalists inside the CNT. This is an old obsession of the

French intelligence, whose consequences were utterly tragic in Algeria in the nineties of the last century.

I wonder whether this report was not actually the cause of "second thoughts" among the French officials.[1]

---

[1] The Gulf Today, July 16, 2011: http://gulftoday.ae/portal/cd920830-f344-4fcc-8752-4fa5fd23b8d0.aspx

23

# WHO RULES SYRIA?

A little time after the Syrian revolution started, I was having a dinner in an Arab country with a personality who happens to know President Bashar al Assad closely, for he met with him several times. As we talked about Syria, he said: "Bashar is a novice in politics. When I advised him to consider opening up a dialogue with the Syrian elite, his answer was: who are they? They are nothing. Clearly, he despises the intelligentsia of his country. He thinks he would be able to rule the country a long time without people's consent."

The opinion of that Arab political leader (who is also a brilliant academic) is that Bashar has been used by his entourage and so became a kind of "hostage" of the security apparatus. His experience in politics was equal to zero when he took over. He could try to improve himself by calling to help some credible intellectuals and experienced political leaders with an unstained past, but he did not.

My point is Bush Jr. was almost in the same situation before he runs for president, although he had managed to get elected as governor and thus acquired some experience with government business. Yet, he understood that the job of president is quite different, involving complicated issues. Bush Jr. called to help people like Condoleezza Rice, Dick Cheney, Karl Rove, Karen Hugues, Colin Powell, Donald Rumsfeld, Paul Wolfowitz, etc... Like Bashar al Assad, Bush had also the father's heritage to manage in order to make his own way to leadership, but unlike him, he was willing to learn. Humbly, like any student, he would listen hours and hours to Condoleezza Rice (and other experts) lecture him on a wide variety of issues.

Bashar al-Assad, according to my source, would never listen to those who were willing to give him a disinterested advice. Maybe was it too late for him anyway. Being raised in a cocoon under the paternal warm shade, he has been accustomed to thinking that there is only one way to rule the Arabs of Syria: al-Assad's way (the family, that is). Thus, once president, he was just unable to make his own way to leadership by responding positively to the demands of the elite. Instead, he walked in his father's steps, remained fully loyal to the Baathist-family dictatorship, and opened his ears exclusively to the paranoid security apparatus that stayed unchanged, while the entire world was changing. How could such a characterless man lead a democratic reform? Clearly, the system was locked up from the outset and he would not dare to change it, even with the full powers he was endowed with as president. Therefore, the question is: who rules Syria actually? Is it Bashar or those groups of interest that manipulate him in order to gain time, for saving whatever could be saved and leaving the sinking boat?

It took 11 years, hundreds of protests, thousands of prisoners, tortured and injured, more than 1,600 dead since March 2011 and several condemnations from the international community (Human rights groups and UN included), for the juvenile and naive president Bashar Al Assad to issue a decree authorizing multi-party system in his country. Thus, while the people revolution is tearing down his rule and making a jest of his decrees, he authorized himself a little hope. Why not? After all, hope is for everybody, even for the naive whose vocation is to become dictator.

The decree allows political parties to be established and to function alongside the Baath party, in power since 1963 with the constitutional status of "the leader of state and society." The Syrian government adopted a draft law on multiple political organizations last month. Ostensibly, neither the president nor his entourage got the message the streets are sending them. The decree Bashar issued Thursday, August 4, would have made sense a few months ago (not to say a few years), before he unleashed his security forces and his army giving them license to kill.

Prior to the ongoing revolution, the Syrian regime was considered by some Arab parties (states, political movements and Arab League included) as a "necessary evil" even when they disagreed with its politics. Though everybody knew its legitimacy has long been eroded (since the massacre of Hama in 1982), its Arab "supporters" maintained the fiction that this was the "only" regime opposing resistance to Israel. They just could not consider it possibly replaceable, because if the "Baath" goes away, who on earth would resist, help the Palestinians, and liberate the Golan?

Those people must be blind. For if we combine together all the Arab wars against Israel in which the Syrian Baathist regime took part, the performance of the Syrian forces during the ongoing revolution against the disarmed people of Syria would by far outdo any other performance against the Israelis in any time. Honestly, if the Syrian forces have shown the same courage, the same talents in the killing business they have been showing us since March 2011 against their own people, not only the Golan would have been liberated but Palestine too.

This revolution is not to be ended so easily. One might be mentally handicapped to believe that Bashar al Assad could still save the furniture while the whole house is being carried away by this irresistible tsunami sweeping the Arab autocracies. The Syrians are disarmed and yet standing to a regime that gave them the unmistakable proof that it was able to survive only because they were afraid of its repression. While fear is normal, recent examples as well as crowd sociology show that it can be easily forgotten and bypassed in a just confrontation with an unbearable evil.

The "Damascus spring" (2000-01) has preceded the recent wave of Arab uprisings. Upon the death of Hafiz al Assad, the opposition forces have pressed for political reforms. Bashar, who was then freshly appointed president, could have listened to their voices and issued the decree he has just issued last Thursday. Not only he would have won a popular leadership and a new legitimacy in his country, but he would have appeared as a precursor and a model for the Arab world.

Unfortunately, he missed the appointment History gave him, and thus failed the only mission that could give a sense to his presidency.[1]

---

[1] The Gulf Today, August 6, 2011: http://gulftoday.ae/portal/83374514-9766-4117-a6f0-3b676cd9dff9.aspx

24

# THE SPIRIT OF THE TIME

With all the joy and the pride of the people who made their way to freedom through sweat, tears and blood; who are still holding their banners, chanting their slogans, sticking to their demands, sitting in places and squares transformed into huge freedom meetings , demonstrating on the streets, fighting against zealous pro-dictatorial troops and security forces sometimes with old rifles if not bare-handedly...With all their joy, their pride, their enthusiasm, and their great hopes, in all those little Arab villages, those cities that used to be, not so long ago, the realm of fear and despotism... With all their sacrifices... the cruelest catastrophe would consist in losing contact with that innocent legitimate initial flame that spurt out of their suffering: the craving for freedom.

When we see the Arab despots falling one after another, like the pieces of a domino game under the irresistible popular surge, we can only figure out the birth of a new Arab world. But after the rush of adrenaline that a dictator's downfall - live on TV or on the streets - procures us, comes the reflection. And with the reflection, the problems left behind as a legacy of several decades of dictatorship, many of which may be framed or reduced to just one word: mindset.

Then we realize that toppling a dictator is much easier than building a democracy.

None of the countries where an uprising recently tumbled the dictator was prepared for such a day. Therefore, it is obvious that we are not witnessing a long prepared revolution according to the French and American tradition, although we have to concede that the struggles against despotism have engendered more or less an obscure spectrum of leaders and ideas, more or less scattered in the press and the political literature. But how can we ascertain that those are well the men and the ideas the Arabs just need to rise and stabilize democracy?

In Europe and America, not only an important revolutionary literature had accumulated across the years, thus paving the way to the new system, but those revolutions have been led from the beginning to the end by faithful, dedicated, well-learned, open-minded men whose mission consisted in guiding and explaining to their fellow-citizens the spirit of the time. The post-revolutionary systems that have carried up and perpetuated that spirit (i.e. the craving for freedom), would not have been possibly conceivable without the historic contribution of such men. Progress on the path of freedom is not just a post-revolution product. Such a hypothesis could not even be contemplated to men like Voltaire, Rousseau, Montesquieu, Benjamin Franklin or Thomas Jefferson. As far as human freedom is concerned in any of today's big democratic countries, the work for democracy has long preceded the beginning of its construction.

Montesquieu's "Considerations on the Grandeur and Decadence of the Romans" or "The Spirit of the Laws" have been published many years before the revolution of 1789. Although he was a liberal conservative, arguing in favor of a limited, balanced, constitutional government, (i.e. on the English model), the influence he exerted on the shaping of democratic institutions in the West is beyond doubt. Montesquieu's ideas, like Voltaire's, were reformatory rather than revolutionary. Nevertheless, both men's ideas had a great influence in both the political revolutions of the eighteenth century: the American and the French.

My point is once an idea is in the air, it cannot be contained anymore. Call it the "spirit of the time" or the "spirit of revolution". Call it the "craving for freedom" or "for social and political justice." Call it "political liberty" or the "Spirit of laws." It is always about universal values, not about sectarian or religiously inspired ideologies.

When it is there, gripping a whole nation, the rulers must either put up or give up. For "the spirit of the time" is kind of "despotic" in its own way. It does not allow another ruler to overrule the freedom of the citizen and the sovereignty of the people.

Indubitably, revolutions do not invent or create that "spirit." It is rather the other way around. Revolutions become possible only when ideas of liberty, democracy, social-economic and political justice, grow and take shape as "the spirit of the time." That is why you do not have to mind who make revolutions as long as they spurt out of the spirit of freedom. You just have to worry about so-called "revolutions" made in the dark or rode by, either ambitious military or ideologues, who will become soon your "saviors."

When the idea of freedom takes hold in a country, even the most powerful ruling class can but serve it, though unwillingly. Suffice it to recall that it was the French aristocracy, which first started the revolution. Indeed. In 1787, the Parliament opposed the monarchy's efforts to effect needed reforms. Instead, they insisted on the calling of an Estates General, which they thought the aristocracy would control. When the Estates General met in 1789, it was the people, not the aristocracy, which came into power. So, instead of balancing the state, the aristocracy had helped to overturn it.

Such an event would not have happened without the contribution of what they called "the philosophers," who like Voltaire, Rousseau and Montesquieu, have formed an "atmosphere of reasoned dissent." Likewise, many of the men who made the American Revolution and drafted the Constitution and the Bill of Rights have been under the spell of "the spirit of the time" that seized philosophers and scientists in Europe and America. In 1688, the English Whigs, or Liberals, deposed King James II on the grounds that he had disregarded man's natural rights of life, liberty, and the possession of property. John Locke gave the natural rights theory classic articulation in his famous "Treatises." No wonder that many years later, Jefferson wrote: "We hold these truths to be self-evident, that all men are created equal, that they are endowed by their Creator with certain unalienable Rights, that among these, are Life, Liberty, and the pursuit of Happiness."

"Self-evident." These are the keywords.

What is self-evident in the ideologies struggling to shape the post-revolution landscape in the Arab countries?

To me, great revolutions are guided by universal values, not political ideologies craving for power. To be blind to this truth is to be blind to the essential, held by Jefferson as "self-evident," and thus universally undeniable.

If we exchange universal values for local ideologies, let us not wonder if we are paid in monkeys' currency.[1]

---

[1] The Gulf Today, August 27, 2011: http://gulftoday.ae/portal/ac201025-f3c2-4808-8368-1aa938d2bdfd.aspx

25

# CLOSER TO THE FINAL STAGE

At the sight of the Syrian revolution unfolding everyday with more popular determination, despite the repression, the question that seems to me urgent to answer is not "how much longer will Bashar manage to stay in power, " anymore, but rather: "is he still in power?"

Bashar al-Assad's rise to power in June 2000 came at a critical moment for the Syrian regime. Inside and outside the country, the feeling that the Baath system, which had ruled Syria for close to forty years, had reached the end line, was taking hold as the regime was gradually growing more irrelevant, anachronistic and disconnected from the reality.

The praetorian dictatorship model of state that prevailed in the Arab world, built on repression, relying on policies that stifle not only dissent but also other unauthorized expressions of political opinion by social actors, was stuck in an impasse everywhere in the region. This model was quite ordinary in the 1950s, 1960s and the 1970s. In the 1980s, it has started to show signs of overall weariness, while producing its monstrous antithesis, expressed by radical and violent groups of jihadists : i.e. what was al-Qaeda initially if not a network of global jihadists mobilized by Arab autocracies in full cooperation with the CIA, with the proclaimed goal of liberating Afghanistan from the communists? Yet, at the time, nobody ever figured out that the political change would come into that form of urbanized protest that we saw happening in the Arab cities. The only change considered was then either a coup or nothing! Reform as a prospect was just talk.

In Syria, the model has been often depicted as a military regime committed to radical social, economic, and foreign policies; eager to suppress civil rights and seal the country off from foreign influence, while displaying basic hostility toward the West.

This regime rose to power in November 1970 under the leadership of Hafiz al-Assad, after the Baath party – from which Assad's dynasty sprang – had led a successful coup in 1963. Much like other states following the same pattern (Qadhafi's Libya, Saddam's Iraq, Bourguiba and Ben Ali's Tunisia, Sadat and Mubarak's Egypt, A.A. Saleh's Yemen…) the regime, while still fresh, thrives on populism, perpetuating the myth of popular participation in order to survive. Over time, the populism gradually loses steam. The formerly inclusionary state grows exclusionary. However, if one cannot impute to historical genesis, per se, the longevity of these autocracies, the key is how the institutions of repression evolve. From the moment the inclusionary state becomes exclusionary, institutional political violence settles down, and the countdown starts. Mutual mistrust and suspicion account for much of the relations between the state and the society. Fear becomes the political "stabilizer," used by the police- state. Nevertheless, it is never a guarantee of longevity. Politicians know it. That is why many of those who serve dictatorships at posts of responsibility, try to keep escape routes secretly open (and well-funded) with the exterior world, just in case…

When Bashar accessed power, many Syrians asked themselves whether he was able to distance himself from his father's legacy. Unlike the father, accustomed to unrealistically boasting about the country's "good" situation, Bashar did not hesitate to acknowledge the difficulties he was facing and seemed much promising in terms of reform and political participation. However, soon it became clear that he lacked the wherewithal to bring about the necessary changes. The breaking point was during the outpouring of political liberalization – at least by Syrian standards – in 2001. The old guard, reposing on a coalition of Syrian power bases, content with the status quo and liable to be hurt by the political and economic liberalization process, opposed the reforms and called Bashar to order. Succumbing to the pressure, he reneged on his promises, and that was the beginning of the end.

This is a feature common to all the states that practice exclusionary politics. Faced with important political or economic demands, their impulse is to tighten the reins of repression rather than adopt liberalization as a survival strategy. When those who were excluded identify "Achill's heel," the displayed "might" of the state crumbles down under the conjugated thrusts of the protests in no time. No dictatorship is invulnerable. The Syrians who continue to demonstrate in the streets know it perfectly.

In his masterful "From Dictatorship to Democracy," Gene Sharp identified seventeen weaknesses of dictatorships. I am not going to enumerate them (: read the book). Still, many of them seem clearly adaptable to the Syrian regime in these days (as it was the case for Tunisia, Egypt, Yemen, and Libya previously). Thus, we may say that if all the regimes following the pattern formerly described have a life expectancy of some phases, more or less reckonable, yet varied according to every country's specificities, they tend to resemble each other when they get closer to the final stage, which is now the situation in Syria.

This is a situation where the system is unable to quickly adapt to the social scene; where personnel and resources normally used to support the government are less available; where officials start breaking up with the government and joining the protests; where the regime is less and less able to trust its normal bases of power; where the ideology is of no help whatsoever; where the bureaucracy is at its zenith of incompetency and inefficiency; where internal conflicts within the regime reach a dangerous degree; where the "public fear" is no longer an effective factor of control; where the instability of the hierarchy inside the regime is at maximum level; where subordinates do not obey anymore and sections of the security and military forces become uncontrollable; where the top of the hierarchy is completely blinded and intoxicated by its own propaganda; where regional and international allies distance themselves from the regime while the streets are invaded by the population...

The Syrian regime is agonizing. The question whether there is still a power in the country to which Bashar is clinging is clearly answered if you take time to reflect on the above description of the final stage. To me, the bases of the power are collapsing, and it is now just a matter of time before the protesters invade the presidential palace.

So, what should we do about Syria? Help them in every possible way to put an end at this sorrowful tragedy.[1]

---

[1] The Gulf Today, September 3, 2011: http://gulftoday.ae/portal/7fc52e30-4514-4c58-89ab-ffd2470ccff8.aspx

26

# KINGS WITHOUT KINGDOMS

The problem of changing regimes, necessarily linked to "appropriate" behavior towards opposition groups (assumed to be in this perspective leading the change), has always occupied the heart of US Middle East foreign policy. Contrary to popular belief, it was not the prerogative of the neoconservatives. The latter used and overused the concept under Bush Junior, but they did not create it. Anyway, the concept has created overtime a very bad reaction that has settled permanently among the elites of the Arab-Muslim world to the point of reversing the tide: if despotism is the problem, regime change has become part of the problem not of the solution.

Regime change (sometimes with military intervention) has been a game practiced by various US administrations, Republican and Democrat. In the context of interaction with the Muslim world, several factors come into consideration. Washington cannot - for example - decide to actively support the leaders of the opposition in any country, without considering the eventual consequences of such a support and the possible reactions against it (especially when weaponry is involved) in the Muslim world. Besides, US support for the opposition assumed to lead the change is rarely accepted as the "correct" position, particularly when it involves funding and high-level coordination between US officials and local leaders. This is so because of the historical legacy of the colonization and the mindset it has created among the Arab elites. The charge of US or Western "dummy" is so easy to come to the lips. Some members of the Arab elites are still unable to hold a debate clean of such innuendos in their interventions in the media or even in political meetings. This is an explanation for many of the current impasses of Arab politics, in the times of revolution.

Take the Syrians: many of the opposition leaders have made clear they do not wish any US-led intervention in their country, even to protect the population crushed everyday by the blind repression. Why did the Libyans accept what seems to the Syrians unacceptable? Did the NATO intervention in Libya undermine the future of the country? Did it form such an enormous obstacle to democracy?

These questions deserve to be honestly answered by the Arab elites in the countries where the population is being slaughtered.

Indeed, to raise the issue this way does not entail any assumption about the intentions of foreign powers. Any state has its own interests in view even when it declares acting on behalf of moral values. Yet, it is not necessary to address each powerful state namely in order to get humanistic assistance. The United Nations Organization has been precisely created with such a design, and it is correct to assume that it is still the institution authorized to give help during crises like the Libyan, the Syrian, the Yemeni, as it has done in the past, from Congo to Bosnia-Herzegovina and Kosovo, etc. Nonetheless, the international community that any party addresses a complaint to or a call for help is a community of states. The UN has no armed forces to compel any despot, any "rogue state," any criminal party to give up. Hence, the necessity to enforce the UN resolutions by means and institutions that are essentially those of the states.

That is also the dilemma some Arab elites are unwilling to solve or incapable to face, while their fellow-citizens endure the harshest punishment in the country.

Whereas the elites hesitate, loiter, and indulge into infinite palaver about the way out, the despotic governments can gain time and turn the disarray of the opposition to their benefit.

It is indeed easy for any government facing a mounting popular pressure, with the declared support of the USA and the Western world (as it just happened), to deflect political issues – like democracy and power sharing - to the "religious" stance, the sectarian divide, and the irrational. Such was the case with the Baathist secular regime of Saddam, after 1992, which under international pressure, turned to Islam, not to seek spiritual solace, but to mobilize the masses against a "new crusade," while the Shiites in the South and the Kurds in the North were rebelling. Such was also the case with Iran in the wake of the 2009-2010 electoral protests. And we saw almost the same pattern recurring with the embattled Qadhafi.

In Syria, the Assad's regime did not use the same discourse, with an emphasis on Islam, maybe because nobody would accord it any credibility. Still, it is apparent that for the government, the USA, Israel, and the West are those who want regime change, not the people of Syria.

In Yemen, Ali Abdallah Saleh coming back from his forced short exile in Saudi Arabia, clearly intends to break the will of the population, which continues to shout against him in the streets. Contrary to Assad, Saddam, and Qadhafi, Saleh did not engage in anti-US rhetoric as a way out of his crisis, because he did not build his own political discourse and popular influence on such a basis. Nor were Saddam, Bashar and Qadhafi the leaders of any resistance against the US imperial hegemony. Several recently unveiled documents revealed to the world how much every one of them was ready to sell his soul off to the "devil" they had damned if the "devil" was willing to buy it. But it did not happen.

Wishful thinking made Saddam Ben Ali, Mubarak, and Qadhafi figure out they have become absolutely "necessary" to the Western interests: Saddam for fighting his own war against Iran on behalf of the Arabs (who did not ask him), the West, and the "civilization." Ben Ali, for making France and the USA "confident" he was their "friend" and the protector of "their" interests in

Tunisia ; Mubarak, for keeping Israel's relations with Egypt "safe" and "out of trouble"; and Qadhafi for selling off his network of mercenaries, terrorists, and international pariahs to MI6 and the CIA, and dismantling his WMD program.

All of them imagined they were striking a deal with the West that would grant their offspring and families to be kings without kingdoms in their exhausted republics.

When they discovered that their dreams were pipedreams, it was too late.[1]

---

[1] The Gulf Today, October 1, 2011: http://gulftoday.ae/portal/5525afbf-d0a3-4753-ae76-f1b0374cdb24.aspx

27

# ARAB LEAGUE...STILL IN THE REAR?

The Arab world is apparently changing too quickly for the Arab League, unable to help Syria and Yemen. Let us be honest and acknowledge that this old institution has never been much of a vanguard leader, although we are told that its mission was to promote concord and facilitate agreement between its member-states. Actually it did; but always in expressing the realities of the prevailing mood among the most influent governments, not the popular mood.

During the fifties and a part of the sixties in the last century, the prevailing mood was Pan Arabism: Nasser was the most influential Arab leader; and neither the Saudi kingdom eastward, nor Bourguiba's Tunisia westward, could change this fact. Both were resentful of Nasser's growing power, and persuaded that he represented a threat to their own authority. Yet, the Arab league was then almost acquired to the Egyptian views of the struggle opposing the Arabs to Israel. The statements of the Arab summits in that period show clearly, how the diplomatic discourse of the League was shaped in the Nasserite mold, although the Arab leaders opposing Nasser continued to oppose him, showing through their Western alliances and other discernible behavioral distinctions where they stood.

The 1967's war broke the spell. While revealing to the Arabs their impotence and the hollowness of a political discourse that relies on line shooting instead of facts, it allowed the conservatives aligned behind Saudi Arabia to point out to the defects of the system settled by Nasser and the Panarabists. The political trends that were hampered in their self-deployment by the Nasserite period, self-centered around the Western notion of nation-state, started emerging from the limbo. Represented in Lebanon by the Phalanges, in Tunisia by Bourguiba's fanatics, in Algeria by the Boumedienism, in Egypt by an old school going back to Lotfi Sayyid and Salama Moussa, which will find a way to the top through M. Anwar al-Sadat...Etc... These trends will grow slowly as a timid response to the biggest defeat in the contemporary Arab history.

In the seventies, after Nasser passed away, they emerged with a new discourse merging a new brand of state-capitalism with the same autocratic rule that distinguished the previous period. The war of 1973 followed by the Arab oil embargo gave them "official credentials." From that moment onward, taking the reverse positions of the Nasserite period did not entail guilt or shame. Quite the contrary.

In Tunisia, Bourguiba even made a point of honor at reminding the Arabs of his famous discourse of 1965 in Jericho, when he urged the Palestinians to accept what the UN has offered them in the 1947's partition plan, and received a shower of eggs and tomatoes. Actually, he did not believe that they could win if they continued to rely on the "Arabs": i.e. Nasser! He was convinced that Palestine would never be free if it was not represented by a strong nationalist movement, completely independent and devoted to the Palestinian "nation." At the time, even Yasser Arafat himself could not hold such a discourse that would challenge the belief of the Panarabists: Palestine was the cause of all the Arabs.

In Algeria, Boumediene was triumphant with his third-world pseudo-socialist discourse, self-centered around the great Algerian nation. In Lebanon, the Phalanges movement was constructing its ideology on the idea that Lebanon was something "special" and that it was more connected to the Phoenicians (i.e. maybe because they were pagans) than to the Arabs (i.e. Muslims). It was inevitable that this movement would clash with the Palestinians who were in Lebanon also because their problem was acknowledged as the "Arab cause." In Egypt, Sadat was looking for a way to build his own leadership, and thanks to his army's performance in war, he soon felt enough strong to challenge his predecessor, still present in the Egyptian mind. In that decade, Egypt slipped from the influence of Pan Arabism to the old pseudo-liberal ideology, remindful of the ancient grandeur of this country.

Meanwhile, in other parts of the Arab world, the nation-state ideology was getting more importance, even without having any substantial meaning in the depth of our societies. Whereas the Baath party gained power in Syria and Iraq, it failed to show any difference distinguishing the Baathist rulers (supposed to be ideologically and politically more concerned about the Arab common interests) from the leaders of the self-centered "nation-states." The struggle for power was and remained for years to come just that: a struggle for power, with its procession of conspiracies, coups, counter-coups, and its innumerable victims, assassinated or convicted to heavy sentences, jailed or hanged after a parody of judgment.

In Saudi Arabia and the then-newly Gulf monarchies, the state was gaining ground with an ideology focused on the fulfillment of a religiously based identity. The oil boom and the wealth it accumulated in a short period made these states feel even more sensible to their own weaknesses as they were to that of their region and the entire Arab system. They made choices, which seemed challenging the old and waning left-wing/Panarabist alliance. They were aware that they depended on the West for their trade, as the West depended on them for its energy. The alliance with the West was therefore dictated by the necessities and the conditions of life in the modern time. No ideology would be strong enough to challenge the realities of economy, finances and trade. These choices were often misunderstood or misinterpreted. Anyway, the "ambiguities" of the seventies were also expressed through the statements of the Arab League, which has moved from Cairo to Tunis. Bourguiba was triumphant. However, does that mean that the Arabs have finally adopted the "real-Politick" view he had advocated?

The eighties of the last century showed the growing influence of Saudi Arabia and the Gulf monarchies, which particularly appeared in the offers of peace (Fahd plan). Thus, the Arab League has followed up the prevailing mood. It will continue to follow through the nineties, which turned out to be the decade of global military alliances. The Arabs were divided by Iraq's invasion of Kuwait. The Arab League was at its lowest moments, ever.

Yet, the first decade of this century showed them even more divided and the Arab League powerless, with the US invasion of Iraq. The League was unable to help or control what happened in Iraq. The Iraqis felt isolated and resented the League, and we know what the price of the Arab inertia was.

Today, with the liberation of Libya, thanks to an Arab-NATO alliance, are we witnessing the triumph of the system that made possible the liberation of Kuwait? So, what about Yemen? What about Syria?[1]

---

[1] The Gulf Today, October 29, 2011: http://www.gulftoday.ae/portal/5f36c5c2-302d-4a3b-ae23-ecab9c52bb9a.aspx

28

# TIMES ARE CHANGING

The Israelis are again trying to sell a war off to whoever would buy. At first sight, nothing new: such has been their behavior since the forties of the last century. Their preferred "clients" used to be the world media, and particularly the Western mainstream, some of which participated eagerly in forging the legend of the military "prowess" of the Hebrew state. The targets of the politico-military-media campaign (bluntly called propaganda) were and remain the peoples of the Middle East, from the shores of the Atlantic to the mountains of Afghanistan. It is no secret that war business could be much more profitable to certain social groups than peace. These groups detain billions of shares at the biggest stock markets of the planet, from Wall Street to the City of London, to Tokyo, to Singapore and beyond... During tough times in the big industrial centers, nothing may be more boosting to the "morale" of the market than a rumor that turns into clamor about big changes in the making, preferably a revolution, a coup, or better, a war... That means many new possibilities for businessmen, creation of thousands of new jobs, relocations, reconstructions, contracts, and a flowing river of gold... especially "black gold."

Many in the Middle East, a region deeply influenced by religion, have accepted the notion that these little endless wars are somehow the expression of a mysterious destiny; and since the struggle for survival is part of their life on this earth, they would better adopt it as a principle. That is how they would explain the concept of "Jihad" in Islam, which has never been properly understood in the West, except for the elite of learned specialists. From this perspective, the wars the Israelis have been selling for decades have not changed much in the mindset of the inhabitants of this region: today in 2011 like yesterday in 1947, the Israeli – either civilian or soldier – is still an "alien." He might be born in Tel Aviv, Jerusalem, or Jaffa, after the birth of his state... He might have learned Arabic, because his neighbors were Palestinians; might even like some aspects of Arab culture and arts, relish Egyptian movies, enjoy Syrian pastry and Lebanese cooking; and if he was a Sephardi, feel nostalgia for the beaches of Tunis, the walls of Marrakesh, and the Kasbah of Algiers... In other words, an Israeli Jew, either born in Israel to an Ashkenazi or a Sephardi family, might feel at home in the Middle East, completely attuned with his close environment (i.e. family, friends, community)... Still, he will never be at home as long as his government does not recognize to the Palestinians their right to be at home too on the land of their forefathers. Moreover, this denial based on a historic injustice is ingrained in the mind of every Arab born after 1947; and this will be so as long as Israel works as a war merchant and its leaders as warmongers.

The first generation of Israeli leaders wished to make of Israel an "outpost of civilization" (according to Herzl) defending the values of the West and its liberties against all kinds of despotism and Barbary. Obviously, this highly ambitious project lamentably failed. Instead of an "island of freedoms and peace" in a sea of "darkness," we have seen the erection of a military establishment disguised into a democracy, unable to hear the voices of peace and reason. Like all the dictators that oppressed people and forced them to fight wars, the Israeli leaders imitated those whom they pretended to fight and competed with them in tyranny to an unimaginable extent. And while Israel expanded its control over Arab territories, building everywhere settlements for newcomers and new generations of Jewish colonists along with prisons for thousands of dispossessed Palestinians, the Western mainstream media (fortunately with some exceptions) continued to depict Israel as a democracy, omitting to stress at the same time the solid bonds linking the Western governments to those dictatorships of incompetent elites.

Today, times are changing.

The new generation in the Middle East is ambitious and in a hurry. A generation that does not identify to the old incompetent elite of cranks and crooks that ruled these countries as if they were the family orchard. This generation wants freedom and dignity, and it wants it now. It is not willing to accept the beatitude of the fatalists. If the situation seemed to this generation so unbearable that everywhere the youth raised nearly the same slogans, with a total readiness to fight for them until death, maybe should everyone understand that we are henceforth getting into a new age for the entire Middle East.

In this new age, the old legends and myths will not work. The wiser will be those who grasp quickly and anticipate change, not only in discourse but also in behavior. Warmongers will continue their sinister business; but this time, the old military establishments themselves will have to adapt to the tide not to be carried away.

In Israel, Benjamin Netanyahu, completely bypassed by the recent and brilliant Palestinian victory in the UNESCO, may just be trying to get himself and his government out of the diplomatic isolation (exteriorly) and the dangerous crisis (domestically)by trying a military venture: he is said to be working to persuade his Cabinet to authorize a strike against Iran's nuclear sites. That may happen. He may get what he wants.

Of course, the objective of a surprise attack similar to the 1980's strike against Iraq's reactor, if successful, is to reassure the Israelis about their military capacities, their ability to keep the power balance undisturbed and give Netanyahu enough time to absorb the popular anger against his government, while showing the Palestinians and the Arabs that Israel is still "master of the game," on the ground, not international diplomacy.

Nevertheless, if such a plan was devised and executed prior to the Arab spring, its chances of success would have been bigger than they are today. Actually, the Arab spring not only shows

Israel as a caricature of democracy, but its effect on the mid and long terms may even upset the power balance without war.

The Arabs may not need to fight another war with Israel in order to change the relations (unless they are forced to). These relations are already in the course of changing with the Western countries that are the true "masters of the game" Israel was playing since 1948. What happened in the UNESCO recently is full evidence of the new rules of this age.[1]

---

[1] The Gulf Today, November 5, 2011: http://www.gulftoday.ae/portal/d003b5e9-1a9b-48ac-9253-cbe2e3274e4e.aspx

# 29

# NEW OUTLOOK...OLD STRUCTURES

I am entirely convinced that the Arab League is doing its possible to deflect more a catastrophic development in the Syrian crisis. Yet, it is not enough. Whatever the good intentions of the Arab leaders, the way they chose to tackle the crisis is flawed. The heavy inertia of the bureaucratic apparatus of the league is definitely not adapted to handling local problems. The fact that the League decided to suspend Syria is in itself an acknowledgement of the fundamental right to oppose and even revolt against the regime, if we do not consider it squarely as a condemnation of the official narration of the crisis (the so-called international conspiracy). This is already not a little affair: the Arab League is an official body representing states, not the population or the civil society. It is rare when it leaves its diplomatic and polite bits and bobs and venture in statements antagonizing member-states. It happened once, in 1979, when the Arabs condemned Sadat's lonely agreement with Israel (the peace accords) and decided to suspend and isolate Egypt. The case was serious. Yet, it was far from being an internal issue. The League was still playing on its own ground: diplomacy. In 1975, when it decided to mediate in Lebanon by sending the "Arab Deterrent Force" (which actually was the Syrian army), the crisis was hardly describable as local or internal, for there were at least two camps – each with its own allies from inside and outside the country - facing each other, and one of them (i.e. the Palestinian) was part of the civil war and foreigner at the same time. The League was then still fulfilling its function:

diplomacy and mediation between Arab officials. In 1990, when Iraq invaded Kuwait, the League condemned Iraq unanimously and played its role...

We can enumerate the examples that show the kind of work the Arab League has been doing since its foundation in the forties of the previous century. The point is clear: Diplomacy is the key word here; and as far as I remember, the League has never interfered in domestic affairs; neither was expected to do so. That is why the new outlook of the League is somehow surprising not only to the Syrian regime, profoundly upset by the ultimatum, but to all of us.

We are not surprised because the Arab League reacted after what seemed to be centuries of inertia... We are surprised because it proposed a plan which is actually a kind of "crisis management," although nothing in the League's past experiences and infrastructure and organization predisposes it to handle such a plan and see to its implementation. Absolutely nothing.

This is amazing. Let us put it this way:

The Arab ministers of foreign affairs that gathered twice in a few days (on 12 and 16 November) and made the decision of facing the Syrian regime with both the carrot and the stick issued a clear message: this may be the last chance to save Syria from the chaos following the internationalization and the militarization of the crisis. If the Syrian regime rejects the Arab League mediation and stubbornly sticks to its version of an Arab-international conspiracy to overthrow Assad, therefore it would have to face the unknown. The Arab League has voted on the first meeting to suspend Syria, then on the second meeting to offer the regime a way out by signing a protocol to allow 30 to 50 Arab observers to enter the country and report their testimony. Economic and political sanctions would be implemented in case the regime fails to live up to its promises.

The point is: while this plan seems "perfect" at the first sight, it would become absolutely vain in the practice. Why? For several reasons among which:

1- Admittedly, Assad agrees on signing the proposed protocol for the entry of 30 to 50 observers, what would these observers do to cover an area of 185,180 sq. km with a population estimated at 22 million people, and a wide variety of ethnical and religious communities? Where would 30 or 50 or even 100 fit in this picture? And how would they do their job of witnessing and reporting the atrocities happening right now? Does anybody know the answer?

2- On November 12, the Arab League offered the Syrian regime four days to answer positively its request before the suspension becomes effective; then on November 16, in Rabat, it offered three other days to sign the protocol. What about the suspension if Damascus accepts to sign? No answer. Nevertheless, we know that there will be economic sanctions (although these words were carefully avoided in the written statement of the League). Are the Arab leaders aware of these inconsistencies? And how would the Syrian regime interpret them?

3- If the Syrian regime decides all the same to play the game and accept the observers, would that mean that the Arab league has taken control of the situation on the ground so to impede further killings and atrocities? Absolutely not. The League has no means to control the field. The Syrian regime can still kill and lie and mask; and most of all, the Arab League has no means of knowing what is going on really and no means for reacting adequately. Therefore, the protection of the civilians, which is the purpose of this action, cannot be achieved by these defective proposals.

It seems obvious that while the coordinated action of the Arab league is wished and welcomed by both the population and the opposition, it is still far away from reaching the level of political efficiency we want to see. For this to be achieved, the League has to be re-thought, restructured, and reorganized in order to respond to the new requirements of the Arab societies today. However, the paradox here is patent: on the one hand, this is not the kind of work to be done on the short-term. On the second hand, the urgency in the case of Syria and Yemen requires a new dynamic of the Arab common political action; and it is not obvious that we could head toward the announced goals with the old structures.[1]

---

[1]     The     Gulf     Today,     November     19,     2011: http://www.gulftoday.ae/portal/99fe15b3-fed4-4f32-b34a-2cac8bb27adb.aspx

30

## THE MASTER OF THE GAME

Has the Egyptian revolution taken a bad start or a bad turn?

If the answer is: "a bad start," this is a disaster, for it means that the Egyptians have been deceived or even betrayed. The next question would be subsequently: are the present events going to fix it? Are the demonstrations in Maydan al-Tahreer and most of all the clashes with the security forces, and the blood spilling, the "right way" to do it?

If the answer is: "a bad turn," it is even worse. For it means that the revolution was a complete success and the democratic change underway; but some bad guys tried to exploit the ambiguous situation of a transitory period preceding the announced elections to advance their own interests, and the result is the current mess. The next question would be then: is it a defeat for democracy?

I will not try to answer these complicated questions in such a short column. Yet, I do think that the right answer may be halfway between the first and the second hypotheses.

Let us assume that the people of Tahreer square who made the revolution against Mubarak regime were completely wrong in trusting the military to protect them while moving smoothly toward a democracy. Those who hold such assumptions argue that, unlike Tunisia, the military have actually ruled Egypt since 1952. All Egyptian presidents (Nasser, Sadat, and Mubarak) came from the military. It is normal that in sixty years of unquestioned rule, the Egyptian state becomes gripped into a collusion of vested interests to the benefit of the ruling class, which is a combination of military, businessmen, and politicians. This elite has ruled Egypt and formed the backbone of its system. The revolution that overthrew Hosni Mubarak and some of his cronies, offered them to the crowd maintaining a fiction of revolutionary justice. That seemed to suggest that the revolution succeeded in toppling the regime. The Supreme Council of the Armed Forces (SCAF) vowed to "ensure a peaceful transition of authority within a free and democratic system that allows an elected civilian authority to take charge of governing the country." Yet, the system itself has not profoundly changed. The only fact that the SCAF – and not a civilian body (a transitory government) - was in charge of monitoring the political process in a country where a democratic revolution occurred, is evidence that the game was wrong from the outset.

Some would contend that nothing proves that the SCAF seeks to continue ruling the country after the parliamentary elections, or return it to a unique-party system. No, of course, the SCARF cannot impose such a scenario; not after such a revolution; not after the new move toward Tahreer square. Nonetheless, we have several examples of countries, where the military, without appearing in the picture, would impose their choice discreetly, and continue all the same to pull the strings from behind the curtains. In such a case, the military apparently subordinate to the civilian rule, are actually the masters of the game. Of course, the Egyptian military are not so stupid as to pretend ruling the country directly and publicly. Such a behavior would provoke criticism, mobilize the people against them, and destabilize Egypt.

The SCAF had initially announced its plan to rule the country for a transition period of six months, at the end of which presidential elections would be held. This time frame was later changed, with parliamentary and consultative council elections rescheduled. The current transition period could be extended, with the time of the presidential election becoming uncertain.

Moreover, the generals have not shown much wisdom in some of their decisions. If you do not consider the fact of trying 7000 people ( mostly civilians of course ) before military courts in itself as an aberration almost ignored by the media, how about the announcement made in May 2011 by General Mamdouh Shaheen (on behalf the SCAF) purporting that the military should be granted "some kind of insurance" under Egypt's new constitution, "so that it does not fall under the whim of a president"? He went to the extent of stressing that the military should not be investigated by the parliament!

In other words, they were asking for immunity.

Such a claim is not only weird in the wake of a popular revolution; it is also against the very spirit of democracy.

Does it make sense to build democracy while allowing the military to be "above" the laws that govern everybody? What are they? Angels? Saints? Supermen?

When in July, they announced the adoption of guidelines for drafting the constitution, their propositions were seen as paving the way to give them a legal ground enabling them to interfere in domestic politics, under such or such circumstance, with such or such excuse. This behavior was also considered as possibly indicating the retention of the decision in matters related to Egypt's foreign policy. Any civilian government, even democratically elected, would then run the country under the supervision of the SCAF, which is the real master of the game. Under such a system, democratic institutions would work in such a way that would always preserve the power balance between the military and the civilians for the benefit of the former: the power of the military would remain safe as long as no political group is able to challenge it.

The revolution has demanded political and economic change, and both spheres fall beyond the reach and the competence of the military. The alternative to the Mubarak regime cannot be constructed on the marginalization of the demands of Tahreer square. This is the first time in the Arab world's modern history where the commandment of a revolution does not come from the top but from the basis. The people of Egypt have proved that they have a will of their own; but so far, their revolution seems heading nowhere, for a will is nothing without a well-organized head.[1]

---

[1]     The     Gulf     Today,     November     26,     2011: http://www.gulftoday.ae/portal/9666c2c7-712f-478c-ac17-fddf0ace27cc.aspx

# 31

# IRAQ, IRAN AND THE SYRIAN STRUGGLE

As the US military are proceeding to complete their retreat from Iraq, speculations are going wild about the future of the country, on a background of exploding bombs in Baghdad and renewed security threats. Some policy analysts have already hinted to a potential massive shift in the regional balance of power, with Iran moving toward more an assertive role as a dominant power. Such a role is not much welcome in the neighborhood, for fears of Iran's whimsical policies growing into a new status quo hard to changing without another  costly war that nobody wishes. The withdrawal from Iraq comes at a time of an overall crisis in the region, over how to deal with Syria (the most reliable ally of Iran), and how to deal with Iran itself. The big question is: would the economic sanctions recently decided against Syria and Iran have enough strength and impact to smother the regimes without asphyxiating the population? Are they enough to weaken the position of both governments and precipitate their downfall?

Nothing is less hazardous than wishful thinking. So many examples show us that autocracies and dictatorships do not fall because of economic sanctions, from North Korea to Saddam Hussein and Qadhafi. The first is still alive and kicking; the two others have collapsed after a military intervention orchestrated by major Western powers left them no other choice.

Resisting Western pressure is actually the ideological basis of these regimes. For so many years, they have indoctrinated troops, militias, and civilians with such a dogma that has become a system of belief and behavior. The zeal the Syrian troops and Shebbiha deploy in killing and torturing their own people can only be explained (although it is not a justification) within this ideological and political framework. On the one hand, the US Middle East half-blind policies have turned the populations of this region bitterly against the West helping dictators becoming the defenders of the Palestinian rights and the champions of resistance against Israel colonial aggressiveness. On the other hand, the more the support of the West to the Israeli expansionism was perceived unfair to the Palestinians and the Arabs, because it is the support of the powerful not the weak, the deeper the logic of resistance took roots in the traditional ground of anti-imperialist fight. Both practices have grown so entwined that it is superfluous to add: they have typified the current Middle East and cemented the socio-economic and military basis of the regimes to the point that democracy and human rights values were considered secondary compared to the fight against Israel and the western imperialism.
Some scenarios may seem merely frightening to the West. Imagine Iraq falling completely under the Iranian influence, with its huge human and material potential. Imagine several years with the Syrian and Iranian regimes surviving the sanctions thanks to this strategic asset, which is an Iranian dominated Iraq. This prospect would allow Iran to extend its reach westward within a sphere stretching from Afghanistan to the Mediterranean.

However, as big an issue as it may appear, it is not easy to prove. For, why should the Syrian regime survive sanctions? Why should Iraq fall necessarily under the Iranian dominance? Is it a fate? Certainly not. However, objective conditions are determining.

In both Libya and Iraq, the dictators have been able to resist the siege just because they maintained the population under the yoke of fear. In Syria, ordinary people are resisting repression. The regime's credibility is almost inexistent. The Arab League and the Islamic Conference's positions in support of the popular demands have boosted the morale of the opposition and the demonstrators continue to challenge the regime. This has not happened in Libya and Iraq under the sanctions. The Arab League role here is a key to the future of Syria.

Concerning Iraq, the problem has been created by the Americans themselves. Bob Woodward reported that in 2006 Prime Minister Jafari was no longer acceptable to the United States and the United Kingdom. "Jafari's support came from the Iranians and the detested Moqtada al-Sadr (...) The worry was if Jafari was elected prime minister for four years he would become Moqtada's pawn". Moreover, "the Iranians started saying openly and emphatically that Jafari was their candidate". The situation grew untenable. However, the alternative was not much different. When Jafari stepped aside on April 20, and the Iraqi parliament selected its first permanent Prime Minister Nouri al-Maliki, the Bush administration did not have a clue about him, except that he had spent 23 years in exile between Syria and Iran. In a meeting in the White House (May 12) where ten former secretaries of state and defense were invited, Colin Powell said: "I'd like to offer you caution about Mr. Maliki, because frankly I don't think any of us heard anything about him or knew anything about him until he was announced last week. And we pushed Jafari aside, but he is a deputy of Jafari out of the Da'wa party. And I have to have a little bit of caution about somebody who spent most of the last 20-odd years in Iran and Syria."

Is Maliki the man of Iran? Let us not play the sectarian game and believe that being Shiite, he is necessarily pro-Iranian. Not so easy. After all, his direct rival, Ayad Allawi is also Shiite. Yet, as Prime Minister of the interim government, Mr. Allawi offered the Arab neighbors more a reassuring image than other Iraqi politicians. Why? Because he was "well known for his pan-Arab credentials, for his orientation towards security and intelligence work, economic and social liberalism, and caution towards Iraq-wide federalism. His Shiism was of a strictly non-political variety, while his relationship with the Najaf hierarchy was correct, though distant. He was also perceived to be a foe of Iran", which probably explains why Teheran used of all its influence to support al-Maliki against him in 2010.

Now if we put aside the problems of power distribution that the Iraqi constitution may lead to in the future, and focus on those eventually rising from the Iranian influence, would it be wrong to assume that Iran is the winner of the war that George W. Bush led? The answer of this question may be in the outcome of the Syrian ongoing struggle, for Syria is indubitably a key to both countries.[1]

---

# 32

## DEAD MAN WALKING

The State Department official, Frederic Hof, told Congress on Wednesday 14 that Assad's repression may allow him to hang on to power but only for a short time. Urging the Syrian opposition to prepare for the day when it takes control of the state in order to prevent chaos and sectarian conflict, he added: "Our view is that this regime is the equivalent of a dead man walking." Hof compared Syria to North Korea and said it was difficult to determine how much time Assad has left in power but stressed, "I do not see this regime surviving."

Part of the US objective in the course of manipulating both the Iranian and the Syrian issues is to deter Iran from completing an arc of influence from Iraq, after the US military withdrawal, through Syria and Lebanon, thus controlling a large field between the Gulf and the Mediterranean. Syria is an old ally of Iran. If the regime collapses, the interesting question is: who would occupy the ground? In the US assessment, whoever will rule Syria after Assad, would be under pressure from Iran throughout Iraq, whence the necessity to control the consequences even of the old alliance's falling apart. A post-Assad Syria does not need to collide with a heavily "influenced" Iraq. The borders between these two countries may become an area of arms smuggling and infiltration of pro-Iranian militias. This could be just the opposite of the ideal

American scenario wherein a democratic-secular and liberal Syrian republic, preferably ruled by a pro-occidental (not necessarily pro-US) elite, would punish Iran as the main ally of the dictatorial regime by associating itself to the US-led policy of sanctions and isolation; extend its hand to a pro-US government in Iraq (if it remains friendly), and most of all cut off the support to the Palestinian factions considered radicals and −of course − to Hezbollah, while engaging in negotiations with Israel for a peace package.

Therefore, if such a hypothesis happens to be valid, and if the regime continues the blind murderous rampage while rejecting the Arab League's offers, a US-led external intervention to help toppling the regime would not surprise many observers. Yet, so far, it is unlikely.

Financially, such a war would be very expensive and, as Syria is unlike Libya deprived of big oil resources, the West − still striving with its own economic mess − is quite understandably reluctant to provide the Syrians with the same military means that were given to the Libyan rebels. For, who would pay for the war? Moreover, following the September 2007 Israeli air strike on a Syrian nuclear reactor, Damascus has invested in air defenses; and according to some intelligence assessments, attacking it may cost human casualties and money. Therefore, the only incentive that may convince the West to intervene may be a kind of big deal with the Syrian opposition, whereby the US and Western interests would be granted in the post-Assad era. Now, whether the Syrian opposition is ready to strike such a deal with the West, after the precedent of the Iraqi opposition, remains to be seen.

In the present conditions, a major military operation such as the one led against Qadhafi or Saddam, is hardly imaginable and hazardous. For if the West is still keen on isolating − and maybe striking - Iran, why would they begin by waging a war on Syria in order to attain Iran? Actually, even a war against Iran may cost a lot more than its possible rewards if it leaves the regime intact. So, why risk the shot?

Maybe the "safe" tactics from the US perspective would be to weaken both regimes without confronting them directly: no need for their opposition to be bound by a strategic alliance to the USA. In this context, the opponents would be considered "useful" as long as the showdown with the Syrian (and possibly the Iranian) regime continues. Day in, day out, the regime of Damascus, blinded by its own incapacity to understand correctly and answer positively the Arab League's offer, is digging a deeper grave for a rule that has become unbelievably fascistic in an era of generalized sympathy for the Arab spring protesters.

Hof is right to say: this is a dead man walking. For Bashar al-Assad so far acted as if he were his own enemy, not only the enemy of his people: he is just incapable to see and acknowledge that the Arabs were trying to avoid him the same doomed fate than Saddam and Qadhafi. Such an endeavor from the Arab leaders is explainable only in the context of the Arab spring by the acknowledged centrality of Syria's regional role. In 10 years of Assad's unpopular rule, few events could have better underscored the centrality of such a role than his visit in July to Beirut and his meeting with Lebanese Prime Minister Saad Hariri who had repeatedly charged him of killing his father. That charge had generated an international pressure forcing Syria out of Lebanon. Assad was joined in Beirut by Saudi Arabia's king Abdullah, who together with Sheikh Hamad Al-Thani, prince of Qatar, held a summit at which they pledged their cooperation in the effort to ensure political stability in Lebanon. That summit was meant to show the strong commitment of Saudi Arabia, Syria, and Qatar to achieving that objective.

After the beginning of the protests in Syria, the Arab League remained a long time hesitating and trying to help Bashar al-Assad with the kind of "empty" discourse that angered the Syrian population to the point that they said: Assad is killing us with the blessing of the Arabs!

Why was that? Because the Arabs know perfectly what is at stake in Syria: this is not just a country like Tunisia, with almost no external problems, no wars, no occupied land, and no heterogeneous population... a country just striving for democracy and dignity. Syria, even without oil, is a strategic prize, because it commands: the struggle with Israel, the struggle with Iran, and the amazing mosaic of the Middle East population.

Unfortunately, the only people today unable to understand what is at stake, are those who are no longer fighting to stay in power ( is there still a power in Syria?) but for their survival in a regime that seems definitely doomed and condemned to be a dead man walking.[1]

---

[1] The Gulf Today, December 17, 2011: http://gulftoday.ae/portal/49a19bb8-c944-4ff6-9a4a-b338ec42e3a1.aspx

# 33

# 12 MONTHS OF SPRING

"May you live in interesting times," says the old Chinese dictum. These times we are living in are probably a significant sample. 2011 has been certainly one of the most "interesting" years ever lived and witnessed in the Arab world. It was so breathtaking, so surprising, so full of an unexpected concatenation of events that it will go through history referred to as merely... a season... the best at all: the spring! Moreover, even if actually only a handful Arab states were concerned, the change was so striking that a new conviction has appeared among the youth: the change is still coming and it is overlapping, not to say overwhelming the entire Arab nation. This is for the introduction.

Now, what about the development? Should we say it might still take another dozen months to show whether these are true and genuine democratic changes or fake? What if 12 other months are not enough? How about 12 years or more, much more? Am I pessimistic? Not at all, but simply realistic. Indeed. The Arab world has lived long centuries under dark autistic leaders. Out of the blue, people angered and fed up took to the streets, and the heads of government started falling off. How did that happen so quickly? Is it a mood? Is it a true social metamorphosis? Is it going to last?

I am willing to believe that the communication boom and the new technologies conjugated with globalization have literally atomized time and exploded the pace of change. Yet, I am not sure that these variables have also affected the mindset and the belief system of the Arabs in a non-return way. Not sure because of the infancy of the democratic revolution, the stammering of the experience in Tunisia, the looseness of politics in Libya, and the disorientation of people and the continuation of violence and chaos in Egypt, Yemen, and Syria.

The fight for democracy that has just started in the Arab world is not going to be easy, for both internal and external factors.

The internal factors: the Arabs may pursue their groping for democracy or its simulacrum in 2012, just as Plato's chained people groped for the delusion of truth in their cave, or venture to go out and find the real light. The whole matter is about knowing the difference: where the delusion is and where the truth is!

They may as well put another half a century to understand that they were actually deluded and betrayed, as they did when they started understanding that the newly independent post-colonial states were another system of servitude. That's why many are so skeptical about the newcomers, not only because they are complete novices with no experience in government, but also because of their political background as ultraconservative Salafists and other ex-militants of the right-wing Islamism (Nahdha and Muslim Brotherhood). The test of government is particularly revelatory of the true nature and character of any person, any ideology. To defend democracy when you are in opposition or jailed or exiled is one thing. To fight for it when you are in power is another.

We have seen in the modern history of the Arab countries great heroes of the anti-colonial struggle and defenders of the rights of people to choose their own rulers, becoming merciless tyrants when they grabbed power. Therefore, if history has a sense, it would be this: do not believe them until they prove they are true democrats.

The external factors: revolution is contagious, everybody knows it. That's why revolutions have always been fought by unsatisfied neighbors and outside powers allied to unsatisfied locals. The craving for freedom is a state of the mind. Yet, it is a dangerous one, not for the individual or his community, but for the rivals or the parties that are afraid of what it may bring onto them if it is allowed to prevail.

Much of the violence we see in Egypt, Yemen, and Syria is largely caused by anti-revolution reaction. It is understood that revolutions are seldom peaceful. They may even happen despite the governments being willing to reform. Sometimes reforms become part of the process that leads to revolution, either because they are incomplete or because they were sabotaged. Many cases suggest that collective violence is likely when discontented people are offered unfulfilled hopes that their discontent will be remedied.

Contagion is most feared by those who do not wish any change to happen, because it has been evidenced many times throughout history as the most efficient channel of regime change. A call to revolt seems less effective than news of its occurrence in the neighborhood. The demonstration effect is apparent in the revolutionary contagion that spread across the Arab world since the success of the Tunisian revolt and the flight of the ex-president. This is not new. A similar effect has been shown in the revolutionary contagion that spread from the North American colonies to Western Europe to Hispanic America between 1776 and 1820; in the series of unsuccessful communist revolutions in Europe after 1918; in the infectious anticolonial nationalism of Africa and Asia after 1945; and in the wave of anti-communist revolutions that shook Central and East Europe in the wake of the Polish insurrection led by Solidarnosc in the 1980s.

Therefore, the assumption that the anti-revolutionary, anti-democratic forces in the Arab world have already mobilized, might not be inaccurate. If the fight for freedom is so uneasy in countries like Yemen, Syria, and Egypt, where people continue to die daily, as if it were a banality of life, it is not only because of the "solidity" of these regimes. Much more powerful regimes (like the former communist states of Europe and the USSR) have collapsed under the thrust of a determined population. It is because those Arab regimes are being supported (secretly or openly by different political maneuvers from outside allies) that they are still standing against the free will of the people.

Last, but not least, 2011 has carried a hope to the Arabs everywhere. Let's pray that 2012 will make that hope achievable at least in the countries where people suffered and sacrificed their lives for it.[1]

---

[1] The Gulf Today, December 31, 2011: http://gulftoday.ae/portal/b58f8888-189a-4458-b315-92b37c26eb60.aspx

34

# CHANGES THAT DID NOT OCCUR

The ongoing crisis in the Gulf continues to spill a lot of ink. Let us hope that it remains with ink and nothing else. Some speak of a "nuclear" Iran as if it were expected to change the face of the world. They forget that, by all accounts, Iran is a small developing country. The noise they are making around its nuclear program has so far failed to hide the truth, which is: Israel, not Iran, has surely the deadly arsenal of nuclear weapons; and Israel, not Iran, occupies Arab territories by force, and is again threatening its neighborhood of war.

Indeed, nearly three decades ago, Iran became the center of an important phenomenon, called: political agitation. Yet, it changed nothing in the Arab world. The autocracies continued to live as they have always lived. They survived the Iranian seism ...until the "Arab spring". Today, something is changing in the Middle East; but it is hardly connected to Iran.

The Iranian revolution was certainly one of the most sweeping events of the last century. It has been compared to the 1917's Bolshevik revolution mostly for the shockwaves both events unleashed. Yet, the Iranian influence could not change regimes, although it inspired movements across the Arab world in the 1980s:

In Egypt, on October 7, 1981, a splinter from the Muslim Brotherhood called Islamic Jihad assassinated president Sadat. The group was subsequently found to have hatched the assassination plot with Al Gamaa al-Islamiyya, a Brotherhood offshoot that would , in the mid-1990s, develop ties with al-Qaeda and be chiefly responsible for the 1997 terrorist attack in Luxor on Nov. 17, 1997. Oddly enough, the Muslim Brotherhood (with its Islamist allies) is today the winner of the first Egyptian elections after the revolution. Is this phenomenon less important than Iran's nuclear file? I doubt it.

In Syria, the Muslim Brotherhood initiated a rebellion against the regime of Hafiz al-Assad. Today, it is the entire people of Syria in revolt against the same regime. This has nothing to do with Iran.

In Lebanon, the Hezbollah considering Israel and the USA as two sides of the same coin, sought to deal both a massive defeat in the country. Iran nurtured Hezbollah and Hezbollah served Iran's Islamic Revolution. However, both fear the collapse of Assad's Syria, and are helpless about it.

In Afghanistan, Jihad was directed against both internal and external enemies, i.e. the communist government and the Soviet invaders. Today, it is still directed against two "enemies": the ex-ally (USA) and its local "protected". The "enemies" have changed, not jihad; and Iran has nothing to do with it.

In Gaza and the West Bank, Islamists called for a long armed struggle to liberate Palestine and establish an Islamic state. Today, it is still the same discourse, and better: Hamas and the Islamic Jihad intend to build an alliance. Who is responsible for the political impasse? Iran? No. Israel.

And in all MENA countries, in the eighties, Islamists seemed rising as a force ready to topple governments and take over. In Afghanistan and Lebanon, they surely succeeded in driving foreign troops outside, but that victory did not lead to the ideal Islamic states that their ideologues had hoped for. Both countries remained mired in civil wars long after foreign troops retreated. However, Islamist organizations were drawing adherents across the region and their code of behavior was shaping societies and making Islamic symbols more visible in the public space. Was this due to the influence of the Iranian revolution in the region? Only partly, because many Islamist organizations in the Arab world have preceded the Iranian activism not followed it. And today, with the Arab spring, they reached their goal: they are in power. Who is responsible? Iran? No. The stupidity of those who supported dictators for so many years.

True, a number of Islamic movements in the 1980s, taking their inspiration from the success of the Iranian revolution, have launched armed struggles and attempted to topple secular rulers or to repel foreign invaders. This is what we call an "ideological preponderance," which is a sociological phenomenon also noticeable in the wake of many revolutions, from the 1848's European wave, to the 1917's Bolshevism, through to the 1989 East European uprisings, and up to the 2011 Arab uprisings.

But what is at stake today is more than Iran upgrading its nuclear program. This cannot be of any real influence upon the societies of the Middle East. The real challenge comes from inside these societies themselves, as we cannot predict yet how Egypt, or Tunisia, or Libya would evolve with the Islamists at the top. How are they going to handle the internal and external issues? Do they really understand the "realities" of a complicated international game? And above all, how the revolution in Syria and Yemen would develop, whereas we have the impression that these countries are on the eve of implosion, because of the type of social order that so far has prevailed.

Although socially diversified, the Middle East in not yet a pluralistic society in which a subordinate group does not have to forsake its lifestyle and traditions. Pluralism is based on mutual respect between various groups in a society for one another's cultures. It allows a minority group to express its own culture and still to participate without prejudice in the larger society. Unfortunately, violence and even civil wars have destroyed the civil peace in several countries of the region because of the intolerance and the manipulation of social groups against each other. On such a large scale, this may be hardly the consequence of the only Iranian meddling in internal conflicts.

In Lebanon, the fifteen-year civil war started well before the Iranian revolution. In Algeria and Morocco, there was a Berber problem since the independence. In Egypt, Copts and Muslims did not wait the Iranian revolution to clash. In Sudan, the civil war between southern Christians and northern Sunnite Muslims lasted for most of the second half of the last century, made thousands of victims, and ended up in partition. In Yemen, the tribes and ethnic groups were just incapable of living together. In Syria, Turkey, and Iraq, Kurds, Shiites, Sunnites, and other ethnic and religious groups are at the throats of each other since so many years that it is ridiculous to say the Iranian revolution pushed them. In Iran itself, the Arabs of the Khuzestan (called Arabistan), the Sunnites, the Kurds, and other social groups – women included – face the same problem, which might have been aggravated since the revolution.[1]

---

[1] The Gulf Today, January 21, 2012: http://gulftoday.ae/portal/b73a8863-8a2c-4cf0-8754-7347a49466b5.aspx

35

# OLD ISSUES FOR NEW RULERS

When one consults the most recent researches preceding the revolution, one would find a prevailing opinion saying that Egypt confronts simultaneously the challenges of economic and political structural adjustment in this century. While it is true that no study, as far as I know, has predicted the revolution, some findings are all the same still interesting to remember and understand. What some researchers called "process of political adjustment" – implicitly emphasizing the value of political participation – has probably been quite metamorphosed by the biggest event in Egyptian modern history, since Nasser and the Free Officers came to power, (Suez nationalization excluded), which is: January civil democratic revolution. As the political process engendered by this event is still in the making, considering the magnitude of change expected to touch on every aspect of the Egyptian society, we will not comment the unknown.

However, there is an aspect that needs to be brought into the light, which is the fact that any political change (or adjustment) would have no substance or effect if we do not found it on the economic realities. Now, on this level, let's admit that any new government issued from the recent elections, whatever its credentials or ideological inclinations, will have to deal with the same reality that the former government (prior to the revolution, that is) would have dealt with. Even with a worse reality, considering that the Islamists propelled to the forestage in the last elections, might not be exactly the kind of reassuring asset for the touristic sector, for example. Of course, this sector is not the whole economy. Yet, it is not clear how the new government is going to deal with the need of economic adjustment that has been identified in recent researches on Egypt.

I heard the leader of the Muslim Brotherhood saying in an interview on Al-Jazeera that if all or some of the Egyptian funds that have been embezzled by the corrupt elite, are allowed to return to the country (from abroad), we won't need to borrow!

Well, this is the kind of beautiful and hollow bla-bla, based on half-truths, half-lies. I don't mean that those funds are not important. They are indeed, and the people of Egypt should, by all means, try to recuperate them. However, to pretend that this alone would free Egypt from borrowing, is just naive. The biggest industrial societies are also the biggest borrowers. Egypt is not outside the world capitalist system.

The point is the challenge Egypt faces today on this level is almost the same that it faced in the last days of Mubarak's regime. Nevertheless, let us not cut off politics from economy. It doesn't make sense to do so, even without a revolution on the hands.

The first aspect of the polity requiring adjustment, in order to reach good governance, is that a considerable amount of new political infrastructure should be built, for the present one represents the vestiges of the 1960s' socialist era.

Recent researches have pointed out to the components of this outdated infrastructure, including: 1 - Constitutional/legal framework within which politics is conducted; 2- - Political and governmental organizations and institutions; 3- Information dissemination and opinion formation systems that surround the political process.

For the first point, the real work has not yet started. The announcement that the emergency Law was to be abolished is a good step forward. But it is not everything. Some of the worse effects on Egypt's political life were due to the imbalance between the executive and the legislative branches. This has to be constitutionally fixed.

For the second point, the revolution would have to build its own institutions and organizations with, however, a different objective. To keep an optimistic faith in the capacity of the revolution in implementing its own choices, one should exclude the transformation of the current Islamist majority into a new "ruling party" devoted to controlling the civil society and the bureaucracy as well. Most of all, the "new rulers" should consider that the best economic and political asset of Egypt is its modern culture, which has served as a model for the entire Arab region. Disturb that model, and Egypt will go bankrupt. Leave it alone, even if you don't like it, and the country would survive.

The third point does not need to be overemphasized. Its importance is the same than democracy itself. Assumedly, we should not expect to see the state-owned media (for example) being controlled by an all-mighty ministry of information. Such a department should not exist at all. Nor does it make sense to abolish this ministry just to give its prerogatives to the Interior ministry. Once, this point is clear for everybody, the new system should softly settle down as simple management, not thought-control institutions or a religious police.

The second aspect of the polity that needs to be cared about concerns creating a dynamic, outward-oriented economy. Here, the problem is obviously the highly centralized nature of the state itself. How to downsize it, with the objective of rendering it more efficient, without imposing too much hardship?

The human factor is Egypt's first asset. The new rulers – notwithstanding their ideology – should understand that they would not be able to run Egypt, and much less to succeed in the political and economic adjustments required, without creating a consensus. However, no consensus would be reached without respect to the fundamental rights that the revolution sought to make obviously respected. We live in a complicated world, where the old slogans like "Islam is the solution" would not work to providing people with their basic needs, let alone welfare, without internal and external compromises. Make of the liberals, the Nasserites, the leftists... your enemies, instead of your political rivals, and your success, as a new majority, is already compromised. Make of the West your foe, and you put your country on the same path than Iran.[1]

---

[1] The Gulf Today, January 28, 2012: http://www.gulftoday.ae/portal/52a47994-9555-4dde-a37e-67d2b3ae52a2.aspx

# 36

# RUSSIA: BACKING LOSERS

Russia showed contempt for the entire Arab world, not only because it chose willingly to support an Arab regime involved in crimes against the humanity, but also because it literally spat on the Arab League's initiative, which – despite its shortcomings – is still an attempt to ease the pains of the Syrian people. Russia sided with the losers out of an apparent resentment toward the Arab spring. Why "losers" and why "resentment," would you ask? Let's begin with the second...

## Why the resentment?

Moscow has taken what is rightly described as a counter-revolutionary stance in Syria and seems voluntarily siding with a doomed despotic government. Is this a rational choice? Is it dictated by Russia's interests or by other considerations?

Ostensibly, there are much more similarities between Russia and Syria than Moscow may be willing to admit.

First, although it professes a commitment to democracy, Russia is still far away from it. The corrupt bureaucratic structure of the Putin- Medvedev regime is beyond doubt a receipt for democratic failure, resistance to modernization, and rejection of peaceful reforms. We won't be surprised that a revolution (of the Arab kind) spreading over to reach Russia, whose power elite is still convinced of a plot against Arab dictators. Remember Medvedev's first take of the Tunisian and Egyptian revolutions. He was shocked: "We must face the truth," he said. "In the past, such a scenario was harbored for us, and now attempts to implement it are even more likely. In any case, this plot will not work."

The Russian narrative of the conspiracy theory implicated Western intelligence services in hatching Arab revolutions through the manipulation of social networks. This is also, what is still officially admitted in Damascus. Yet, when they move away from the paranoid discourse, the Russian leaders adopt a despising attitude toward the Arab peoples. This seems crystal-clear when Putin describing Qadhafi's regime as « warped and ugly monarchy », yet argued that « on the whole, it satisfies the local public mentality and political practice. » For the last inheritor of Stalin, to imagine that "the local public mentality and political practice" could be fed up and hoping for a better government was too much.

Yet, there is more than the simple "solidarity" between two corrupt authoritarian regimes. Moscow might well be afraid of these revolutions occurring in the Arab world. After all, Islamists are today the new majorities in Tunisia and Egypt, and who knows where else, next? Why should this wave stop at the borders of Iran? What would prevent it from spreading over towards the Caucasus in the north and Central Asia populated by Muslims? Violence in the north Caucasus has preceded the Arab spring, and the images of protesters in the streets of the Arab cities may strike the imagination of many people in the Caucasus and trigger the rebellion. The same may be said about unrest in Central Asia: southern Kyrgyzstan since 2010; an almost imploding situation in Tajikistan; and an Uzbekistan on the verge of revolt because of the despotic regime.

Add to these concerns, the panic about losing such a good "client" as Syria, a key-player in the Middle East geopolitical game. This is not new. The former Soviet Union was a long-time ally of Syria and a main supplier of arms to the Syrian military. Soviet advisers and military personnel were welcomed by the late Syrian president Hafiz al Assad, even as Soviet relations with other Arab governments, such as Egypt, deteriorated after successive Arab defeats in the wars with Israel. It is estimated that the Soviet Union provided Syria with up to $26 billion worth of arms until 1991. Between 1999 and 2003, Russian-Syrian military relations revived. In 2005, while cancelling most of Syria's $13.4 billion debt from previous arms agreements, Russia was still and remains to date its primary arms supplier. In May 2010, Russian president Dmitry Medvedev visited Syria, and a little later, reports appeared about new arms agreements. Today, the regime is using this Russian arsenal against its own people.

## Why Russia is losing?

Before the widespread unrest that broke out on January 26, 2011, Syria's brand of authoritarianism sounded well established. Protesters called for political reforms and the reinstatement of civil rights, as well as an end to the state of emergency which has been in place since 1963. However, it is clear today, that a robust security response may never succeed to stem the tide of popular discontent, as the Syrian regime seems unable to find an alternative strategy that might achieve this objective. In short, many observers agree that the regime is now beyond the point where it might be possible to implement a program of peaceful and gradual reforms.

According to several surveys and reports, the signs are not good for the regime. The increasingly united front in the West against the regime of Assad emphasized the political vulnerability of its trade dependence on the West, becoming Achilles' heel. The economy is crumbling, as the combination of a crashing tourism sector, falling foreign direct investment, and the tightening of western sanctions has dried up foreign currency flows. Some reports suggest that the reserves of the Central Bank of Syria are being depleted at a rate of $70 million-$80 million per week as part of an effort to stem the depreciation of the pound in the parallel market. The situation is not going to improve even with Russia and China blocking the move of the Arab League in the International Security Council. The most painful blow to the economy has been the restrictions imposed on the trade with the EU, previously the destination for more than 90% of Syrian exports. The expansion of the current account deficit (about 6% of GDP) is expected, as the result of these disruptions. Political uncertainty will also discourage investment by domestic businesses, creating the danger of an increase in unemployment that would reinforce any decline in consumer spending.

If these tendencies continue, and nothing in the current situation suggests that the regime is able to halt or slow the pace of the general collapse, the question that Russia would have to face is: how does it feel to lose with such a stubborn blindness?[1]

---

[1] The Gulf Today, February 4, 2012: http://www.gulftoday.ae/portal/c737c528-6289-4ad2-aa97-bd4e337fa75b.aspx

# 37

# EGYPT – USA: ONE YEAR AFTER

As Egypt celebrates the first anniversary of its revolution, the relationship with the USA is at one of its lowest moments. Tension between the two countries has escalated after Egyptian investigators filed criminal charges against 43 foreign and local activists, including 19 American NGO workers. Egyptian prosecutors raided offices of 10 NGOs in December on suspicion of illegal funding and operating without licenses. The NGOs included prominent democracy-promotion groups, Freedom House, the International Republican Institute (IRI), and the National Democratic Institute (NDI).

Speaking before the parliamentary committee on human rights, Egyptian minister of planning and international cooperation, Fayza Abulnaga said that civil society organizations not registered with the Egyptian government have received $175 million from March to June 2011.

A heated controversy ensued: Mr. Kamal al-Ganzouri, the army-appointed prime minister, said his government will not "back down" in the investigation, despite a US warning that it could prompt a cut to Cairo's $1.3 billion in annual military aid.

Actually, the crackdown and the aid might well be tightly connected. The raid against the NGOs' offices occurred on December 29, just after Congress decided to link the $1.3 billion annual aid package to conditions that include "demonstrating a commitment to Egypt's peace treaty with Israel, progress toward democratic reforms and the protection of free expression, association and religion."

Some observers say the current Egyptian social and political scene doesn't look like it is going to meet these conditions. Behind the present rigidity of the Egyptian government, looms the will to push Washington to waive the conditions for "national-security concerns," for example. However, other observers argue that those who decided to move against the NGOs might well have miscalculated the risks, for the situation could be exploited by the radical-wing of the Islamists that is completely opposed to maintaining Camp David accords. The military establishment itself is not immune against the wrath of an uncontrolled mob move.

US senators John McCain, Kelly Ayotte, and Joe Lieberman said Egypt's government is "exacerbating tensions and inflaming public opinion in order to advance a narrow political agenda." They continued, "A rupture in relations would be disastrous, and the risks of such an outcome have rarely been greater."

The nature and the scope of these relations have often been questioned and criticized in Egypt by a number of intellectuals and observers, who consider them flawed, unbalanced, and responsible for the depreciation of Egypt's stature in the Arab world and on the international stage.

"For nearly thirty-five years," wrote Galal Amin, « Egypt kept saying yes without deviation to whatever the United States asks of it : in its foreign policy, its policy toward the Arabs, its relations with Israel, and its economic policy. The result has been a continuous decline in Egypt's political and economic standing internationally and within the Arab world while Israel has been increasing its gains at Egypt's and Arab expense. »

Such an opinion is far from being isolated in today's country. It is indeed shared by many people among the intelligentsia and different social groups, military not excluded.

There is indeed since the revolution a feeling that Egypt-US relations need to be re-assessed; but this is not a new feeling. It has just been reinforced. Nor is it exclusively the concern of the Muslim Brotherhood and the Salafists who dominate the current parliament. Other political organizations and trends, from the center to the left, may also share it.

Paradoxically, the United States may hardly scold the Egyptian political class for showing "too much" independence. For many years, the matter of Human rights and democracy has often been a "scowling" tool in the hands of the US diplomacy that was used to pressure Cairo into obedience. It is no secret that Washington has had several contacts with the Muslim Brotherhood during Mubarak era, and was frequently pushing for addressing the thorny problem of private and public freedoms.

In the 1990s, President Clinton supported the strategic liberalization of political systems in the Middle East. Officials in his administration spoke of "improved governance", "political participation", "pluralism", and "greater openness". Nevertheless, pro-democracy initiatives were neglected when they conflicted with core "high policy interests." This was acknowledged by then US secretary of State Madeleine Albright: "We did nudge at times, supporting Kuwaiti leaders in their initiative to give women the vote and encouraging the creation of representative bodies in Bahrain and Jordan. But we did not make it a priority."

However, post-9/11 changing international dynamics resulted in US growing more seriously concerned about democracy, because of the linkage between authoritarianism and terrorism. The Bush administration seemed willing to move democracy promotion from low to high-level policy. While developing the case for removing Saddam from power, Bush said for instance: "the world has an interest in the spread of democratic values. A new regime in Iraq would serve as a dramatic and inspiring example of freedom for other nations in the region." In another speech in 2003, he said: "We support the advance of freedom in the Middle East, because it is our founding principle...the hateful ideology of terrorism is shaped by oppressive regimes..."

This policy was criticized as a new cover for an old US policy that was still interest-driven. But this is another debate.

The Obama administration was more seriously confronted to internal dynamics of political change in the Arab world than any other was previously; and it had to take quick and decisive decisions concerning battered rulers that used to be US-supported. It tried to cope with these dynamics of the Arab spring until it was faced with the case of the NGO's in Egypt.

Ostensibly, the US-Egypt relations have reached a turn. It is not an easy one.

Imagine a train full of people launched at a maximum speed. This is the train of the revolution.

If the pilot were good, he would try to control the speed before taking the hard turn.

Yet, what if there is not a single pilot in the cabin, but several men (the SCAF?!) busy trying to defend themselves against a large group of travelers attacking their cabin and asking them to get out and leave the train to them?[1]

---

[1] The Gulf Today, February 11, 2012: http://gulftoday.ae/portal/07d2c12c-1f80-44a2-8365-e30683c706db.aspx

38

# POST-ALI ABDULLAH SALEH'S YEMEN

Are the events unfolding in Post-Ali Abdullah Saleh's Yemen bearing an ominous or an auspicious significance? Is the country, without Saleh, going to be a better or a worse place? In other words, will the Yemeni revolution reach its objectives?

These questions, among several others, related to this issue will be debated for two days in Doha (February 18-19), in a Symposium organized by "the Arab Center for Research and Policy Studies" (ACRPS), on: "The Yemeni Revolution: Historical Background, Local Specificities, and Future Prospects." The meeting is expected to be attended by a number of academics and experts on Yemeni affairs.

The topics are highly important; the context is intense; the expectations are very much elevated, and we surely can understand why. The country has been in turmoil several times and many years before what we call today « the Arab Spring. » A significant part of its pains is due, like in similar cases, to its political elite. But unlike Tunisia and Egypt somehow alike in their political culture and in their social infrastructure, Yemen has a poor performance regarding this aspect of its polity.

Neither in Tunisia, nor in Egypt, has the tribe – as a social organization – had any significance after the independence. Thus, it is not expected to weigh in on the political stage. In both countries, the forced departure of the head of state under the pressure of the people did not raise the same political dilemma that we see in post- Ali Abdullah Saleh's Yemen. Why? Because, in Tunisia and Egypt, the president did not represent an influential tribe, but a political organization (a party). The party – any party – could be dismissed, dismantled, or overwhelmed by a rival organization (s) or pushed out the political stage. Power transition would then be a matter of roles redistribution, according to a new or an amended constitution, and the new balance of forces inside the political spectrum. So far, this is what happened with more or less differences due to the historic specificities of each country.

In Tunisia, for instance, the armed forces have always been a-political. The Tunisian army has been maintained, since Bourguiba, outside the political scene, and it did never seek to exert influence (occult or plain) in this respect. That was indeed one of Bourguiba's best achievements, added to the importance he accorded to public education, women empowerment, and the construction of what he called "national unity" that took over the archaic role of the tribes. Of course, during the fight against the French colonial rule, Bourguiba used the influence of the tribes to gather and mobilize the population for the struggle. However, once the independence won, Bourguiba could not allow any influence to compete with the State. The party that led the struggle for independence became the cornerstone in the construction of the modern nation-state. The tribes were obliged to abide by the law. The law was positive. Thus, tradition has been restrained and remained limited to the family life.

In Egypt, the 1952 revolution also tried to install a modern regime, in which it relatively succeeded. However, the part of the armed forces grew increasingly over time, not only because they have made the 1952 coup, but also because Egypt was at war with Israel, and no other Arab country has held that role of defending the Arab cause (Palestine included) against several hostile forces: 1- Israel, which occupied Palestine and since 1967, parts of other Arab territories; 2- the old colonial empires Great Britain and France, on the decline, and trying to clutch to their "zone of influence » and interests in the Suez Canal ; and 3- the USA, emerging in the aftermath of the Second World War as the most ambitious superpower ready to occupy the vacuum left by Great Britain and France, and striving to keep the rival USSR away of the Mediterranean and the Gulf. So, for Egypt, the stakes have been different since that time, because of the different challenges it faced, which propelled the armed forces to play a role in the Egyptian society and economy that was not allowed in Tunisia (far away from the war scene).

However, if we put aside the difference regarding the role of the armed forces in Tunisia and Egypt, the political culture in both countries would reveal to have more common points than people tend to think. In Egypt too, we would not find a significant influence of the tribes. Nasser's era has molded the society in almost the same kind of bureaucratic, state-directed socialism than Tunisia under Bourguiba. With more emphasis on the pan-Arab cause, and a pronounced inclination toward the struggle of the non-aligned, Nasser has also accorded much importance to education, women empowerment (although less than Bourguiba) and a modernity that pushes tradition and tribalism, almost naturally so to say, away from polity and politics.

Now, if we look toward Yemen, what would we see?

The tribe is still at the center of the political life of the country. Nothing could be more a nuisance to polity and politics than this single fact. For the dilemma of the Yemeni revolution today, unlike Egypt and Tunisia, is not how to make the transition to democracy work, but how to hinder the repetition of the same game, the same policies that brought the country on the verge of civil war several times. Because when we ask: who was responsible for the mess that caused the revolt? To think that it was a man alone (i.e. Ali Abdullah Saleh) who blocked the political and economic life of the country, is to take a wrong turn. If things were so simple, then suffice it to remove him from power, and everything will be fine. This is just wrong. A.A.Saleh, like Z. Ben Ali, or H. Mubarak, was the product of a system, which still needs to be changed in order to make democracy work. Yet, in Tunisia and Egypt, the old political parties that were monopolizing public life have been swept away by new political movements. In Yemen, the party of the president is –to a large extent – the expression of a traditional rule, which is, the rule of the tribe. If it seems relatively easy for the Tunisians and Egyptians to remove a party from power, or dismantle it or overwhelm it under a wave of little newly formed organizations, how would you remove, dismantle, or sink a tribe or several tribes struggling for surviving the rule of A.A. Saleh? To do that, you need to change the system itself, not a single man.[1]

---

[1] The Gulf Today, February 18, 2012: http://gulftoday.ae/portal/302a544a-8a94-4404-a3e7-18783c72689d.aspx

# 39

# TALKING ABOUT DEMOCRACY?

Some incidents happened in Tunisia and Egypt that shed suspicion on the intentions of the Islamist majority. Among other examples: a journalist has been jailed in Tunisia for publication of a woman picture (then released); and the artist Adel Imam is still to face a trial in Egypt for a ridiculous charge.

Should we be able someday to talk about "Arab Democracy" without causing brow rising, suspicious gazes, or hilarious laughter? Will the new rulers show us evidence that they really represent the genuinely democratic turn several generations of Arabs have been expecting?

The national democratic revolutions seem interested in the political culture of liberal democracy and human rights, though. Baathist Pan-Arabism, militarist unionism, Marxism-Leninism, radical-Islamism (Taliban and Iranian brands, for example) have all failed as alternatives on all levels: political, economic, social, and cultural. Only one hope remains: that liberal democracy could achieve what no ideology was able to do for the Arabs.

In the 1980s, the secularist impulse was in trouble under the pressure of the Islamist rising tide. Christian Arabs who played a key-role in the development of modern Arab culture and political thought since the nineteenth-century were, a century later, marginalized. Many of them felt threatened and were, sometimes, forced to seek refuge in Europe and America.

The rise of Islamism has continued, though, reinforced by repression. Today, many people are scared by the perspective that the political life of the Arab world be reduced to a fight between dictatorial regimes and Islamists. The modern Arab culture is much concerned by this dilemma.

Even if the achievements of the post-colonial independent states were scanty and unfinished, they represented sometimes a frail hurdle against barbarism. For after all, men like Bourguiba, Nasser, Boumediene, and even Hafiz Assad and Saddam, before they took the fatal turn toward unbearable dictatorship, have played modernity against backward tradition, secularism against religious totalitarianism, and tried to maintain a minimum level of adjustment to the requirements of our time, while imposing a dictatorial (and –alas- sometimes brutal) rule. Modern culture was not banished in their societies.

The Arab democrats of current times are inheritors of liberal precursors, such as Lotfi as-Sayyid, Salama Moussa, Taha Hussein (Egypt), Taher al-Haddad, Bachir Sfar, Ali Bach Hamba (Tunisia) and many others in Syria, Lebanon, Iraq, etc...

While modern democracy is connected to the liberal trend in political thought, the Islamist thinkers do not agree on giving it the same signification.

The Islamist revivalist prefers to use the Islamic concept of "Shura" instead of democracy. The Marxist-Leninist understands democracy only when it is linked to the dictatorship of the proletariat. The classic Pan-Arab nationalist considered it a secondary objective and did not give it a thought. The liberal meaning has long been obliterated in the succession of dictatorships throughout the Arab world, although several countries have experienced the multiparty system (Iraq, Syria, Lebanon, Egypt, Tunisia...) since the first quarter of the XXth century. Even in the very conservative Gulf, demands for political participation began as early as the 1930s.

In Islamic jurisprudence, not only the "Shura" (consultancy) is not binding but it is also restrained to the elite loyal to the ruler (ahl al-hall wal 'aqd). For Sheikh Muhammad Abdu, who was all the same considered as an influential reformist, "Shura" means the absence of "absolute despotism." Abdu actually believed that the East needed only the rise of a "strong man" whom he labeled a "just despot." Such a man in his eyes "remaining just to his people, would achieve in fifteen years what reason alone cannot achieve in fifteen centuries."

Apparently, such an idea made its way throughout the Arab world in the XXth century as far as we can infer from the multiplication of the autocratic regimes that took over after World War Two and even before it. Several of them claimed to modernize their countries and achieve some sort of economic and cultural independence regarding the great powers of the West and the East. While they succeeded in introducing some social and economic reforms according to the standards of either capitalism or socialism as they interpreted them, they failed in reaching the levels of development promised. They also failed completely in the democratic test. It seemed therefore that Muhammad Abdu's idea about the "just despot" was useful to them, although it poisoned the life of their people.

Democracy was also suspect in the eyes of their opponents among the Islamist groups. For the latter, the sovereignty of the people, which is the core of the democratic rule, is at odds with the sovereignty of God (al-Hakimiyya), the source of all Islamic laws and governments. Moreover, whatever the virtues of democracy, "Shura" is preferable to them since it does not impel imitating the West. That is why the Algerian Islamic Front of Salvation (FIS) stated - even before the announcement of the electoral results that would bring it to power - that it intended "to discontinue the application of democracy as soon as it assumed power."

Some of the Islamist groups might have adjusted their views to fit in the new social trends, particularly since the revolutions that toppled the authoritarian regimes in Tunisia and Egypt (January, February 2011). Thus, the Tunisian leader of al-Nahdha party, Rachid al-Ghanouchi, stated just before his return from exile that their experience has ripened their thought and they became much interested in the Turkish model (meaning the AKP of Erdoğan). The Egyptian Brotherhood also made similar reassuring statements.

Yet, while these new openings remain to be tested, it should be noted that initially the Islamists leveled two arguments against democracy, both based on the notion of Tawheed (the oneness or unity of God). Firstly, they denounced democracy as shirk bi-Allah (attributing partners to God). In their eyes, the right to legislate without being bound by a superior Divine authority contradicts the Koran decree: "The command is for none but God" (12:40). Secondly, human sovereignty, they contend, contradicts God's sovereignty (Hakimiyya). Whereas in democracy the legislator is the people, according to the Tawheed of Islam, sovereignty (Hakimiyya) is the sole prerogative of God, and any usurpation of the legislative authority from God undermines that Tawheed. From this perspective, democracy is considered a form of ignorance (Jahiliyya). We see this in Banna's rejection of Egyptian parliamentary politics and suggestion that the Umma must be directly represented through adherence to Islamic precepts.

How far is the standing of today's rulers in Tunisia, Egypt, and soon in Libya, Yemen, and probably Syria, regarding the political culture that shaped the Islamist thought remains to be seen and tested.[1]

---

[1] The Gulf Today, February 25, 2012: http://gulftoday.ae/portal/0c2b184a-dafc-4d44-8ee7-bb443375edf0.aspx

# 40

# OPTIONS FOR SYRIA

We live in the wake of two important revolutions that unleashed a wind of freedom that observers everywhere have dubbed « the Arab Spring »: Tunisia and Egypt. Something happened in this region that cannot be undone, denied, ignored, forgotten; and we cannot continue to live as if it does not concern us, "because it is in the other countries." The Arab League, with its monumental bureaucratic spirit, has fortunately been quick to understand what was at stake and how to adapt to it. The efforts made to help Yemen and Syria get out of their "crisis" are, in this context, honorable, although not sufficient. The situation in Yemen may reverse, because of the continued meddling of Ali Abdullah Saleh and his cronies where they should not meddle. Saleh was offered immunity against judiciary prosecution, against the will of many people in his country, for whom he still must face trial. Yet, he is not satisfied with such a "luxurious exit" and he shows it around. Shouldn't they have subordinated such an "exit" to the condition of abstaining from any political activity in Yemen? I think they should.

In Syria, the situation is worsening every day because of the inability of the international community to act quickly and cogently. A few days ago, I attended a debate at the Brookings-Doha about the options for regime change. First, I was surprised that the experts were already discussing the military intervention as an option. I thought the Obama administration was unwilling even to raise such an issue, after the withdrawal from Iraq and the bloody stalemate in Afghanistan. Moreover, in an election year, what benefit could any candidate for the presidency draw from calling for a military operation in Syria? However, several options have been actually discussed, and regime change by invasion (Iraq style) or by bombing Assad (Kosovo style) were just two of them.

Let us stick to the facts.

The diplomatic efforts led by UN and Arab League new envoy Kofi Anan may fail, because of at least two enormous obstacles: Russia's refusal to drop Assad and the inability of the diplomatic community ( Arab League and Friends of Syria included) to force Assad to leave power. What is left then? Some experts from the Brookings suggest putting the pressure on the regime through concerted coercion: isolation, economic sanctions and non-military support to the opposition. But they are aware that this option too may fail. Even with a similar coercion, Saddam Hussein stayed in power for more than a decade. Moreover, the "maritime blockade" the experts suggest, to "stop goods from entering Syrian ports" would be just as harmful to the Syrian population as inefficient, because the regime receives logistic support, weapons, and aid through its terrestrial borders. By the way, the Arab Summit that is expected to gather in Bagdad this month, should pressure Iraq to watch its borders with both Syria and Iran. Everybody knows how easy it is to smuggle weapons and all kinds of merchandise to Assad across those borders.

The experts also suggested a possible reliance on Israel to remove Assad from power. They say, "Israel could posture forces on or near the Golan Heights and, in so doing, might divert regime forces from suppressing the opposition. This posture may conjure fears in the Assad regime of a multi-front war, particularly if Turkey is willing to do the same on its border..." In their opinion, this would convince the military leadership still loyal to Assad to drop him.

This will not work, even if Turkey accepts to do the same thing. Something is missing in this analysis. It is the fact that Israel is actually an invader in the Golan. How could we imagine that the

Syrian opposition would accept "help" from Israel, which is still occupying a Syrian territory by force? Furthermore, would the Arab League accept such a scenario, implicitly meaning that the Arabs would work "hand in hand" with the Israelis, in order to topple Assad? The last point is that Assad, not the opposition, would have more political leverage, if Israel enters the game. His "phantasmagoric" scenario of a huge American-Zionist conspiracy against his regime would thus find ground in the reality.

We are therefore left with the hard scenarios.

Arming the Syrian opposition in order to avoid the worse, which is the invasion scenario, or the air-force "liberation bombing" (Kosovo) that would end up into a humanitarian disaster.

Is it realistic to arm the opposition?

Yes, it may be, not because this is the best option, but because not doing it, would anyway not hinder the regime from continuing the rampage. Therefore, providing the opposition with weapons to defend itself and the population, is the choice of those who have no other choices.

But beware! The Syrian opposition is weak and hardly united. If you want to create another Afghanistan in Syria, go ahead, give the opposition groups all kinds of weaponry, and you will end up with a new "jihadi land," a haven for al-Qaeda.

In Syria today, there is only one recognized opposition organization, which is the Syrian National Council (SNC). If you have to give weapons and military assistance to the Syrian opposition, make sure you will have at the other end people who are responsible, reliable, and accountable. Most of all, it would not be acceptable or even moral to bypass the SNC and offer direct military assistance to the FSA (free Syrian army), for you would be thus paving the way for the rule of the "best armed" in post-Assad Syria.

Without a supervising political organization, - and you just got the SNC – this option (i.e. arming opposition) would end as a nightmare for the Syrians, the neighbors, the Arabs, the Americans, and the Europeans...

The choice that is made these days would mark the future of Syria and the neighboring region. Be sure Russia is and will be anyway against such an option. If along with arming the opposition, no efforts are made on the diplomatic side to convince Russia and China to join the other nations in a just and honest condemnation of the Assad regime and maybe a concerted course of action to remove him from power, we would be opening the gates to a prolonged civil war.

At the end of the day, it turns out there is no single option in Syria, but maybe several to be implemented at the same time on several fronts.[1]

---

[1] The Gulf Today, March 24, 2012: http://gulftoday.ae/portal/1512ee36-4e47-44d0-a135-018af00b3ad4.aspx

41

# IRAN AND THE REGIONAL CHANGES

As I have already hinted,[1] Iran has enormously profited from the upheaval in the Arab countries at least on one aspect: it has delivered it momentarily from the international pressure regarding its nuclear program. Iran has officially welcomed the revolutions in Tunisia and Egypt while trying to recuperate them ideologically, pretending they were "Islamic" or "pro-Islamist" revolutions, "anti-imperialist," "anti-American" revolutions. This kind of discourse was probably intended for domestic consumption. Yet, those very uprisings the Mullahs have welcomed would boomerang reminding the Iranians that they have not been less abused by their government than the people of Tunisia, Egypt, Libya, Yemen, and Syria: On February 2011 , thousands took to the streets in Tehran and other major Iranian cities, demanding democracy and freedom...The protests were quickly silenced. Iran is today the main supporter, with Russia, of the Syrian regime – a position that reveals the duplicity and the irrationalism of its policy.

Prior to the Arab uprisings that expanded from North Africa to reach Syria, Iran - not any Arab country - was under pressure and there were war-drums and much talk about more sanctions. WikiLeaks diplomatic cables have made public what was intended to remain in the secret vaults of diplomacy. Comment from pundits and observers about an "Arab-American conspiracy"

---

[1] See: The Sectarian Divide.

against Iran filled up the TV shows and the press columns. As the Obama administration was still reluctant to make another presidential doctrine out of another war, Israel seemed well designated and even happy with the eventuality – still possible by the way - of striking Iran, encouraged by the rising fear in the Gulf and the positions of the Arab leaders complaining from Iran's awkward and adventurous behavior.

At such a time, a series of uprisings burst out and Mr. Ahmadi Nejad was just too happy to welcome those who - involuntarily - relieved him from his greatest worries: to give up the nuclear ambitions or face war. He did not imagine that the revolution would soon rock his most important ally in the region.

That was hardly an advantage, yet a frail one, to be added to some others. As Barbara Slavin put it, "over the past three decades, the Islamic Republic of Iran has shown remarkable endurance. It has survived an eight-year war with Iraq, mounting economic sanctions, and serious domestic unrest. It has benefited from the missteps of adversaries, which have created opportunities for Iran to expand ties to militant movements in Iraq, Lebanon, and the Palestinian territories, and to increase its influence in Afghanistan."

Iran's conservative ruling elite proved to be particularly lucky since the day it started leading an adversary course with the United States, opposing plainly its role in the region, for war or peace. This behavior has become so obviously systematic that some observers talked of a "rivalry" between both states. I do not agree.

This is, for example, the approach of E. Abrahamian (2008) who suggests that "Iran's emergence as a regional power has brought it into a collision course with the other major powers in the region - the United States, especially with the latter's occupation of Iraq and Afghanistan, as well as establishment of military bases in the Caucasus and Central Asia, not to mention the earlier ones in Turkey and the Gulf region." Furthermore, he hypothesizes that the US-Iran relations have been "complicated by the fact that Shiites in the region - in Iraq, Afghanistan, and

Lebanon - look toward Iran as their main protector against local and external threats."

However, Abrahamian does not provide evidence in support of his hypothesis. Actually, it would be more plausible to say that Iran since the 1979 revolution, was the self-designated "defender" and the main sponsor of the Shiite sectarianism in the region, as it tried to give substance and scope to its suspicious claims by sponsoring sectarian dissent and luring Shiites into a kind of state-clientelism, whereby Teheran became the "patron" providing money and varied assistance.

In Lebanon, this endeavor gave rise to Hezbollah, which soon became a real state within the state. In Iraq, after the 2003 invasion and the demise of Saddam, the Shiite opponents who were exiled in Iran returned home. They have been during years trained and supported by the Islamic Republic for the main objective of toppling Saddam's regime and taking over. However, this Iranian interference with the internal problems of its neighbors (also in Yemen, Saudi Arabia, Bahrain...) might not be considered as a rivalry with the US as much as it is with other regional powers, like Saudi Arabia, Egypt, or Turkey.

I say this for at least two reasons: 1) The Americans knew Iran was sponsoring some Iraqi Shiite groups and the Bush administration all the same helped propel them to power. 2) No matter how we would describe the American presence in the Middle East, the USA would never become an "insider" in the sense of a "regional power." Sure that the USA is a global super-power, but certainly not a Middle-Eastern regional power. Hence, it is irrelevant to talk of "rivalry" between the two countries. A rivalry exists, though, but between Iran and Saudi Arabia, Turkey, or Egypt (not with Iraq anymore).

The second aspect of the "US-Iran rivalry" according to Abrahamian is related to the issue of nuclear energy. He opposes the Iranian insistence on developing such technology, "citing international law, the need to find energy alternatives, and the inalienable right of developing countries" to access the modern world, to the US insistence "that Iran should not be trusted with nuclear technology (...) because its real intention is to develop weapons of mass destruction."

Here too, it is inappropriate to talk of "US-Iran rivalry," for admittedly Iran could get a nuclear weapon, which country would feel threatened? The USA or Iran? The balance of power between the two countries is too unfavorable to Iran. Everybody knows it.

The nature of the US-Iran relations is different from the one that characterizes the relations between Iran and the Arab neighbors. That is why Iran should be more concerned with pacifying its relations with the Arabs. Yet, its position as supporter of the Syrian regime, condemns Iran to further hostility in the Arab world.

It is no secret that many Arab Sunni consider Iran the main beneficiary from Saddam Hussein's toppling, since it has extended its influence to the Shiite groups that were unreachable previously. However, Iraq does not represent the "Arab spring." The hope of democratic and peaceful change is still meeting armed resistance, from Iran, and those who speak the language of "revolution" and "freedom" and perform the role of anti-democratic forces.[1]

---

[1] The Gulf Today, March 31, 2012: http://gulftoday.ae/portal/1b602dad-586a-427e-afe8-503f0456b4f8.aspx

42

# MOSCOW FIGHTING ARAB SPRING

Apparently, it is not Bashar al-Assad and the Baath Party that are ruling what remains of Syria today, but Vladimir Putin and Russia. From the moment Moscow decided that the protesters in the streets of the Syrian cities are a threat for its stranglehold on this Arab country, it became obvious that the struggle is not opposing al-Assad to the Syrian revolt any more, but opposing the latter to Russia.

Russia has no solution for the crisis. It simply wants the Syrian protesters to give up their claims, to forget their dead, and to accept the man Russia imposed on them. Left to himself, without Russian political and military support, how long could he survive? Is Assad more powerful than Ben Ali, Hosni Mubarak, Muammar al-Qadhafi, or even Ali A. Saleh? All of these men were professional military officers. They relied on a complicated intelligence and security apparatus. They had powerful allies among the most powerful nations of this world. Until the eve of the revolution that toppled them, they were downright untouchable. Moreover, they have accumulated the experience of a very long rule that made them believe they were uncrowned kings who could leg their "conquered territories" to their offspring or relatives. How could a greenhorn, with no political experience, no military or intelligence knowledge, no particular talent, outrun them and stay in his palace despite the raging country outside? Is that possible thanks to his own resources and talents? Would anyone of those reasoning bass-drums who rely on the TV channels the voice of their master, explain to us, by the power of what mystery, what magic, al-Assad is still "triumphing" on his people, while much more powerful and experimented Arab presidents were unable to resist the same groundswell that devastated their respective countries?

I'll tell you what! This "mystery" is not a secret anymore: it is Russia. Putin took over the country that gave the Arabs their first and greatest revolution against the Ottomans during the First World War; the country that has always been the hub and the cantor of the Arab dream; the heart of the Arab world...Russia is using Al-Assad as a pariah for its own strategic interests, not giving a single thought to the consequences of this dangerous policy, not caring about the thousands of victims falling in this madness full of violence and blood. Russia thus revealed to be the enemy of the Arab people. The enemy of its dream of honorable life.

In its thirst for power and conquest, Russia seems ready to crush millions of Syrians if necessary, as it had crushed their brothers in the Caucasus.

There is not a single statement made by the Russian officials, from the beginning of the revolt, which did not defend Assad while condemning the protesters labeling them "armed gangs." Russia sided with Assad, although he is a criminal, and gave up any compassion, any sympathy for his victims among the population. Is Russia still neutral? Is Russia still objective and credible?

What is all this "love" for Assad? How did Russia decide that the "ruling family" in Damascus deserves to sacrifice for its safety and survival the population of the country, and to lose any respect, any credibility among the Arabs? How could you imagine even for a second that such madness is for the sake of Assad and his regime, not for the sake of the Russian desperate ambition in the Middle East? For sure, Russia has nothing to lose anymore. It had already lost every Arab country where it had imagined its foothold would stick forever: beginning with Egypt (a shameful and blatant expulsion); Yemen (a normal collapse in the wake of the world communism crumbling); Iraq (the wrong country to bet on); Libya (the wrong dictator to support); and now... Syria? No, No... It is too much to bear for the progeny of Ivan the terrible!

Decidedly, a bad luck had struck Russia in the Arab world. It has always bet on the wrong horse. It has always lost. True, Russia can pretend that, unlike some Western nations, it has never occupied an Arab country; it has no colonial past. Nevertheless, despite their deceitful policies since Sykes-Picot (revealed by the Russians!), their hypocrisy and double-dealing, their blind support to the Israeli occupation of the Arab territories, the Western powers are more accepted in the Arab world than Russia! This is a truth. An incomprehensible truth for the Kremlin, which watches the West applauding the Arab Spring, with the same easiness, the same hypocrisy used in applauding the "dictators" who were its "friendly allies." There is indeed in this Arab ambivalence and in this Western luck, something that drives Moscow mad.

However, the Western powers, although no less interested than Russia and, regarding the problem of Israel and Iran, showing more stupidity in their positions than the Russians, have also managed to keep an honorable exit, when they understood that this revolt wind crossing the Arab world is not to be calmed easily. They made a choice. They have always made the same choice by the way. Remember other "friendly dictators" they dumped when the population could no longer bear them. The West, specialized in selling "freedom" for whoever wishes to buy, and supporting "young would-be dictators" until they become useless old rugs, proved to be enough flexible, enough wily to get himself a seat in the locomotive of any revolution against the autocrats he had himself supported during long decades.

This is called strategic interests.

Seemingly, it does not exist in Russia. For if it existed, Russia would not cling with nails and teeth to a crumbling dictatorship at a time a wind of liberty is changing the whole scene of the Arab world.

I said, in the beginning of this paper, Russia is apparently ruling Syria. Well, I apologize. Now I think that Russia is not exactly ruling Syria, but ruling itself out of Syria and the Arab world for an inestimable period of time.

An old Arab dictum says: time will tell...[1]

---

[1] The Gulf Today, April 7, 2012: http://gulftoday.ae/portal/f753783f-788b-4bcc-8d79-9865cb9c2843.aspx

# 43

# IS BUSINESS APOLITICAL?

Israel and Egypt officials are both downloading the decision to cancel the gas deal contract, claiming that it has nothing to do with politics. Thus, they probably think it is the best way to ease the tensions between them.

However, the realities are there, and the denial may turn to be self-delusion.

The fact is that Israel is unhappy about the revolution that toppled Hosni Mubarak, while Egypt is unhappy about so many Israeli attitudes that their listing could make a whole book.

The Camp David accords and the subsequent Egypt-Israel Peace Treaty were mentioned several times in the public space, both in Israel and Egypt, since the revolution. They have provided the formal framework under which Egypt has conducted its relations with Israel during the Mubarak presidency. The normalization has always been subject to criticism in Egypt. It is undeniable, though, that while for many the treaty is just unworkable and in need of adjustment or cancellation, the strong opposition continues to exist alongside an acceptance of the Camp David Accords as the instrument that ended the state of war between the two states.

As it has been noticed several times, Israel's security strategy in the region for decades has been based on the existence of autocratic regimes that were able to maintain relationships with Israel, irrespective of any popular feeling against such relationships, and at the same time to ensure that no threats to Israel's security emanated from their territories. This is no longer the situation and Israel has certainly perceived the change. There is a new element in the politics of the region: the Arab public opinion. Henceforth, legislators and presidents are elected. They have to respect their constituencies in order to reach office and stay in their post.

Since the revolution, there was anxiety that a new Egyptian regime under the influence of the Islamists would cancel the Camp David accords ending the state of "cold peace." Israel's security arrangements in the region depend heavily on that treaty.

The SCAF expressed its commitment to the Camp David accords. But held under "fire" from the protesters of Maydan al-Tahreer, the military may feel much in need of popularity. Some of their recent attitudes cannot be understood outside this context.

Some moths after the uprising and Israeli force entered Egypt's territory in pursuit of what they claimed were Palestinian militants, and in the process killed five Egyptian soldiers.

Egypt demanded an apology and compensation from Israel, as thousands of protesters demonstrated outside the Israeli Embassy in Cairo, burning an Israeli flag and demanding that the ambassador be expelled and the Embassy closed.

Feeling the danger, officials in Egypt and Israel tried to save the situation.

On October 11, Israel issued a formal apology to the Egyptian government and took responsibility for the shooting that killed the Egyptians near Eilat on August 18. This apology coincided with news of the Egyptian-brokered release of Israeli Sgt. First Class Gilad Shalit. On October 18, after five years in captivity, Shalit returned to Israel after Israel and Hamas, with Egypt serving as a mediator, completed a prisoner exchange deal. In exchange for Shalit, Israel agreed to free a total of 1,027 Palestinian prisoners in two phases.

On October 27, 27-year-old Ilan Grapel, an American law student from Queens who also has Israeli citizenship and was arrested on espionage charges in Egypt in June, was released in exchange for 25 Egyptians held in Israel.

A report for the Congress noted that for Israel, its foreign policy toward Egypt is in a difficult phase. Now, more than ever, Israel depends on a positive relationship with the Egyptian military to ensure the preservation of the 1979 peace treaty. Though it expressed its concern over the storming of its embassy, Israeli officials were careful not to harshly criticize the SCAF.

Now, to come back to the gas affair, it is obvious for everybody that if this is a business decision, its consequences are highly political.

It is a business decision indeed, because Jordan, which receives Egyptian gas through the same pipeline - and previously paid $3 per million BTUs -, agreed earlier this month to sign a new contract at prices closer to the global average ($ 6-7). But with Israel, this cannot be only a business decision.

Recently, an Israeli columnist (Zvi Bar'el) acknowledged, the issue is also "supremely political. Because in Egypt, as in Israel, the pipeline has become a symbol. A symbol of disgusting normalization with an occupying country; a symbol of the corrupt government of former Egyptian President Hosni Mubarak, whose sons are suspected of having received commissions of 2.5 percent to 5 percent of the total billion-dollar transaction; and a symbol of the abandonment of the interests of the Egyptian public, which pays a higher price than Israel for the gas it consumes."

Knesset Member Binyamin Ben-Eliezer, who signed the gas deal with Egypt during his term as infrastructure minister, said the deal's termination is yet another indication that a conflict between Israel and Cairo is possible. Opposition Leader Shaul Mofaz called the Egypt's decision a "flagrant breach of the peace treaty between Israel and Egypt." He added, "Egypt's actions require an immediate response from the US."

Lastly, the international shareholders of East Mediterranean Gas (EMG) for whom the decision to halt Egyptian natural gas exports to Israel was not due simply to commercial differences.

"Any attempts to characterize this dispute as a mere commercial one is misleading," shareholders in East Mediterranean Gas Co. (EMG) said in a statement to Reuters. "This is a government-backed contract sealed by a memorandum of understanding between Egypt and Israel that specifically refers to the [1979] peace treaty."

Thus, enter the Camp David accords and the peace treaty on the stage. Ostensibly, the cancellation of a commercial deal is twice significant: it is about trade and finances, and it is also about policy and politics.

Better, it has been interpreted as 'retaliations': "Egypt canceled the natural gas deal with Israel as a strategic move in response to Ampal American Israel Corp's lawsuits against the Cairo government," the Israeli company's finance VP said at a meeting with bondholders. Ampal's main holding is its 12.5% stake in Egyptian gas exporter EMG.

The announcement, therefore, has raised speculation that it was intended to force Israel to call off a $8 billion lawsuit.

The above picture shows the extreme anxiety that characterizes today the relationship. In such a context, nothing is apolitical, especially when it involves bilateral or international relations.[1]

---

[1] The Gulf Today, April 28, 2012: http://gulftoday.ae/portal/da3bebf0-1788-4449-b209-dd8091e7f143.aspx

44

# REVOLUTIONS AND COUNTER-REVOLUTIONS

In the mid-1990s, the German social scientist, Gunar Heinshon, coined the term "Youth Bulge Theory," to describe a trend in demography. The theory will eventually be developed by American political scientists, Garry Fuller and Jack Goldston. They argue that "developing countries undergoing demographic transition or those moving from high to low fertility and mortality rates are especially vulnerable to civil conflict." As we know since the great Ibn Khaldun, the conjugated effect of social and economic oppression and political repression is the gravedigger of any regime.

Lionel Beehner opines "the theory contends that societies with rapidly growing young populations often end up with rampant unemployment and large pools of disaffected youths who are more susceptible to recruitment into rebel or terrorist groups. Countries with weak political institutions are most vulnerable to youth-bulge-related violence and social unrest."

I wonder how the Arab ruling elites could be so irresponsibly blind to these truths.

In the beginning of the 1980s, Brzezinski then "grand wizard" of the US foreign policy, coined the concept "arc of crisis" while arguing that from Afghanistan eastward to Morocco westward, this region constitutes a potential "powder keg" that might explode any time. The National Security adviser of President Carter was actually hinting to the elements that have already exploded literally to the face of Mohamed Ridha, Shah of Iran in 1979, and the US could do nothing to stop the revolution.

What happened then could tell us a lot about how a great popular revolution could be dragged far away from its objectives and even take a very dangerous turn with the capture of a foreign embassy- a precedent in the annals of diplomacy that would put Iran on the bench of international terrorists and pariahs.

The revolution that has been achieved by different secular and non-secular parties, ended up completely overtaken (actually stolen) by the Shiite clergy to its own benefit. That was a coup against the revolution of the people whose first victims were the liberal elite and the left.

In the Arab world, where the majority is Sunnite, some are now scared that the revolution in Tunisia, Egypt, Libya, Yemen, Syria, may also be stolen, for the benefit of an ultra-conservative brand of Islamism.

Remember that such was also the case in Afghanistan.

Actually, when he coined the term "arc of crisis," Brzezinski seemed more concerned by Afghanistan than by Iran. The latter has then completely escaped the American lap and has even grown dangerously hostile. But in Afghanistan where the red army has not been welcomed by the population, Brzezinski saw in the eventual organization of an armed resistance the tool to destabilizing the URSS and forcing it, if success is achieved, to recognize its biggest defeat in history, without direct confrontation between the two Superpowers. The "arc of crisis" means for Brzezinski that this region could be turned into a potential strategic depth for the Afghan resistance, with the help of "good-willing" Sunnite authorities, whose role would be to call the Arab Muslim youth to Jihad.

Brzezinski's plan has been successfully implemented. The Arab youth that started flocking to Afghanistan to take part to the "holy jihad" against "the Empire of Evil" (as Reagan dubbed the USSR) were far from imagining that they were actually helping the CIA dig the grave of the Soviet reign. Meanwhile, the plan helped the Arab regimes entangled into innumerable social and economic difficulties, to get rid of an army of unemployed youth.

Let us remember that in those years (1980s) several revolts burst out in Tunisia, Egypt, Sudan, Algeria... and were severely repressed. The repression has achieved its goal in suppressing the protests, relatively because the war in Afghanistan had siphoned a great number of those unemployed youth. (Nothing of this kind happened in 2011.) At the same time, the Arabs who took the lead in organizing the Afghan resistance, with the assistance of the Pakistani military intelligence and the CIA, succeeded in imposing their radical conception of Islam to the Afghan people as well as to the Mujahedeen, included those dubbed "Arab Afghans." Weapons and cash were flowing. The Soviet Reign in that country was thus granted a perfect doom.

Brzezinski was not blind, but just "one-eyed."

In manipulating the Muslims in his "arc of crisis," the USA really succeeded in pushing the USSR to its last ditch: the defeat in Afghanistan turned to be fatal to the Soviet empire. The decade of the 1980s also witnessed the first great popular unrest in Poland, which would shake the Warsaw Pact and not just Jaruzelsky's rule.

Nonetheless, Carter's adviser was all the same unable to forecast the developments that would take Afghanistan from a country of moderate Islam, as several still were in the "arc of crisis," to a country of radical Islam, where ideology and barbarism are the same thing.

Therefore, if the Afghan revolt against the communist occupant was worth the sacrifices, the result was unfit and unfair to the population. The Afghan did not revolt because they could not grow their beards, throw half the population (the females) behind closed doors, and force an outdated anachronic body of laws on a contemporary society. Yet, that was exactly what they got.

Similarly, those in the Arab world today who express their fear may not be wrong. Revolutions could be stolen, manipulated, betrayed, and lead to another system of dictatorship, using the very slogans of the revolution: justice, fairness, freedom, human rights, private and public liberties, etc...

After all, one could see what became the ideal of socialism under Stalin and his heirs. "Popular democracies" as the communist regimes dubbed themselves were a jest of history.

Many people do not know that the French nobility in 1648 was the party who opened the way to the revolution, by renewing the Fronde against the king. That's why the French historian Lefebvre says "it was an aristocratic revolution." However, when Louis XVI was forced to yield and agreed to the calling of the Estates General, and the nobility thus conquered the parliament and the king, it lost the nation. For the nobility was unable to give up its social privileges in return for political power. Yet, even after all the really talented nobles - Lafayette, Mirabeau, Talleyrand - passed over into the camp of the third estate, it would be too late. The French revolution will also inexorably provoke a counter-revolution, like so many revolutions, when it instituted the "government by terror."[1]

---

[1] The Gulf Today, May 6, 2012: http://gulftoday.ae/portal/6919be12-8b2e-4ea6-bb5e-eee506375a16.aspx

45

# ELECTORAL DEBATE: THE ART OF WAFFLING

Anyway and whatever the opinion one bears about Egyptian politics and Egyptian electoral candidates in the post-Mubarak era, many Arabs - not only Egyptian citizens- were happy with the first ever presidential televised debate organized in Cairo, between Mr. Amru Moussa, former Foreign policy Minister and Secretary General of the Arab League, and Mr. Abdel Moneim Abul Futuh, former militant of the Muslim Brotherhood (MB). Indeed, after watching this debate, those who are still skeptical regarding the scope and the authenticity of change in Egypt, know today that something really important is happening in this country.

The difference in the answers of both candidates is a matter of opinion and sensitivity. Each of them has a political record that determines to a large extent his present attitudes. Somehow, each is right when reminding people of the fact that the recent past of his rival could not be dismissed or omitted. Really, Amru Moussa was a statesman of the former order, and although we suspect that no minister in such an order could challenge the president or have his own policy, Moussa, in the eyes of many Arabs, has certainly more a positive record as a Secretary General of the Arab League than as Egypt's Foreign affairs minister. As he has himself reminded his rival, when he charged him of being the "symbol" of the Mubarak era, he had resigned 10 years ago. Yet, even if he did, he could hardly be described as a man of the opposition.

As to his rival, Abul Futuh certainly represents the opposition to all the governments that ruled Egypt since the free officers established the republic, through his affiliation to the MB. Yet, that does not presuppose he is the ablest for the job of president. A good militant is not necessarily a good statesman. And although Abul Futuh resigned from the brotherhood one year ago, his mind and his attitudes have been shaped in those years of militancy, so that he could hardly be described as a man in complete rupture with their ideology and worldview. True, he has managed to present himself as a man who could gather some moderate Islamists along with hardliners and maybe even some elements of the liberal trend. Yet, the post of president requires much more than the simple electoral tactics of the ongoing campaign. It requires merely being even above those political tactics in order to unify all Egyptians for a great project of society.

On this level, so far, it is difficult to say that all the presidential candidates have succeeded in such a task. Actually, they did not have enough time to come out with a convincing project of society. For just a year ago, nobody was even imagining that the days of the regime were near the end.

The debate on domestic social and economic issues was disappointing for its lack of precision, and its populism. None of them provided clear answers about what they intended to do if they win the election, although both tried to "politicize" and "ideologize" the questions they were unable to answer, by lack of a social project. So, on this level, we watched two men trying to "hypnotize" the eventual voter with old tricks, instead of giving facts and figures and arguing about them. And when they happen to talk about the hardship of an important part of the population, they gave promises that cast doubts about their ability to ever fulfill them, for they never said how they would do or where exactly they intend to find the funds.

As the debate shifted to foreign policy, it seems that both men wished to be closer to the average Egyptian citizen who, as it is known from the simple scanning of the newspapers, does not bear Israel and the Camp David accords in his heart. For most Arab observers watching the debate, it was not surprising to hear Abul

Futuh qualify Israel as "enemy" and argue that it is a dangerous state for the security of Egypt. Nor was it odd to hear Moussa reminding the viewers of a clause in the accords providing for their review and assessment each five years by the parliament, - a task that has never been performed so far. Yet, Moussa was more cautious about the consequences of any awkward treatment of the issue. In his eyes, international accords could not be abrogated for "electoral reasons." There is ostensibly a demagogic and hypocritical attitude in making a promise that could be interpreted as downright belligerent, while Egypt is not ready to go to war, he contended. It is also dangerous to indulge in such a belligerent discourse just to obtain the voices of all those who feel the plight of the Palestinians as their own. Here, he revealed more tact and finesse in the art of diplomacy than the militant of the Muslim brotherhood.

Conversely, Mr. Abul Futuh was not convincing when he kept stressing that Israel is Egypt's enemy and must be treated as it is. I was wondering: if this guy becomes Egypt's president, how would he do to talk face to face with Netanyahu and the Israeli leaders after what he said? Should he reverse the tide then in order to stay diplomatic and describe them as "partners" in peace? If not, would he abrogate the Camp David and the peace treaty with Israel? Would Egypt be then better positioned to obtain from Israel what it would not obtain otherwise? Then, what about the Palestinians? If Egypt is no longer able to negotiate on their behalf with Israel and the US, in what consists the progress?

On the other hand, neither Amru Moussa nor anybody can ignore that the Camp David accords and the Peace treaty, were born in a historical context. The present conjuncture is merely different as it emerged out of a popular revolution that would propel an elected government up to the political stage. That means that the Egyptian citizen has for the first time in contemporary history an opinion to voice, which whatever its consequences, has to be heard. Diplomacy as an art of "blah blah" and void speeches and demagogic rant is over. This is another era, where diplomacy should not be confined to the spheres of a small elite of initiated, but be open to the scrutinizing gaze of the elected representatives of the people. Legislators would have their opinion about how their country should deal with regional and international issues. Therefore, it is advised to avoid old waffling in political speeches.

Unfortunately, we are still there. As far as I can judge from this debate, waffling is still considered a good mean to dodge precise and rational answers to complicated issues. Let's hope they'll do better next time.[1]

---

[1] The Gulf Today, May 13, 2012: http://gulftoday.ae/portal/180387f1-759e-4f40-8320-9c716d912733.aspx

# 46

# SYRIA, USA AND ISRAEL

The dramatic events in Northern Lebanon, last week, obviously related to the Syrian crisis, elevated a little more the level of insecurity and provoked anxious questions about the plans of Assad and his allies in Lebanon. The extension of the conflict to the fragile neighbor is not a mere philosophic speculation. Syria has always been an influential and much feared actor in Lebanon. When they remember the civil war, the Lebanese link it systematically to the occult role of the Syrian Mukhabarat.

Although the civil war erupted in 1975, the seeds of this explosion were long embedded in Lebanon's history. The domestic factors were directly related to the political confessional system that governed the country since its independence, formalized through the National Pact in 1943.

The demographic changes in the country made this system outdated because of its structural inadaptability to the changes. The Syrian society contains similar cleavages that until the outburst of the revolution, have been muted by the Assad minority regime.

Minorities are not just a source of cleavages in society, but, as Jon B. Alterman pointed in his testimony before the US Senate Committee on Foreign Relations (April 19), their anxieties "can make them cling to ruling governments. The twelve per cent or so of Syrians who are Alawite, the ten per cent or so who are

Christian, and the smaller Kurdish, Druze and Armenian populations, are all a source of strength to Assad, for they fear dominance by the Sunni Arab majority." That makes him assume: "in many cases, they will fight to death for the ruling government, because they fear ruin if it is deposed."

But the gradual militarization of the conflict and its possible extension to Lebanon, provoke other considerations, some of which are related to Israel.

The militarization of the Syrian crisis, with the emergence of the Free Syrian Army, is not much of a surprise in a country where the successive governments since the fifties of the last centuries have all resulted from coups and counter-coups. The modern history of Syria itself is that of an endless series of military meddling with political affairs, and since the coup that brought Hafiz Assad to power, that of a ruthless dictatorship.

True, militarization was imposed on the Syrian revolution, which was initially peaceful, as the murderous and immoral rampage of Assad and its clique of assassins caused anger and mutiny among the military. However, some among influential US observers are skeptical regarding the military way as conducive to the triumph of the revolution.

Two examples recently illustrated this mind-frame.

1. David Ignatius wrote in the Washington Post on May 24, about the growing instability in Iraq, Jordan and Lebanon, that "fear of blowing up the region – and spawning even more Sunni-Shiite sectarian war – is one reason the Obama administration has refused to arm the Syrian opposition. Officials fear that militarizing the conflict, without reliable Syrian allies or a clear endgame strategy, could produce unintended consequences much like those of the Iraq war."

2. Alterman, in his testimony said to US congressmen: "Understand that militarization helps Assad. The more the protest movement looks like an armed insurrection, the more it will play

into the hands of a relatively well-armed and well-trained Syrian army."

How to reply to both arguments?

1. If the point made by Ignatius is true, then what is the use of staying in Afghanistan all these years, with the unbelievable consequence of being forced to yield to the Taliban? Would it not be wiser to withdraw after destroying the enemy, which the Americans did when they launched the war that dismantled the Taliban regime? But in Afghanistan as well as in Iraq, the US military were pursuing a strategy based on the fictive notion of "nation-building" as a necessary post-war responsibility. The "unintended consequences" have always been a result of such a strategy. The US successive administrations could simply not bring themselves to accepting the idea that Omniscience is only to God, and the US is not God: it cannot destroy and create at will. It has to choose between war and peace. If it chooses war, the logical consequence is that of destroying the enemy. The enemy would resist and fight. This is expected. Therefore, it is not "unintended consequences" that the US has been facing in Afghanistan, Iraq and in any country where its troops intervened.

2. Militarization helps Assad? Absolutely not. Nothing is more scaring for any despotic rule than to see people ready to die, guns at hands, for their freedom. And no army in the world, whatsoever the level of its training, has ever been able to defeat a handful of well-armed men, determined to bring down a hated regime. These are simple facts of history. Just read history; what does it say about revolutions? Have they always been bloodless, peaceful demonstrations? And when have such demonstrations been enough to topple dictatorships?

If the US is not willing to arm the Syrian opposition, it is not because it fears more instability, but because Syria represents presently zero threats and zero interest to Obama.

Even Israel is more comfortable with such a regime that has never been considered menacing than with a new one where the Islamists may win a majority and rule the country. So, the real instability for the US-Israel alliance may result in the defeat of Assad with no "reliable ally" to run Syria and reassure Israel.

Meanwhile, who cares about the probability of Syria tilting toward civil war? The US? Israel? Unlikely. Both of them have been able to live with 15 years of civil war in Lebanon. As long as the Arabs fight each other, external powers watch. It may even be a source of joy for some. Obviously, some Arabs are always willing to do the dirty job that would otherwise be Tsahal's. The performance of the Syrian government is actually a crystal-clear example.

The truth is, there is no interest for the US in arming the Syrian opposition, so far. Maybe the day such an opposition pledges to strike a deal with Israel, funds and weapons would flow endlessly and consequently, the US would use all its means – and we know they are powerful – to topple Assad and end the plight of the Syrian people.[1]

---

[1] The Gulf Today, May 27, 2012: http://gulftoday.ae/portal/561d53ea-71b7-40d8-9106-702124ed2b66.aspx

47

# MORE THAN A DEATH SENTENCE

The post-revolution trial of the former head of the Egyptian state is not supposed to be the opportunity to seek revenge and proclaim the right to vendetta live on TV. It is really painful and sad to see people giving way to such violent emotions and asking for blood, besides the fact it is against the very spirit of the revolution. Why did the peoples of Tunisia, Egypt, Libya, Yemen, and Syria revolt? Was it not because they sought justice, honesty, and the rule of law, which would guarantee them respect, freedom and dignity? Well, this has nothing to do with revenge.

The free expression of one's emotions is understandable, but the respect of the law must prevail. It does not serve the goals of democracy and justice to start this new era by spilling the blood of the former president and his men, even if their responsibility for the repression is fully established. Think of what happened during the great French revolution of 1789. Gustave Le Bon, one of the best writers on the psychology of crowds, said: "The motto of Liberty, Equality, Fraternity, a true manifestation of hope and faith at the beginning of the revolution, soon merely served to cover a legal justification of the sentiments of jealousy, cupidity, and hatred (...), the true motives of crowds unrestrained by discipline. This is why the Revolution so soon ended in disorder, violence, and anarchy."

Clearly, the danger that threatens all Arab revolutions is the same that has been thus diagnosed: it is when the rational ceases to dominate the instinctive, and the effort of the instinctive to overpower the rational becomes successful.

A society cannot exist without restraining some instincts men have inherited from their "primitive animality." It is important to overcome these instincts, which can bring overall destruction on the society. The need for the democratic elite here to show the crowd, prisoner of its passions, a sense of discipline, respect and abidance by the law, is patent. There is no other way to cement the national unity than to convince people that one of the goals of the revolution has been reached by the mere fact of presenting Mubarak and his men before a law-court. What else could be considered as the expression of the people's will? A life sentence, in my eyes, is much more terrible than death. No other sentence could be heavier.

While acknowledging the President's responsibility, it is all the same obvious that the system was faulty, not just a man or a dozen. How to judge a system? Revolutions reform systems or replace them. The men are just tools in a broader machine. Egypt has been subject to the autocratic rule of Mubarak and the National Democratic Party (NDP) since he took office in 1981, following the assassination of Anwar al-Sadat.

The historian Kai Bird, said describing Mubarak at the moment he accessed power: "He was then a nonentity." Other observers said about him: "Cautious and unimaginative, the former air force commander has never in his (...) reign come close to filling the shoes of his predecessors.
It soon became apparent that he was simply an apparatchik of the Egyptian military establishment. He never attempted to create for himself the kind of popular legitimacy that came naturally to Nasser. His one talent was that of a "Machiavellian survivor," as Kai Bird put it. He marshaled all the usual tools of repression— and more than $60 billion of American aid stemming from the Camp David Accords—to sustain his power.

This man (i.e. Mubarak) was not the only responsible for what happened; the real responsible, as I said, is the system. But as in all revolutions, the head of state becomes the object of hatred and anger, mostly because power is always personalized. We must remember that Mubarak was really facing the fate of Nouri al-Said (of Iraq), torn to pieces by a maddened crowd.

On February 11, Egypt was on the brink of an abyss. Thousands of demonstrators besieged Mubarak in his presidential palace, heavily guarded by army tanks. "The potential for a small group of impatient protestors to sooner or later try to force its way through the gates and trigger a sudden downward spiral into bloodshed and chaos was all too real," remarked an observer of the events.

That was the moment the Egyptian Supreme Council of the Armed Forces chose to step in to save the country at the climax of 18 very long and difficult days.

A policy briefing of the Council of Europe then described the situation is these terms: "in Egypt (...) the military is in the driving seat and has assumed responsibility for steering the country's transition to democracy. Just as pre-revolutionary Egypt was described by scholars as a 'hybrid regime' that had elections but no democracy, its revolution has also taken on a hybrid form. The revolution was neither fully democratic, as in Tunisia or Indonesia, nor was it entirely authoritarian, as in Gamal Nasser's 1952 coup or the Iranian Revolution of 1979. It was fundamentally democratic in impulse – the protests and an early referendum on amending the constitution have clearly been expressions of the people's will – but it has also been characterized by a number of authoritarian features, not least the role of the military, with its summary and often brutal way of dealing with continuing dissent."

Thus, if you want to be fair, many other people were responsible for the death of protesters. However, the trial of Mubarak offered them the opportunity to stay in the shade.

For when a neutral investigation about the killings, then? The question is still there.[1]

---

[1] Published under the title "President to Prisoner," in The Gulf Today, June 3, 2012: http://gulftoday.ae/portal/2266531c-fbaa-47b8-9edf-75f0d600e284.aspx

48

# THE 'KOSOVO ROAD' TO SYRIA

The Syrian situation is heading towards a full-scale conflict, with partisans and allies on each side. On Thursday last week, former US ambassador to the UN Bill Richardson said the US would have no choice but to start arming Syria's rebels if indeed Russia is sending attack helicopters to President Assad's forces.

Several members of the Congress – including Senators John McCain (R-AZ), Lindsay Graham (R-SC), and Joe Lieberman (I-CT), as well as Rep. Sue Myrick (R-NC) – had already shown support to the idea of arming the Free Syrian Army (FSA). Last March, a congressional briefing by Myrick featured a presentation by James F. Smith, former director of the controversial Blackwater (a military contracting firm), to discuss potential ways to establish a "liberated" zone in northeast Syria, to allow US military and intelligence agents to operate freely.

On April 2012, Senators John McCain and Joe Lieberman visited the Turkish-Syrian border and met with General Mustapha Al Sheikh and Colonel Riad Al Asaad, leaders of the Free Syrian Army, before paying a visit to a refugees camp. "Make no mistake," the Senators said, "the situation in Syria is an armed conflict. This is a war. Diplomacy with Assad has failed, and it will continue to fail so long as Assad thinks he can defeat the opposition in Syria militarily."

But the inconsistency of the Obama administration over this issue is alarming.

Last Tuesday, US State Secretary Hillary Clinton accused Russia of sending attack helicopters to Syria. Although both Putin and Lavrov denied arming Bashar, a declaration from Rosoboronexport Deputy CEO Igor Sevatyanov, on the same day, confirmed that Russia's state-controlled arms trader intends to fulfill its contract for the supply of armaments to Syria (RIA Novosti, June 12). "The contract was signed long ago," said Sevatyanov, "and we supply armaments that are self-defense rather than attack weapons, and there can be no talk about any violations by Russia or Rosoboronexport either de jure or de facto."

However, the oddity is not in the fact that Putin continues to provide weapons to Assad, but in that, the Pentagon is buying Mi-17 helicopters from the same arms trader: Rosoboronexport!

The story is reported widely on June 14: the state-run weapons broker signed a $367.5 million deal with the United States in May 2011 for delivery of 21 Mi-17 V5s. Twelve more were reportedly added. They are now talking about a $900 million deal, including engineering services and spare parts.

Can you believe the Pentagon needs Russian helicopters seemingly for the Afghan military, while the State Department is charging the Russians with delivering helicopters to Assad? What is this cacophony just after the massacre of Houla? Then who to blame?

US commentators have focused on the mercenary reasons for Russia's support of Assad. Herve Ladsous, the UN's peacekeeping chief, acknowledged on Tuesday that Syria was now effectively in a state of civil war. Ostensibly, Russia is part of the sinister game Assad is attempting to survive the earthquake. Thus all efforts to slow down the slipping towards a full-scale war, is deflected by

Putin's rigidity. Although, Washington policy-makers seem undecided, Hillary Clinton has already announced that the USA would be joining an international effort – led by Arab countries – to finance and equip the Free Syrian Army (FSA).

The talk about arming the FSA is not new. The Wall Street Journal reported in March about a meeting in Riyadh between the Saudi and the Jordanian kings whose object was to permit weapons shipment into Syria through the border, "in exchange for economic assistance to Jordan."

The fact that an ultra-conservative Saudi Arabia supports a revolution in an Arab country, while the Americans seem still reluctant, is in itself a sign that times are really changing in this region. "Saudi Arabia has argued strongly for weapons supplies to Syrian rebels despite US concerns," says the WSJ. The option of arming the FSA means that not many people among the most influential Arab states think presently that it is still possible to resolve Syria's crisis diplomatically, as was the case in Yemen.

However, the question today is not about whether "they" will arm the FSA, but rather what kind of weapons will be delivered to match the heavy weaponry used by Assad.

In a meeting with Dr Burhan Ghalioun, former president of the Syrian National Council in Doha a few days ago, I asked him whether it is true that there is a scenario resembling the fight against the Soviets in Afghanistan: funds from the Arabs, and weapons from the USA and its allies for the forces resisting Assad and his Russian allies.

He said something like "the Arabs are helping with funds" and "we still have meetings to coordinate our efforts"; and he added something that confirmed the state of enmity with Russia now prevalent among the Syrians. He said: "We will declare Russia an enemy of the Arab people if it continues its support to Assad." That means that Russia would likely lose all its assets in the Middle East, after the fall of Assad.

The ambiguous point is now about the kind of weapons needed by the FSA and that the US would permit its circulation. Insofar as Saudi Arabia is concerned, high-end US weaponry such as F-15 fighter jets, Patriot air-defense systems and Abrams main battle tanks seem unlikely to be delivered to the Syrian rebels. Yet, even smaller US-made weapons, such as anti-tank missiles, are covered by strict terms that prevent re-export.

Saudi Arabia arsenal also includes rocket and missile systems, grenades and field artillery. Nonetheless, we can imagine a situation where the US Congress would waive the restrictions concerning some weapons and allow their delivery to the FSA. For example, if Assad makes full usage of Russian helicopters and other weaponry to commit more genocides, it is useless to ask the UN Security Council for a condemnation and much less so for a military intervention, because of the Russian veto.

We have seen cases where wars and regime change are conducted as undercover operations, sometimes with the full knowledge of powerful Congressmen. This may happen again, not to mention the Kosovo crisis when NATO launched a military intervention against Russia's strongest objections...[1]

---

[1] The Gulf Today, June 17, 2012: http://gulftoday.ae/portal/dca003a2-2e28-429a-874d-2173a452dbc4.aspx

# 49
# SCENARIOS FOR EGYPT

Some observers considered the runoff opposing Muhammad Mursi to Ahmed Shafiq, as actually opposing two institutions that have been fighting each other for most of the period covering three presidential eras: i.e. Nasser, Sadat, and Mubarak. J. B. Alterman pointed in "Foreign Affairs" (June 5, 2012) to "the most hierarchical institutions in Egypt", meaning the Muslim Brotherhood and the military, which in their recent struggle, resorted to mobilizing their "traditional bases" instead of "finding creative ways to attract the center". But why should the Muslim Brotherhood or the military seek to attract the center that is not necessarily attracted to them anyway? How would they coax liberal-minded, educated, and Westernized Egyptians, if neither Abdul Moneim Abou el-Fatouh nor Hamdeen Sabahi has been able to weigh in the balance? Not to mention El-Baradei.

Other observers dramatized the situation prevailing today in Egypt to the point of predicting a civil war. This was particularly a hostile Israeli viewpoint emphasized by Barry Rubin, who put a question: "what do Egyptians want" to which he could but bring an insulting answer: "a democratically elected Islamist dictatorship". In a second article, the director of GLORIA center (an Israeli think tank) described Egypt in a state of civil war following a coup similar to that of the Algerian generals after the victory of the Islamic Salvation Front in 1991.

Both authors, Alterman and Rubin, failed to see the complexity of the Egyptian society, which led them to oversimplifying the situation, reducing it to an opposition between the Army – wrongly assumed to be secular, like in Turkey – and the Muslim Brotherhood, as if its politicians are incapable to grasp the nature and scope of Egypt's regional and international standing.

I do not pretend that the risks of slipping toward violence, extremism and chaos do not exist. They may even be made up to prevent some unwished political developments. Yet, it is not necessary that the situation is either "white" or "black". Other colors, tones and shades also exist. Actually, I would rather describe the Egyptian society as a kaleidoscope rather than a black and white picture. This does not exclude uncontrolled or dramatic scenarios.

I would then make the following assumptions:

1- Egypt's political system has been described as "authoritarian" and indeed, "pharaonic." The important issue that has to be examined after the fall of Mubarak and the new reorganization of the system is whether this revolution is able to change profoundly and durably the structure of power in Egypt or not.

2- Although the military is not eager to rule directly, circumstances have sometimes forced them to leave their barracks and help stabilizing the internal security. The bread riots in 1977 and the police conscript riots of 1986 for example called on the military to restore order. In the aftermath of much disputed elections, if the military leaders think the country is slipping toward chaos, they will feel compelled to take over. However, considering the present Egyptian frame of mind, such takeover would be of relatively short duration.

3- It is believed that in case the Muslim Brotherhood becomes really the government-dominating force in Egypt, the US and Israel would be faced with a nightmare. The peace treaty with Israel may be scuttled, and the border with Gaza opened and weapons would flow without restriction to help Hamas. This scenario would be rendered even more threatening to the US-Israel alliance, if the Egyptian military itself split, with a faction supporting the Muslim Brotherhood.

4- The previous scenario is not as unrealistic as it sounds at first sight. It may take shape if both, the Muslim Brotherhood and its military allies feel that the street is favorable to them. At that point, a conflict may emerge with the secular officers, but they would be put under huge pressure from the pro-Islamist masses mobilized in the public places for that effect, and forced to comply with the new masters of the country.

5- The conflict may end up momentarily with a compromise whereby a more or less declared Islamist-oriented military council rules behind the curtains, supporting the Islamist civil politicians in the government. The military officers, who do not agree on such a development, would be discreetly moved apart. The others would feel that their interest is in supporting the new regime.

6- It is unlikely that such a conflict over power would lead to the kind of civil war that has been recently predicted by the Israeli writer Barry Rubin (Gloria Center, June 15). Because, first, if some members of the Egyptian military hierarchy would resort to violence, in order to "save" the relations with the USA, over a considerable period of time, the US Congress and parts of the US administration – not to mention the media and the public opinion – would probably call to cut military aid to Egypt anyway. Second, the military officer corps in Egypt reflects the ideological currents of the middle class, including a conservative persuasion. It has nothing to do with the Turkish military. Some of the original free officers (Sadat is the most prominent) were close to the Muslim Brotherhood. One must then assume that the military establishment has not been excluded from the wave of "conservative Islamism" that encompassed the country since the eighties of the last century.

7- Some elements of the Egyptian military would not like to cut off US ties completely, even if they support a Muslim Brotherhood-led government. Because of Egypt's weight in the Arab world and its key-role in the Middle East political processes, it is hard to imagine this country sliding toward the status of "pariah" similar to that of Iran, or Iraq under Saddam, or Libya under Qadhafi. Egypt is not Egypt without its complexity, its hybrid culture and its Mediterranean leanings. The Westernized elite would fight to keep Egypt in the modern camp. That would not be possible with cutting off ties with the West.

Finally, I would advise those who wish to grasp the Egyptian spirit to read its great authors and to look closely into its modern culture that truly shaped the contemporary Arab world. If after that, they think such a culture could easily be thrown to the dustbin, because the Islamists came to power... we have then a big problem.[1]

---

[1] The Gulf Today, June 24, 2012: http://gulftoday.ae/portal/62513033-01e3-4a5a-901e-0b1fd0336843.aspx

# 50

# ASSUMPTIONS ABOUT DIFFERENT CASES

Since the beginning of the « Arab spring », many assumptions were made about the possible spread of the revolt throughout the Arab world, which assumedly would topple all the regimes-members of the Arab League, one after another. The naivety of such assumptions hardly needs to be overemphasized. The people who made them seemed to exclude the fact that even though the Arabs constitute virtually a single nation, they have always been determined and ruled by varied and contrasted interests, due to the accumulation of multiple historical experiences.

Yet, the logic behind such hypothetical notions is that the Arab regimes are, despite their differences, almost similar. They are assumedly authoritarian and corrupt, and react in the same manner, hurrying up with repression as soon as a problem rises on the streets. As they suffer from a deficiency of democracy, they would end up fighting against their own population fed up with their autistic behavior.

However, as time elapses, such assumptions become harder to prove, for many reasons.

Firstly, the revolution that signaled the beginning of the change happened in Tunisia. This country, with due respect for its history, has never inspired - and much less commanded the Arab world. Since its independence in 1956, Tunisia has rather lived on the "edge" of the Arab world, turning whole-heartedly toward the northern shore of the Mediterranean. The elite that run the country under Bourguiba leadership were westernized and felt more attached to the West than to the East. Under Ben Ali, the picture did not change on this level. I am not inclined to thinking that while Tunisia needs the help and assistance of the rich Arabs, it still can inspire revolts in their countries. This is quite irrational.

Secondly, if there is a country able to inspire the Arabs, it is well Egypt. Yet, in Egypt, the revolution has not upset really the regime. The military is still running the country and the real power is into its hands. Therefore, I very much doubt the assumption that even Egypt could inspire a revolt everywhere in the Arab world. It did not happen under Nasser – and we all know whom the man was and what he was trying to do. It will not happen under Mohamed Morsi either.

Thirdly, maybe there is an "Arab spring", but even in the few countries wherein the revolt succeeded to topple the head of the state, the reactions were not the same. The time the revolt took to bring down the president was different from a country to another. The transition period is showing up many unexpected problems that question the very direction they are taking.  So, are they similar? The answer is obviously: no.  Are they really heading steadily toward democracy? That still needs to be proven. Therefore, if between the countries wherein a revolt burst out, there is not much similarity, why should we expect the same to happen everywhere in the Arab world? I strongly doubt it.

Fourthly, the basis of the above assumptions may be that the Arab countries participate of the same culture, the same sensitivity, and the same "Arabo-Islamic" personality. Therefore, it is assumed that the Arab citizen and his ruler are expected to clash everywhere the same way it happened in Tunisia, Egypt, Libya, Yemen, Bahrain, and Syria. However, admitting the common cultural and psychological ground as true, does not rule out accumulated differences. Precisely, what is happening in Syria shows that we do not constitute a single country, nor do we have a single character. A regime can be authoritarian and give up under the popular pressure, as it happened in Tunisia. It may find a way to manipulate the revolt and retain power, while sacrificing a man (Yemen) or more (Egypt). It may kill, and the extent of the killings may impose exterior interference (Libya and Syria, and Yemen). Briefly, there is no single way and no single reaction, but many differences that impose caution in assessments.

Fifthly, what is there common between the rich Gulf countries and Tunisia, Egypt, Libya, Yemen, or Syria? The answer is not much; apart from speaking Arabic, praying five times a day (for the observing), watching the Egyptian TV series in Ramadan, and sympathizing with the Palestinian people. Really nothing, that may inspire or trigger a revolt. The key-element that pushed the Tunisians and Egyptians to express their anger on the streets is deficient in the Gulf. I mean the wretched condition of the majority of people. Look at the countries wherein a revolt burst out: people out there are bound by poorness and misery. The oil-rich Libya was not an exception. Corruption is a real scourge; yet it is common to many countries in the world, included the most developed. But anger accumulates over the years when people feel they are excluded, not only from policy-decisions (because of democracy deficiency), but also from the dividends that enrich a small circle.

Sixthly, I live in the Gulf since almost a year. The streets are full of foreigners. You go to the malls, you see Europeans, Asians, Americans, Australians... if you see Arabs, 8 on 10 cases, they turn out to be Egyptians, Algerians, Sudanese, Lebanese, Syrians... anything but nationals. If the latter happen to pass by, wearing dishdasha for the men, and long dresses for women, be sure they are going to shop from the greatest brands of the world. You go to the malls; you find the shops of Paris, London, New York city...The same coffee shops, the same restaurants... Are these countries wherein a revolution is about to happen? Against what? Against money and wealth? Who would do it? Not those who are populating the malls and the streets, because either they are better off or they are foreigners. So who?

Seventhly, while living here, I discovered that the problems of the Gulf are really different from those of other Arab countries. I am not saying like Voltaire's Candide, "everything is at its best in the best of the worlds," but the problems here are different. They are actually related to big interests of international corporations, with a particular focus on the geopolitical configuration and the strategic games of regional and world powers.

In other words, the Arab countries and regions have their specificities. Obviously, we cannot apply the same criteria to different – even opposed cases. We just cannot find the same answers to the same questions. I will go further and pretend that we cannot even put the same questions to all the countries without more distinction.[1]

---

[1] The Gulf Today, July 1, 2012: http://gulftoday.ae/portal/58294b4e-52d9-4c8a-859f-dbc899ed3c8c.aspx

51

# ARAB SPRING: NEW CULTURAL VALUES?

Are there new common values shared by people in the countries where a revolution recently occurred? If yes, what are those values? How are they expressed?

I will make my assessment based on the genuine and still unpublished data from the Arab Opinion Index Project conducted by ACRPS in 12 Arab countries, representing 85 % of the population in the Arab world, through 16,173 face-to-face interviews. In this paper, I focus only on two countries where a revolution occurred (Tunisia and Egypt,) with the purpose of assessing whether really we can talk of "new values" emerging from these revolts which would be described as the "political culture" of the "Arab spring".

The interviews have been performed as follows:
Egypt: from 30 May to 7 June 2011,
Tunisia: from 30 May to 30 July 2011,

## Definitions

I define values as shared beliefs about the goals toward which humans should strive.

If one talks of "new cultural values," it is implied that they must reflect a profound change in the perceptions and attitudes.

Neil j. Smelser suggests a definition of culture as "a set of values, views of reality, and codes of behavior held in common by people who share a distinctive way of life."[1]

Clifford Geertz calls culture "a set of control mechanisms – plans, recipes, rules, instructions... for the governing of behavior."[2]

However, while emphasizing the function of culture in social control, one would be ill advised to pretend it is all mighty. Actually, if culture shapes human behavior, a number of factors limit this ability, among which I can mention: biological limitations,[3] physical environment,[4] and the need for a stable social order.[5]

Hence, I would fairly talk of "**cultural relativity**"[6] and, in the same context, of "**relativity of change**." Thus, on the one hand, my understanding of culture and cultural values stands against the essentialist attitude that for many years has smothered social sciences, hampering qualitative and quantitative variation.[7]   On

---

[1] Neil j. Smelser, Sociology, Prentice-Hall, Inc., 1984, 17.

[2] Clifford Geertz, The interpretation of culture,  New York: Basic Books, 1973, 44-45.

[3] There are biological limits that hinder us from leaping tall buildings at a single bound, cramming a huge amount of knowledge in a single brain, and according to some sociobiologists, even complex behavior such as fighting and generosity may be genetically inherited. See: Smelser, op.Cit. 21.

[4] Environmental factors for example limit the ability to develop certain cultural patterns: droughts, volcanic eruptions, tropical rainforest may interfere with the way people live and use the soil. (Ibid).

[5] As it has been noted, "if societies are to survive, cultures cannot value such acts as random murder, theft, or arson..."(Ibid).

[6] The culture of the past and that of the present are different, as they may be so in space too, it is because a culture always selects some aspects of behavior and experience as well as institutions. Cultural variation is boundless. The sense of the works of Clause Levi-Strauss is to make us understand that a culture can be understood only in terms of its own values and in its own context.

[7] " Since variables, and only variables, can be measured, only theories sensitive to variation can be tested according to the standard methods, quantitative or qualitative." See: Stephan Fuchs,  Against Essentialism, a theory of culture and society; Harvard University Press, 2001, 15.

the other hand, what is induced by social change[1] in contemporary societies stresses its relativity so that we cannot talk of "new values" in the absolute. What is "new" may be "old" from other aspects or for other parties.

## Hypothesis

I assume that if popular revolutions of the kind that happened in 2011 in the Arab world may be described as a moment of "rupture" that moves a country from an "ordinary time" to another "conception of time,"[2] such a "rupture" cannot be definitely established as an historical fact before the occurrence of another change, which is *basically cultural, in the sense that it brings new*

---

[1] Anthony Giddens underlines this relative aspect of the social change in the contemporary world. In his eyes, a "satisfactory approach of the problems of social change (...) has to give prominence" to certain notions, like: "1- Relations of autonomy and dependence among societies or nation-states (...) 2- The uneven development of different sectors or regions of social systems (...) 3- Critical phases of radical social change, in which the existing alignment of major institutions in a society becomes transformed, whether or not this involves processes of political revolution (...)4- A 'leapfrog' idea of change, according to which the 'advanced' in one set of circumstances may inhibit further change at a later date; while on the other hand that which is 'retarded' at one point of time may later become a propitious basis for rapid advancement." See: Anthony Giddens, Central Problems in Social Theory; University of California Press, 1979:225-230.

[2] For Azmi Bishara, they just did. "It is the time of revolutions," he said. "The president has departed in a hurry, leaving behind him a reversed pyramidal structure. In these regimes, the pyramid was standing on its top." See: Azmi Bishara, Al-Thawra al-Tunisiyya al-Majeeda [*Tunisia's Glorious Revolution,*] ACRPS Books, Beirut 2012, 39.

*values affecting the perceptions and the attitudes of the citizens.[1]*

My guess is that such a change is still in the process of happening. It may as well reverse and take the country back to some kind of dictatorship,[2] or take years or decades to transform the behavior of the Arab citizens in these countries.

To test this hypothesis empirically, I will confront it to the results of the ACRPS Opinion Survey in two Countries: Tunisia and Egypt.

---

[1] Although A. Bishara is enthusiastic and optimistic about the Tunisian revolution, he showed caution regarding the flaws of the political class. He observed for instance that "the political parties have never trusted the permanence of the revolution, let alone its final victory." (Op.Cit. 41). In another book, he distinguishes perfectly between "political revolution", "scientific revolution," "industrial revolution," and "social change," stressing that "social change may need a revolution or more, and it may as well happen gradually without political revolutions." See: Azmi Bishara, Fi al-Thawra wal-Qabiliyya lil-Thawara [ On Revolution and Revolutionary Potential] ACRPS Books, Beirut 2012, 41. In my eyes, social change is basically cultural, for it necessitates a metamorphosis of the perceptions and the attitudes, which shape the behavior. Farther, A. Bishara reminds us that "the revolution for freedom does not always guarantee the construction of democracy, which is a complicated process..." (Op.Cit.49).

[2] The French Revolution of 1789 and the Russian Revolution of 1917, both testify, each in its own logic, that there is a difference between toppling a hated regime through wide popular protests and establishing a new order based on the principles of freedom, democracy and social justice for all. Both reverted to dictatorship after a brief glimpse of hope for democracy. While in Russia, the process was irreversible toward dictatorship, in France it took more than a century to settle democracy in the country, which means that "democracy is not necessarily directly created by revolutions." This was also observed by A. Bishara, On Revolution and Revolutionary Potential, op.Cit. 82-83.

I will start with the question of political identity,[1] because the way people define themselves reveals the cultural values to which they accord primacy.

## Political identity

Today, we can account at least for a simple fact, which is: **after the Tunisian revolution**, there would be **a new attitude concerning the way people should deal with dictators in the Arab region.**

Such an assumption may raise the question: Why? Is that because of the strong and clear emergence of shared beliefs of injustice in the Arab world prior to the uprisings? The answer is: Maybe; but it is not enough. Such beliefs would not help people to mobilize on a large scale without: 1- the commitment to a collective identity, solidarity and consciousness, all of which have become clear in the propagation of the revolt across the region. 2- The process of construction of meaning through the social movement. As we have seen during the protests that took place in Tunisia and Egypt, a central task for the groups of participants that constituted the social movement was "the formation of a collective identity."[2]

The collective behavior is the subject-matter of social psychology, which has reemerged in the eighties after a "decade of organizational theory and utilitarian economic models in the study of social movements,"[3] particularly in the United States, although neither in Europe nor in the third world did the theorists feel so

---

[1] "All movements that struggle for recognition," says S. Behhabib, "exhibit complex cultural patterns; the fact that such struggles may be just as fundamental to the development of modern selfhood as struggles for equal dignity are and have been provides us with no criteria of judgment and evaluation in the event of conflict and contestation between these goals and struggles. We still face the burdens of judgment and cultural evaluation." See: Seyla Benhabib ; Princeton University Press, 2002; 58.

[2] Social movements are themselves social constructions. Melucci for example considers " a social movement – or more precisely collective action – as a process through which actors produce meanings, communicate, negotiate, and make decisions." See: Alberto Melucci, Nomads of the Present: Social Movements and Individual Needs in Contemporary Society. London: Hutchinson Radius, 1989, in: Aldon D. Morris, and Carol McClurg Mueller (editors), Frontiers in Social Movement Theory; Yale University Press, 1992: 80.

[3] Aldon D. Morris, and Carol McClurg Mueller (editors), op. Cit.: 53.

urgently the need to escape social psychology in their explanation of collective behavior.[1] Furthermore, "understanding the relationship between group consciousness and collective action has been a major focus of social science research."[2]

The question was: **among the following factors, which one would you rank first in defining your political identity?**

| Factors | Egypt | Tunisia |
|---|---|---|
| 1- Religion (Muslim, Christian...) | 73.3% | 49.8% |
| 2- Ethnicity (Arab, Kurd, etc.) | 15.1% | 15.1% |
| 3- Nationality (Egyptian, Moroccan, etc.) | 8.7% | 26.1% |
| 4- Party affiliation | 2.5% | 7.2% |

First, it is important to stress that the interviewees *were not asked to define their political identity*, but just to *localize* the key-factors that would help defining it. One can thus safely assume that if they were asked to define their political identity, without any suggestion from the interviewer, their answers might have been, to some extent, different. The party affiliation, the leftist or

---

[1] " Hasn't the critique of the collective behavior tradition thrown out the baby with the bathwater," said Cohen, "by excluding the analysis of values, norms, ideologies, projects, culture, and identity in other than instrumental terms?" Jean L. Cohen, " Strategy or Identity: New Theoretical Paradigms and Contemporary Social Movements." Social Research 52, 1985, no. 4:663-716; in: Morris and Mueller, op.Cit.54.

[2] Drawing from a wide range of research documenting the importance of preexisting group ties for movement formation, in a recent review of the field, McCarthy and Zald offered the concept of the micro-mobilization context to describe the link between the macrolevel and microlevel processes that generate collective action. "They view informal networks held together by strong bonds as the 'basic building blocks' of social movements." How these networks transform their members into political actors is another question. European theorists like Touraine, Melucci, Cohen, Pizzorno, Boggs... while analyzing social movements, loosely grouped under the rubric "new social movement theory," offer the concept of "collective identity" as a key to understand this process. See: Verta Taylor and Nancy E. Whittier, "Collective Identity in Social Movement Communities," in: Morris and Mueller (ed.) Op. Cit.:104-105.

rightist inclination might have emerged as the core of that identity,[1] *not necessarily Islam, ethnicity or nationality.*

What happened is that they have been faced with a choice; and they chose according to their beliefs. Nonetheless, we should not mistake the interpretation of these results. *The respondents did not choose a political identity, but a factor among others in its composition.*

Thus, we see that religion is obviously the primary factor that defines the political identity in both Egypt and Tunisia.[2]

Islam is the religion of the majority in Egypt and Tunisia. Is there a correlation between this fact and their definition of the main factor in the political identity? To know more about this issue, a complementary question, **"among the following factors, which one would you rank second in defining your political identity?"** resulted in the following answers:

| Factors | Egypt | Tunisia |
|---|---|---|
| 1- Religion (Muslim, Christian...) | 6.3% | 24.6% |
| 2- Ethnicity (Arab, Kurd, etc.) | 17.4% | 29.4% |
| 3- Nationality (Egyptian, Moroccan, etc.) | 69.8% | 25.6% |
| 4- Party affiliation | 6.5% | 18.3% |

---

[1] To paraphrase U. Beck, one would say, the questions: who am I? What do I want? Where am I heading? (...) lead to a type of political identity that is primarily conservative axed around religion. For Beck, however, "the concept of politics in simple modernity is based on a coordinate system, one axis of which runs between the poles of left and right and the other between public and private. Becoming political here means leaving the private sphere for the public sphere, or, conversely, that the demands of parties, party politics or the government proliferate into every niche of political life. If the citizen does not go to politics, then politics comes to the citizen." See: Ulrich Beck, The Reinvention of Politics; Polity Press, 1997:152.

[2] Such a result is not necessarily excluding modernity from the political sphere, insofar as a German, Italian, American conservative would also define a main component of his political identity on a religious ground (Christian-Democrat, Christian Nationalists, Christian Theocrats, Christian Reconstructionists, etc.) If the fact of founding one's political identity on religion excludes one from modernity, then the US politics would be completely anachronic. For instance, Micklethwait and Wooldridge develop a hypothesis according to which America is deeply conservative, and its conservatism is quite different from that of Europeans, because it is basically religious. See: Micklethwait John and Wooldridge Adrian, The Right Nation, Conservative power in America; The Penguin Press, New York, 2004.

Nationality emerged as the second factor (after religion) in the definition of the political identity in Egypt (69.8%), whereas in Tunisia nationality ranked third behind ethnicity, which was the second factor.

The possible explanation of this result is that there is more polarization about religion in Egypt, because of the existence of the Copts, whereas Tunisia is more religiously homogeneous.

Nevertheless**, Islam not the nationality is the key-factor among the components of the citizen's political identity in both countries.** Clearly, the majority of people sticks to a conservative – *in the sense of religious - definition of the political self that is not much turned towards the modern notion of nation-state*. This gives religion an additional weight in the political life.

This factor is probably known to the Islamist parties in both countries, which capitalize on the religious feelings to mobilize people for the elections.

The fact that a large part of the respondents define their **political identity** in direct connection with Islam may give us **a first clue** to explain the Islamist landslide in the first elections after the revolution. Although the objective of this paper is not to explain the causes of the Islamist victory, but to provide elements to understand what is assumed to be "new cultural values," if any, one cannot ignore that Islamism, since its emergence as a political trend, has created or more precisely "reinvented" cultural values to fit in with its political and social project.

A **second clue** may be provided by the analysis of the **causes of the revolution**.

A **third**, by the analysis of the **relations between religion and politics**.

## Renovated interest in national politics

Tunisia

The revolution brought in politics to the public place[1] again as a new concern for people disenchanted with the public thing through several decades of autocratic rule, under both Bourguiba

---

[1] "If the citizen does not go to politics, then politics comes to the citizen." U. Beck, ibid.

and Ben Ali. Forms of resistance[1] have taken shape and survived either as clandestine opposition or unspecified and silent mass withdrawal, often mistaken by foreign observers for popular submission. Although the January 2011 revolution has been to a large extent unexpected, one of its striking characteristics consisted in the **political motives** of the protesters who, very quickly, directed their demands at political targets. This was clear from the slogans that were chanted in the streets, like: "Ben Ali, leave"; "Tunisia is free and RCD is out" etc...

Given the importance of the event, the interviewees – as one expects - would show a lot of concern with politics. They were asked: **"to what extent would you consider yourself interested in the politics of your country?"**

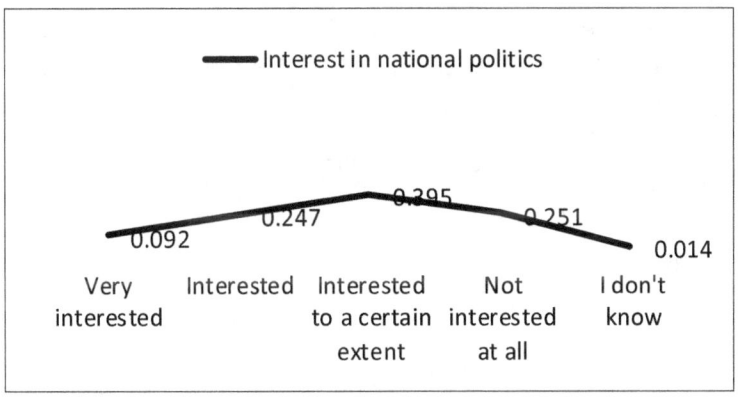

Our sample showed that the Tunisians did not seem "very interested" in politics even after the revolution. The average (39%)

---

[1] Many authors have described or predicted a revolutionary form that rises from previous social orders. "Every social order structured around domination and subordination releases power relations that crush citizen-subjects into positionalities, escape from which only certain kinds of resistances prove effective," writes Chela Sandoval (Chela Sandoval: Methodology of the Oppressed; University of Minnesota Press, 2000, 162) . For Foucault, in order to be liberated from previous modes of social organization, we need to "promote new forms of subjectivity through the refusal of the kind of individuality which has been imposed on us." (See: Michel Foucault, "The Subject and Power," in Michel Foucault: Beyond Structuralism and Hermeneutics, ed. Hubert Dreyfus and Paul Rabinow; Chicago: University of Chicago Press, 1983, 216.)

of the interviewees considered themselves "interested to a certain extent" only, while those who said they are "not interested at all" totalize all the same 25.1% (a quarter of the respondents), which expresses – notwithstanding the importance of the change - the degree to which people, over the years, have grown distrustful of the political class in their country. Yet, the revolution represented a new hope for the 24.7% plus 9.2% of the respondents who expressed a renovated interest in politics.

Egypt

At the time when the field enquiry was performed in Egypt, the country was still in turmoil. Even if people for so many years have lost interest in politics, the revolution brought it back to the public place (maydan al-tahreer).

However, the same question "to **what extent would you consider yourself interested in national politics?**" obtained different answers in Egypt, shown in the graphic below:

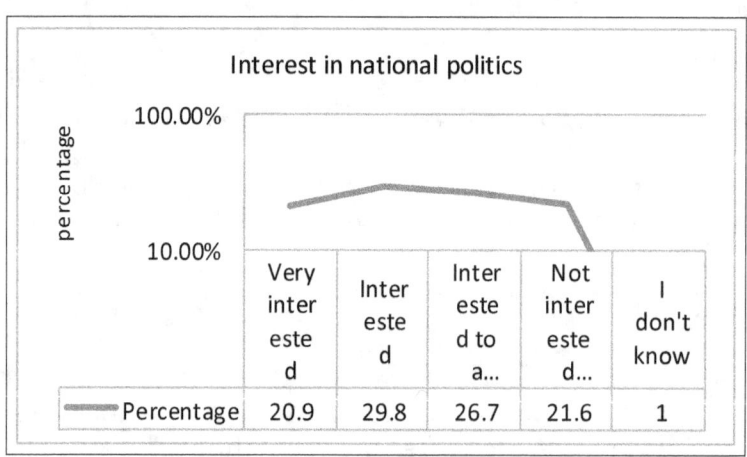

| | Very interested | Interested | Interested to a... | Not interested... | I don't know |
|---|---|---|---|---|---|
| Percentage | 20.9 | 29.8 | 26.7 | 21.6 | 1 |

**Compared to the Tunisians, the Egyptians seem to be relatively more interested in the politics of their country after the revolution**. Between "very interested" and "somehow interested" we have all the same a majority of 77.4 % of respondents saying that the political affairs in their country have become of interest to them ( compared to: 73.4% in Tunisia). The three categories (very interested, interested, and interested to a certain extent) are in Egypt ostensibly closer to each other, whereas in Tunisia the gap is wider between the first (9.2%) and the third (39.5%). Those who do not show any interest in politics are also less numerous in Egypt.

Nonetheless, would we have asked them the same question before the revolution, they would have shown in both countries probably much less interest in politics.

This is somehow what we did in asking them "**Did you vote in the last legislative elections?**"

The distrust of national politics in both Mubarak and Ben Ali's era, expressed itself through the answers, where people showed how much they have grown suspicious of the political elite:

| Tunisia | | Egypt | |
|---|---|---|---|
| **Yes**[1] | **No** | **Yes** | **No** |
| 38.3% | 61.5% | 27.9% | 72.1% |

Obviously, the majority of the respondents (61.5% in Tunisia and 72.1% in Egypt) did not seem interested in the politics of their country before the revolution. That means that the **revolution changed something in their attitudes regarding politics and electoral process. The old suspicion of the political elite is matched by the hope in the future of the change.**

This becomes evident from their answers to the following question: "**Do you intend to vote in the next legislative elections?**"

| Tunisia | | | Egypt | | |
|---|---|---|---|---|---|
| **Yes** | **No** | **I don't know** | **Yes** | **No** | **I don't know** |
| 68.7% | 17.8% | 13.2% | 76.7% | 16.9% | 6.4% |

In both countries, the majority of interviewees answered positively the question. However, from the negative attitudes and

---

[1] Many of them might have been actually forced to vote, in order to obtain some services from the regime they would not be able to get if they did not show evidence of their vote on the electoral card. It was also a mean for the regime to obtain voters while controlling their vote.

the refusal to answer, we deduce that distrust, which still exists in both countries, remained higher in Tunisia than in Egypt.

Now, if political distrust is definitely not surprising under the autocratic rule, the fact that such proportions of the interviewees after the revolutions still show the signs of loss of confidence, means **that, unless they are completely a-politic, they do not yet believe the revolution has really changed the system.** This negative attitude is understandable after decades of dictatorship. One should emphasize all the same the **significant change in attitude**: "Interest in politics" may not be in itself a "new value". However, it heralds a possible hope in the change.

## The way to fight

<u>Toppling the regime through popular protests</u>
The fact that **political change** happens as **a result of a social movement action** is something **new** in the history of the post-colonial state. In itself, this event may create a new pattern for behavior in the future, based on the **shared belief in the people will and the efficiency of collective action**. We can already see this pattern in action through the fast propagation of the revolt across the Arab region. Therefore, if the Arab spring created "new values," it is at this point that they start.

Until recently, political change has been understood either as the result of a coup (generally called revolution) or just as a 'reshuffle' inside the ruling clique, orchestrated by the same structure: the state/party on top of which stands the "leader." Political change in this context never expressed a genuine popular will, and much less the purpose of a social movement, but just the leader's wish. The idea that the regime could be brought to accept a power transition involving a takeover by the opposition was almost alien to the political culture prevailing in those countries. It was almost unimaginable. **The slogans chanted by the protesters in the streets of Tunisia and Egypt (e.g. the people want to topple the regime) were, first, a complete "innovation" in the political culture of the whole region, and second, a testimony to the effect of collective identity and solidarity feelings**. For much less than those claims, people could be shot if they demonstrated on the streets as we know it happened several times in Arab countries (included in Tunisia and

Egypt). Therefore, there seems to be **an important change** *that occurred so slowly and imperceptibly that the observers failed to notice it. The change concerns* **the way people think in the Arab world of the political struggle**. Whether discontent was initially political or became politicized in the course of events, is not here the point. As it has been noticed, "the increasing specialization of roles and functions in modern societies, and the corresponding development of complex social and economic interdependencies over ever-larger areas, have contributed to increased ambiguity about the sources of socioeconomic malaise."[1] However, the political system is most likely to be held responsible, "not simply by default but because of widespread organizational ideological, or elite-generated expectations."[2]

Throughout much of the enquiry conducted by ACRPS, we will find **similar reactions to similar phenomena**. For instance, it would be hard to explain why people in Yemen, Morocco or the Gulf support the toppling of Ben Ali or Mubarak, without the hypothesis that more than the common values and beliefs Islam has provided them; **they actually share today a collective consciousness of their ability to fight a dictatorship and to bring it down.**

Here are the figures:

Toppling Ben Ali through popular protests

|  | **Support** | **Oppose** | **No answer** |
|---|---|---|---|
| **Tunisia** | 96% | 3.9% | 1.8% |
| **Egypt** | 54% | 3.9% | 42% |
| **12 Arab countries** | 71% | 8% | 21% |

Toppling Mubarak through popular protests

|  | **Support** | **Oppose** | **No answer** |
|---|---|---|---|
| **Egypt** | 87% | 10% | 4% |
| **Tunisia** | 89.7% | 0.8% | 9.2% |
| **12 Arab countries** | 80% | 8% | 13% |

---

[1] Ted Robert Gurr, Why Men Rebel; Princeton University Press, 1970, 180.
[2] Ibid.

The high level of support for toppling both autocrats through a social movement, shows that people grew more confident about their ability to resist, fight and win. It also shows a real solidarity between the populations of varied Arab countries in the struggle against autocrats and dictators, which brings us to the causes of the revolution.

## Why a revolution occurred? The trilogy of scourges

Tunisia

When asked about their own interpretation of the reasons behind the revolution, ordinary people – not experts - may differ. The primary causes in their eyes may express the scale of values upon which their assessment is based. If a range of 10 possible answers is suggested to them, since they are comprised in the questionnaire, the choice of the most important is theirs. Through their choice, they tell us about the importance they accord to such or such "idea" or "value" in the polity.

Question: **"in your opinion, what is the main reason behind the popular uprising that toppled president Ben Ali?"**

| | Bad Economic situation | Corruption | Injustice and oppression | Tyranny | Liberties and rights violations | Bad governance | Bouazizi | Something Else | No answer |
|---|---|---|---|---|---|---|---|---|---|
| **Tunisia** | 27.5% | 20.1% | 18.7% | 8.9% | 11.9% | 2.8% | 2.6% | 1.1% | 1.9% |
| **Egypt** | 8.1 | 18.4 | 16.6 | 3.1 | 1.1 | 0.3 | 0 | 0.2 | 52.1 |
| **All the Arabs** | 17 | 15 | 14 | 9 | 7 | 4 | 1 | 1 | 27 |

<u>Egypt</u>

Question: **"in your opinion, what is the main reason behind the popular uprising that toppled President Mubarak?"**

| | Bad Economic situation | Injustice and oppression | Corruption | Tyranny | Liberties and rights violations | Monopoly of power | Bad governance | No answer |
|---|---|---|---|---|---|---|---|---|
| **Tunisia** | 34.2% | 14.9% | 8.1% | 6.2% | 7.7% | 1.1% | 0.1% | 13.1% |
| **Egypt** | 30.5 | 16 | 39.7 | 0.8 | 5.4 | 2.1 | 0.5 | 5.0 |
| **All the Arabs** | 26 | 13 | 16 | 9 | 6 | 3 | 2 | 1 |

The reasons evoked by respondents in Egypt do not differ widely from those of the Tunisians, although the percentages are different.

27.5 % of the Tunisian respondents think that the **bad economic situation** was the main reason behind the protests that ended up in a revolution bringing down Ben Ali and his party that monopolized public life during more than half a century. What worsened the case is the **corruption**, which ranks second in Tunisia amidst the reasons of the revolt (20.1 % of the respondents). Then came in the third rank, **injustice and oppression** (for 18.7% of them). This **trilogy**, not anything else (not even tyranny or violations of human rights) was the most powerful trigger that brought down the regime.

In Egypt, **corruption** is number one, as 39.7 % of the respondents considered it the main reason behind the revolt. The **bad economic situation** is number two (for 30.5%). **Injustice and oppression** is number three (for 16% of the interviewees).

We have then the same **trilogy of scourges** defined as the trigger of revolution. They are all related to the "discrepancy between expectations and the degree of realization of value for the mass."[1]

Let us note that only one factor on three may be indirectly related to the political activity of the opposition: i.e. injustice and oppression. But even this factor comprises a good deal of social frustration.

Now observe that expectations are about the importance we accord to certain values in our life. As Gurr put it, "the greater the discrepancy we see between our expectations and capabilities, the greater is our discontent. The greater the importance we attach to the values affected, and the fewer the other satisfactions we have to fall back on, the greater is our discontent."[2]

Let us ask: what is the opposite of a bad economic situation? It is a situation of **welfare and prosperity.**

What is the opposite of corruption? It is **integrity and uprightness**.

What is the opposite of injustice and oppression? It is **justice and happiness**.

Are these not values to which humans – not only Arabs – accord much importance everywhere in the world? When they are all found missing, or worse, reversed, in a society, is it not logic that the political regime is held responsible for the situation? That is exactly what happened in Tunisia and Egypt. People revolted, because they think they have the right to: welfare and prosperity, integrity and uprightness, justice and happiness. **They revolted because they came to realize the discrepancy between the good they highly value and expect from their rulers (i.e. welfare and prosperity + integrity and uprightness +**

---

[1] Contemporary theorists, like Laswell and Kaplan attribute political instability to this discrepancy. Zollschan argues that "all activity, including revolutionary activity, begins with 'exigency,' defined as ' a discrepancy (for a person) between a consciously or unconsciously desired or expected state of affairs and an actual situation'."(...) Some theorists explicitly use the term "frustration" to represent the impetus to collective violence. Thus, Davies, Lerner, and Crozier talk of frustrating discrepancy between what people want and what they get. Hoselitz and Willner, "extending their distinction between expectations and aspirations, link deprivation with the potential for revolution: ' unrealized aspirations produce feelings of disappointment, but unrealized expectations result in feelings of deprivation. Disappointment is generally tolerable; deprivation is often intolerable." See: T.R. Gurr, op.Cit. 38-39.
[2] T.R. Gurr, op.Cit. 59.

**justice and happiness,) and their actual present (i.e. bad economic situation + corruption + injustice and oppression).**

It is clear however, that these are not "new values," nor are they specific to a community, a social or a political group, among others, suggesting a subculture leading to conflict; but universal values. At this level, the causes of revolution in the Arab countries are the same that push people to protest and revolt anywhere in the world. In other words, even if the Islamists were the group that profited of the regime change, they are not the group that marks the revolution in Tunisia and Egypt with its "brand," ultimately, with its values. Nor people revolted because the Islamists have been jailed and reduced to silence under the rule of the autocrats. **There is no evidence of a direct correlation between revolution in Tunisia and Egypt and oppression targeting Islamists**, since oppression was actually targeting all kinds of social groups and individuals: liberals, leftists, human right activists, etc.

This finding is confirmed by other results of ACRPS enquiry related to politics and religion. These findings convince us that **people in Tunisia and Egypt make a clear difference between their cultural identity and their expectations regarding government affairs and public life.** Here is the evidence:

## Religion and Politics/Secularism

Separation between religion and social and political life
People were asked about their opinion concerning the proposal: "Because of the specificities of the religious practices, they must be separated from the social and political life."
The results were:

|  | Tunisia | Egypt |
|---|---|---|
| I strongly agree | 31.7% | 26.7% |
| I agree to a certain extent | 30.9% | 28.1% |
| I oppose to a certain extent | 11.6% | 16.7% |
| I strongly oppose | 10.0% | 11.0% |
| I don't know | 14.5% | 17.5% |

If we add those who strongly agreed on the proposal of separating religion and social-political life (i.e. 31.7%) to those who agreed to a certain extent – but agreed all the same – (i.e. 28.1%), we would have in Tunisia a majority of 62.6%. That means that **a majority of Tunisians are against identifying polity** (i.e. the organization of social and political life) **with religion.**

In Egypt, the figures are a little different, but we have **also a majority** of people refusing to identify polity with religion: 26.7%+28.1%= 54.8 %.

Another proposal was more direct: "it is better for the country to separate religion and politics?" The answers were as follows:

|  | Tunisia | Egypt |
|---|---|---|
| I strongly agree | 28.3% | 28.0% |
| I agree to a certain extent | 23.8% | 23.8% |
| I oppose to a certain extent | 12.8% | 16.9% |
| I strongly oppose | 14.8% | 13.8% |
| I don't know | 19.1% | 17.4% |

Here too, we have **a majority in Tunisia (52.1%) and Egypt (51.8%) standing for the clear separation between religion and politics.**

Religious influence and vote

Another proposal says: "religious sheikhs (clergy) should not seek to influence the vote of the citizens." The answers were as follows:

|  | Tunisia | Egypt |
|---|---|---|
| I strongly agree | 35.0% | 32.1% |
| I agree to a certain extent | 25.7% | 32.0% |
| I oppose to a certain extent | 13.7% | 12.3% |
| I strongly oppose | 7.2% | 8.1% |
| I don't know | 17.1% | 15.5% |

Thus, **in both countries, a majority of respondents is against religious interference with their political choices**: 60.7 % in Tunisia, and 64.1% in Egypt.

However, these findings are not as striking as, indeed, those of Saudi Arabia, which ranked second to Lebanon and well before

Tunisia, Yemen and Egypt, regarding the refusal of religious interference. A majority of 72% in Lebanon said they strongly agree to the proposal of keeping religious men away from their political choices (plus 10 % saying, yes to a certain extent). In Saudi Arabia, 47% said they strongly agree, and 30 % to a certain extent. That makes a total of 77% of Saudi respondents rejecting the clergy interference with their political choices. This seems, all the same, somehow virtual, since there are no elections in Saudi Arabia, unless we talk about the municipal, which still exclude half the society (women) from the vote, until 2015 (according to King Abdullah promise).

This leads one to deduce that **insofar as the political choice through the electoral process is involved, people in the Arab world are more and more inclined to fight the influence sought by the religious clergy.**

Religion and government

Closely related to the previous question is another proposal stating: **"religious Sheikhs should not be allowed to influence the decisions of the government."** The answers were as follows:

|                              | Tunisia | Egypt |
|------------------------------|---------|-------|
| I strongly agree             | 24.5%   | 28.9% |
| I agree to a certain extent  | 32.5%   | 34.2% |
| I oppose to a certain extent | 18.1%   | 14.6% |
| I strongly oppose            | 6.8%    | 6.4%  |
| I don't know                 | 16.3%   | 15.9% |

Obviously, with 57% of the interviewees in Tunisia, and 63.1% in Egypt, we have a majority opposing any influence sought or exerted by the religious clergy in the affairs of the state.

But if the countries of the Arab spring seem thus to develop a **new consciousness based on the clear separation between their cultural identity and their political expectations**, this trend seems confirmed in other Arab countries as well.

Indeed, in the most confessional of all Arab countries – i.e. Lebanon – a majority of 70% of respondents **strongly agree** with the previous proposal (plus 12% to a certain extent, making thus a total of: 82%), which ranks this country number 1 regarding the rejection of religious interference with the government decisions. Ranking second, just behind Lebanon, comes the amazing Saudi Arabia, long assumed to be the place where religious interference with politics and government is the most acceptable. This turns to be untrue: 33% of Saudi respondents strongly agree with the same proposal, plus 32% to a certain extent, which makes roughly a comfortable majority of 65% rejecting religious interference with the decisions of their government.

<u>No amalgam</u>

Another proposal suggests: **"it is better for the country that religious people get the public offices of the state."** The implied signification is: a religious person makes the best official at the service of the state. That was not accepted either. Here are the figures:

|  | Tunisia | Egypt |
|---|---|---|
| I strongly agree | 6.3% | 12.2% |
| I agree to a certain extent | 25.3% | 23.9% |
| I oppose to a certain extent | 25.7% | 28.4% |
| I strongly oppose | 24.8% | 19.2% |
| I don't know | 16.4% | 16.3% |

In Tunisia, the proposal did not get more than 31.6% of consent, between those who strongly agreed and those who agreed to a certain extent. In Egypt, both categories totalized 36.1%. The results in both countries did not reach the proportion of those who oppose: 50.5% in Tunisia, and 47.6% in Egypt. These last ratios are evidence that, despite the Islamists won the elections, **people make a clear distinction between being a religious person and being a good servant of the state**. That means, for those who seek an answer to the question, "why the Islamists won," that they have to find other reasons for that victory than the political identity, since the latter though it implies Islam as a component is not reduced to it.

If the previous findings confirm the existence of a sound, though inchoate, secularist trend in Tunisia and Egypt, which expresses a strong sense of modernity and social permeability to its values, the following findings will show the extent to which these modern values – including the belief in democracy – have penetrated the minds and shaped the attitudes in the two countries that inaugurated the Arab spring.

## The rules of democracy

Two questions were put to the interviewees. In the first, they were asked: **"if a religious party obtains enough voices enabling it to rule the country, would you support or oppose its coming to power?"**

|  | Egypt | Tunisia |
|---|---|---|
| **I support** | 51.3% | 64.3% |
| **I oppose** | 35.2% | 23.1% |
| **I don't know** | 13.6% | 11.2% |

The second question was: **"if a party making its credo of separating religion and politics obtains enough voices enabling it to rule the country, would you support or oppose its coming to power?"**

|  | Egypt | Tunisia |
|---|---|---|
| **I support** | 55.6% | 61.9% |
| **I oppose** | 29.6% | 22 % |
| **I don't know** | 14.8% | 15.2% |

Two observations are here necessary:
1- In both cases, the respondents showed a fair deal of what we can describe as a "democratic ethos," meaning that whatever the results of the elections, and notwithstanding "my own" political opinion I would all the same support the rules of democracy.
2- Those who would support a secularist majority revealed to be fairly more numerous (55.6% in Egypt; 61.9% in Tunisia) than those who would support a religious-led majority (51.3% in Egypt; 64.3% in Tunisia).

The survey wanted to know more regarding people's feeling about democracy.

The conditions of democracy

It is interesting to compare how people in Egypt and Tunisia define democracy and what they view as essential for its completion in their respective countries. The following table expresses these views.

The question was: **"what is the most important condition in order to consider a country as a democracy?"**

| | Civil and political freedoms | Justice and equality | Democratic regime | Improving the economic situation | Security and stability | Something else | I don't know |
|---|---|---|---|---|---|---|---|
| Egypt | 34.3% | 19.7% | 3.9% | 6 % | 9.8% | 4.2% | 22% |
| Tunisia | 29 | 26 | 13 | 4 | 8 | 5 | 13 |

It is clear from the table above that the respondents in both countries highly value "civil and political freedoms" on their Democracy scale, and prioritize this category over "justice and equality" (second rank), "improving economy" and "security and stability." **The "new values" - if any — of the "Arab spring" are therefore expressing people craving for those kind of the private and public freedoms of liberal democracy.**

As a system, **democracy is widely accepted.**
The next question was: **"do you agree that despite it is not perfect, Democracy is still the best regime?"**

| | **Tunisia** | **Egypt** |
|---|---|---|
| I strongly agree | 19.9% | 20.6% |
| I agree | 51.6% | 35.1% |
| I oppose | 6.8% | 11.6% |
| I strongly oppose | 1.3% | 5.9% |
| I don't know | 19.7% | 26.8% |

The proportion of those who agree or strongly agree in both countries makes a majority: 71.5% in Tunisia, and 55.7% in Egypt. We can surely induce that **the belief in democracy is henceforth part of the new political culture of the Arab spring.**

In the same context, it is noteworthy that a majority of respondents (86%) in 12 Arab countries opposed transferring power to the offspring in the republics. In Egypt, they were 93% and in Tunisia, 92%. This is also expressing new values related to the polity.

Likewise, regarding the question**: "would you accept the rule of a political party with which you completely disagree, if such is the result of the ballot?"** 67.6% in Tunisia said yes; along with 58% in Egypt.

Comparatively, if we take for example a country like Algeria, we would find a majority of 46 % refusing to accept the game of democracy if they disagree with the result of the elections. In Lebanon, these anti-democrats are 60%, and in Jordan 68%.

These findings show mainly two points: 1- Democratic values are not yet the most shared common culture in the Arab world. 2- The countries of the Arab spring are **among the most advanced** on this level, not necessarily the leaders. Number one is Mauritania where 83 % of the respondents expressed acceptance of the electoral result even if they disagree with the winner. Tunisia ranked second. Sudan ranked third with 60% of yes followed by Egypt, then Yemen.

This means that, as I have already pointed, we should always make a clear distinction between revolution and democracy. They are not necessarily linked to each other.

## Attitudes towards the world

Democracy in the world

The study of the "values of the Arab spring" through the analysis of perceptions and attitudes in Egypt and Tunisia would not be complete without analyzing the data about how people perceive the external world, along with some axiological issues related to the distinction between "terrorism" and "resistance," etc...

Let us continue with their perception of democracy.

Question: **"if you can choose a score to rate democracy in a country, where would you rank the USA, France, and Turkey on this scale?"**

| Scores | USA | | France | | Turkey | |
|---|---|---|---|---|---|---|
| | **Egypt** | **Tunisia** | **Egypt** | **Tunisia** | **Egypt** | **Tunisia** |
| 0: Not democratic at all | 5.8% | 3.6% | 4% | 0.7% | 3.7% | 0.5% |
| 1 | 0.5 | 1.1 | 0.5 | 0.7 | 0.5 | 1.2 |
| 2 | 1.1 | 0.9 | 0.8 | 1% | 1.0 | 0.4 |
| 3 | 1.3 | 3.4 | 1.1 | 1.5 | 1.5 | 2.5 |
| 4 | 1.1 | 2.7 | 1.9 | 2.2 | 3.5 | 5.0 |
| 5 | 6.5 | 8.2 | 7.0 | 5.9 | 7.9 | 12.7 |
| 6 | 6.2 | 9.8 | 6.2 | 8.5 | 6.7 | 11.9 |
| 7 | 9.6 | 10.8 | 8.2 | 13.6 | 7.0 | 10.5 |
| 8 | 11.3 | 13.1 | 9.5 | 15.2 | 7.8 | 11.3 |
| 9 | 8.1 | 11.7 | 6.7 | 13.3 | 3.4 | 7.5 |
| 10: really democratic | 11.5 | 16.5 | 6.7 | **20.5** | 3.8 | 8.0 |
| I don't know | **37.1** | 17 | **47.4** | 15.7 | **53.1** | **27.1** |

There is all the same 5.8% of Egyptians and 3.6% of Tunisians who gave zero to the US democracy. It is not an important proportion, but it exists. Curiously enough, the biggest proportion of respondents is not among those who answered positively or negatively the question, but among those who said: **"I don't know."** This phenomenon does not concern the question about the USA, but also about France and Turkey, with only one exception: the Tunisian perception of France's democracy, which turns to be "very democratic" for 20.5% of the respondents. If we add the proportions of the Tunisians who rated France's democracy above 5, we would have **a majority of 71.2% for whom France is a model of democracy.** Comparatively, only 62.8% of them rate the US democracy above the average (i.e. 5). As to Turkey, only 49.2 % of the Tunisian respondents rated its democracy above 5. This finding may be surprising for al-Nahdha party (Islamist), which taking its pattern on Turkey, would like the Tunisians to believe that everything is good in the country of Erdoğan.

Nor the Egyptians are less suspicious. For them, Turkey's democracy made a worse score: only 28.7% of the respondents rated it above 5. The USA obtained only 46.7% of scores above 5; and France 37.3%.

In a complementary question, they had to rate democracy in the same countries, according to four levels: highly democratic, medium level of democracy, low level, and not democratic. Here are the results:

| Levels | USA | | France | | Turkey | |
|---|---|---|---|---|---|---|
| | Egypt | Tunisia | Egypt | Tunisia | Egypt | Tunisia |
| Not democratic | 9.9 % | 5.8% | 8.6% | 1.7% | 9.0% | 2.4% |
| Low level | 5.5% | 8.5% | 7.2% | 5.6% | 12.8% | 11.2% |
| Medium level | 35.4% | 35.2% | 40.7% | 33.7% | 46.0% | 49.0% |
| High level | 49.1% | 50.4% | 43.5% | 59.0% | 32.2% | 37.5% |

France still enjoyed the highest score for democracy in the eyes of 59% of the Tunisians, followed by the USA (50.4% in Tunisia, and 49.1% in Egypt). Nowhere did Turkey obtain such or even a close score.

To me, this means at least that the Islamist propaganda did not work. When it comes to assessing a democratic system, people would look rather toward the West, where democratic traditions are established. Yet even in this case, they do not take it for granted. Liberal democracy is fairly valued in Egypt and Tunisia, and the opposite would sound really incompatible with the wind of freedom that swept away two hard autocracies. Yet, one feels that people's *reticence to accord full trust to the Western countries in this matter is more related to external than to internal issues.*

Obviously, there are many doubts about the degree to which France and the USA may be democratic, expressed by the rates of the category "not democratic" attaining almost 10 % of the Egyptian respondents (USA and Turkey). Whether we should link these results to the US foreign policy, or to the laws on immigration, the perception of Western attitudes toward Islam, democracy in the Arab countries, the Palestinian problem, etc... is probably a question that deserves more exploration.

What about Israel?

Interviewees were asked the same question concerning Israel: on a scale from 0 to 10, how would they rate it?

| Rate | Egypt | Tunisia |
|---|---|---|
| 0: Not democratic at all | 18.6% | 28.8% |
| 1 | 1.5 | 7.7 |
| 2 | 1.8 | 4.4 |
| 3 | 2.6 | 4.8 |
| 4 | 2.4 | 4.3 |
| 5 | 6.8 | 6.2 |
| 6 | 4.1 | 3.1 |
| 7 | 3.3 | 3.4 |
| 8 | 3.4 | 3.4 |
| 9 | 3.1 | 2.8 |
| 10: really democratic | 5.3 | 6.5 |
| I don't know | 47.1 | 21.0 |

The previous table shows us two noticeable facts: 1- the largest part of the interviewees in Egypt (47.1%) did not know what to answer whereas the largest part of the Tunisian interviewees (28.8%) believe Israel is not democratic at all 2- Among those who answered the question in Egypt, the largest part (18.6%) believe also that Israel is not democratic at all.

Asked how would they rate democracy in Israel according to four levels, they gave the following answers:

| How would you rate Israel as a democracy? | Egypt | Tunisia |
|---|---|---|
| Not democratic | 38% | 48.4% |
| Low level | 12.7% | 17.8% |
| Medium level | 27% | 16.9% |
| High level | 22.3% | 16.9% |

Obviously, **the largest part of the respondents in Egypt (38%) and in Tunisia (48.4%) do not think Israel is a credible democracy**. This result has certainly something to do with Israel's treatment of the Palestinians. For this is seemingly connected to Israel's activities mainly in the West Bank and Gaza.

Foreign Policy

The survey wanted to know more about the perception of "the most threatening state."

Question: **"among all the states in the region and the world, which one is the most threatening to your country?"**

| | Egypt | Tunisia |
|---|---|---|
| | Percentage % | |
| The USA | 17.4 | 12.4 |
| Israel | 65.3 | 13.8 |
| Iran (:Egypt)*; France (:Tunisia)** | 1.2 | 4.4 |
| Arab states | 0.5 | 1.5 |
| Arab neighbors or other regionals | 0.6 | 33.7 |
| Others | 0.6 | 0.2 |
| I don't know | 14.4 | 31.8 |

*The Egyptians were asked about Iran.
** The Tunisians were asked about France.

**Israel comes in the first rank**, totalizing 79.1% of the respondents in both countries, with particularly a majority of 65.3 % in Egypt.

If we consider the fact that since 1979, Egypt and Israel are tied by Camp David Accords and a Peace Treaty, and entertain what should be described as diplomatic relations, such a result may sound a bit striking. This is showed by the following question:

Question: **"Do you agree that your state recognizes Israel?"**

| | Percentage % | |
|---|---|---|
| | **Egypt** | **Tunisia** |
| I agree | 11.8 | 1.6 |
| I don't agree | 88.2 | 98.4 |
| I don't know | 11.0 | 1.5 |

Let us observe that no less than 88.2% of the Egyptian respondents and 98.8% of the Tunisians **said they do not agree on their state recognizing Israel.**

One may understand why a proportion of 81% of the Palestinians pointed to "Israel" as the main threat to their country when asked the same question. The numerous Israeli military operations in Lebanon also caused 70% of the Lebanese respondents to say the same thing. But how about a majority of Egyptians? Let us also observe that *those who answered this way do not represent a social group defending a political ideology particularly radical or hostile to Israel.* These are the people of a *large sample*, constituting the social strata and the varied range of persons, chosen according to standard methods of data collecting in similar surveys.

This would lead me to deduce that there is therefore **evidence of continued resistance to the Zionist project**, despite the peace treaties and the peace process. The following table shows it clearly:

Question: **"More precisely, Egypt, the PLO, (and Jordan)\* have signed peace treaties with Israel. Do you approve these treaties?"**

| | Egypt (%) | | Tunisia (%) | |
|---|---|---|---|---|
| | Egypt-Israel peace accord | Oslo Accords | Egypt-Israel peace accord | Oslo Accords |
| I approve | 32.4% | 23.7% | 3.0% | 3.8 % |
| I approve to a certain extent | 15.1 | 12.8 | 4.7 | 7.5 |
| I oppose to a certain extent | 12.3 | 11.8 | 9.9 | 8.9 |
| I oppose | 16.9 | 16.7 | 49.2 | 44.7 |
| I don't know | 23.3 | 35.0 | 32.3 | 34.0 |

\*The table is focused just on Camp David and Oslo accords.

**Nowhere did the peace treaties obtain a majority of approval**. Opposition to them reached 59.1 % in Tunisia (against the Israeli-Egyptian peace treaty) and 53.6 % (against the Oslo accords). In Egypt, the opposition to the peace with Israel reached 29.2%, while the approval was 47.5%. Regarding Oslo, 28.5 % of the Egyptians opposed it, while 36.5% approved it.

It is thus noticeable that **the approval for peace with Israel is higher in Egypt than in Tunisia**, although even in Egypt it does not reach even 50%.

These results express **a weak belief in the chances of peace** with the continuation of the same policies that have so far prevailed. **The Arab spring did not change the perceptions and the attitudes regarding Israel, still considered an enemy of the Arabs**. Like all the enemies, it has to be faced with resistance. This brings us to analyze the attitudes concerning the problem of "terrorism or resistance." It is at this point that one feels the **gap in the assessment of the same phenomenon**, between the West and the Arabs. Whether this gap testifies of a political problem that could be dealt with or a deeper cultural misunderstanding, remains to be seen.

Terrorism and resistance

Question: **"there is a polemic about how to define some organizations between those who consider them legitimate resistance organizations and those who describe them as terrorist organizations. How would you consider the following?"**

| | | Egypt (%) | Tunisia (%) |
|---|---|---|---|
| **Hamas (Palestine)** | -I did not hear about it | - 11.2 | - 4.6 |
| | -Terrorist organization | - 9.1 | - 2.1 |
| | -Legitimate resistance | - 61.0 | - 78.4 |
| | -I don't know | -18.7 | - 14.4 |
| **Hezbollah (Lebanon)** | -I did not hear about it | -12.5 | - 4.1 |
| | -Terrorist organization | -9.6 | - 3.5 |
| | -Legitimate resistance | - 56.3 | - 76.8 |
| | -I don't know | -21.6 | -15.0 |
| **Al-Qaeda in Iraq** | -I did not hear about it | -14.6 | -5.4 |
| | -Terrorist organization | -28.7 | -35.2 |
| | -Legitimate resistance | -30.5 | -36.1 |
| | -I don't know | -26.2 | -22.7 |
| **Al-Qaeda (Bin Laden)** | -I did not hear about it | -10.0 | -1.5 |
| | -Terrorist organization | -30.1 | -40.5 |
| | -Legitimate resistance | -35.1 | -37.8 |
| | -I don't know | -24.8 | -19.4 |

The previous table shows that there is a clear majority that considers **Hamas** (61. % in Egypt; 78.4% in Tunisia) **and Hezbollah** (56.3% in Egypt; 76.8% in Tunisia) as organizations of **legitimate resistance**, while both are considered terrorist organizations in the West.

**Regarding al-Qaeda, the issue is less consensual**. There is obviously hesitation in ranging it either among terrorist or resistance organizations. The difference is between 1 to 5 points. The second observation is that if there is a problem in defining who is resistant and who is terrorist, not only between the West and the Arabs, but also among the Arabs themselves, **this**

**problem is not going to disappear under the rule of the Islamists**. In my opinion, it can be only exacerbated and politically exploited.

On the other hand, these results implicitly reveal **the basic values** upon which such judgment could be made. Are these "new values" brought in to the public space by the Arab spring? The answer is: no. **These are the same values that shaped the minds and the attitudes of the Arabs during the fight against colonialism**, which raised also the problem of "terrorism or resistance."

Let us not ignore that Israel (and by the way, the USA) is considered responsible for the problem. This is made clear by the following question:

Question: **"Would you describe the activities of the Israeli troops in Gaza and the West Bank as justified military operations or terrorism?"**

|  | Egypt (%) | Tunisia (%) |
|---|---|---|
| -I did not hear about it | - 2.7 | -5.0 |
| -It is terrorism | - 86.8 | -82.0 |
| -Justified military operations | - 1.7 | -2.4 |
| -I don't know | - 8.9 | -10.1 |

There is a clear **consensus about the terrorist nature of the Israeli operations**: 86.8% in Egypt, and 82% in Tunisia. This is even likened to the US interventions.

Question: **"Would you describe the activities of the US troops in Iraq and Afghanistan as justified military operations or terrorism?"**

|  | Egypt (%) | | Tunisia (%) | |
|---|---|---|---|---|
|  | Iraq | Afghanistan | Iraq | Afghanistan |
| -I did not hear about it | - 3.7 | - 4.2 | - 2.7 | - 5.2 |
| -It is terrorism | -84.0 | - 81.7 | - 80.5 | - 75.7 |
| -Justified military operations | - 2.0 | - 1.7 | - 4.7 | - 4.6 |
| -I don't know | -10.4 | - 12.4 | - 11.4 | - 13.9 |

In Tunisia and Egypt, the majority of respondents (more than 80%) described the US military operations in Afghanistan and Iraq as "terrorist." For the USA, as for Israel, there is a problem indeed. Their policy is not only unpopular, but also perceived as **"state terrorism."** At the zenith of their reign in the colonies, both the British and the French empires experienced and faced similar attitudes.

Finally, with the possible rise of new democracies in the region, the image of Israel may even get more stained.

## Empirically tested conclusions

Here is a summary of our findings:

After the Tunisian revolution, there would be a new attitude concerning the way people should deal with dictators in the Arab region.

Islam not the nationality is the key-factor among the components of the citizen's political identity in both countries.

Compared to the Tunisians, the Egyptians seem to be relatively more interested in the politics of their country after the revolution.

The revolution changed something in the attitudes regarding politics and electoral process in both countries: "Interest in politics" may not be in itself a "new value". However, it heralds a possible hope in the change.

Behind the fast propagation of the revolt across the region, there is the shared belief in the people will and the efficiency of collective action, which may become a new pattern of behavior initiated by the Arab spring.

The slogans chanted by the protesters in the streets of Tunisia and Egypt (e.g. the people want to topple the regime) were, first, a complete "innovation" in the political culture of the whole region, and second, a testimony to the effect of collective identity and solidarity feelings.

The change concerns the way people think in the Arab world of the political struggle.

The revolution happened because people became aware of the discrepancy between the good they highly value and expect from their rulers (i.e. welfare and prosperity + integrity and uprightness + justice and happiness,) and their actual present (i.e. bad economic situation + corruption + injustice and oppression).

There is no evidence of a direct correlation between revolution in Tunisia and Egypt and oppression targeting Islamists.

A majority of Tunisians and Egyptians are against identifying polity with religion, against religious interference with their political choices. They stand for the clear separation between religion and politics.

A new consciousness based on the clear separation between the cultural identity and the political expectations, emerges.

The belief in democracy is part of the new political culture of the Arab spring, although it is not yet largely implanted in the region.

The "new values" express people's craving for those kind of the private and public freedoms of liberal democracy.

For a majority in Tunisia and Egypt, France's democracy scored better than the US. Turkey is not yet a fully credible democracy. And Israel is considered not democratic.

The Arab spring did not change the perceptions and the attitudes regarding Israel: Israel is considered a threat. A majority does not which it to be recognized by their government.

The approval for peace with Israel is higher in Egypt than in Tunisia, but still not enjoying a majority support.

A majority considers Hamas and Hezbollah as organizations of legitimate resistance. Regarding al-Qaeda, the answers are less consensual.

The attitudes regarding the problem of "what is terrorism and what is resistance" show the prevalence of the same values that shaped the minds and the behavior of the Arabs during the fight against colonialism.

Along with the Israeli operations in the West Bank and Gaza the US operations in Iraq and Afghanistan were described as terrorist.

I am aware that some of these findings (particularly concerning politics and religion) sound odd in countries where the Islamists have just obtained a majority of votes. But as I have already pointed, this is a different problem that should be explored to find out the reasons for such electoral results. My problem here was just to make a first assessment of the values accompanying or emerging from the Arab spring. The best conclusion I can make at the end of this paper is that the Arab spring created a hope, which may possibly turn into a new pattern of behavior, regarding the way dictatorships would be faced with in this region.[1]

---

[1] This essay is based on a presentation made at a workshop organized by Georgetown School of Foreign Service, Georgetown Center, Qatar, April 14, 2012. The Arab Spring: One Year Later.

# AFTERWORD

# ON REVOLUTION

# AND SUSCEPTIBILITY TO REVOLUTION

## Introduction

In the booklet On Revolution and Susceptibility to Revolution, Azmi Bishara presents the main things you need to know about revolutions - in terms of their theoretical philosophy, practice, and history - in a concise and useful manner. In so doing, he shows the strength of the approach adopted by many prominent professors and writers: namely, that the deepest thoughts can be presented and expressed without the need for long amplification. This booklet serves as a reminder of the kind of political literature, known as pamphlet, which spread throughout Europe during the early 20th century and gained a considerable amount of popularity. This was spearheaded by Marxist literature in particular, beginning with that of Karl Marx and Friedrich Engels, and followed by those of other revolutionary theorists.

In this book, Bishara seems keen on two interrelated issues: casting light on what has been happening in the Arab homeland since the self-immolation of that poor young man, Mohammed Bouazizi, in the Tunisian town of Sidi Bouzid, which ignited revolution in his own country and several others, on the one hand; and defining the revolution and the revolutionary situation without resorting to supercilious, superficial or arbitrary applications of foreign theories to a different social and cultural reality, on the other hand.

Although it is possible to include this book within the broader heritage of revolutionary literature, it is distinguished by characteristics that make it unique in the modern Arab literature of social sciences. This is not surprising since although revolution is not a new phenomenon in Arab history, theorizing about it has remained somewhat undeveloped, as most of the books written about revolution, as an idea and a practice in the Arab world, have tended either to be historic, documentary, or narrative writings (such as those about the Arab Revolt against the Ottomans, the Orabi Revolt, the revolutions of Prince Abdel Kader and Ali Ben Ghedhahem, and the national revolutions against colonialism), or to be inspired by Marxist models - Leninist or Maoist - without offering a qualitative addition that makes the Arabs active contributors to this human heritage, not just consumers. When writings have deviated from these two types, they have fallen under the magnetic spell of ideology, and presented a "revolutionary ideology" under the aspect of pan-Arab or Islamic theories of revolution, and certainly not a contribution to scientific knowledge.

Even the Palestinian revolution, in spite of its importance, seriousness, and distinctiveness, has remained a captive of stereotypes, dogmatic thought, shallow pragmatism, and/or pseudo-political reactions that qualify neither as scientific thought nor as social theory. This undoubtedly represents part of the Palestinian dilemma. Palestinians often mention the Algerian or Vietnamese revolutions as models, but the first did not produce a theory and was not based on one, despite attempts to attach it to the theories of Frantz Fanon, who was not Algerian but just a sympathetic writer. On the other hand, the Vietnamese revolution was based from the beginning on Marx's view of history. It is a perception that failed the Arab test and did not have success and continuity in the world.

Bishara's book seeks to offer something different. The way the author has set out his book reflects his research approach. He begins by identifying revolution as a concept, then talks about "novelty and renewal, freedom and revolution," and "the revolutionary situation or the revolutionary potential," moving on to discuss "revolution as a phenomenon with the ability to spread," and concludes his analysis with "democratic revolution and ideology".

## Defining Revolution: a matter of Methodology

In defining the concept of revolution, Bishara does not start from either the theories of the Age of Enlightenment and the philosophers of the French Revolution or the many discourses on revolution in which the sociological thinkers of the 19th and 20th centuries indulged. Instead, he walked in the footsteps of the early Arab philosophers who considered Aristotle as the first mentor, so they translated, explained, and analyzed his texts. The first sentence in Bishara's book begins as follows:

"In his Politics, Aristotle claims that all forms of government are prone to revolution, including his definitions of oligarchy and democracy - which he regarded as the basic forms of government - as well as what he described as "balanced", "constitutional" or "aristocratic" governments ..." (p. 7).

In my opinion, Bishara's aim is not to examine historical information, for his issue is primarily methodological. The importance of this step (referring to Aristotle) becomes clear when it is linked with the general approach that the writer takes in seeking a qualitative Arab illumination of the concept of revolution. Although he does not declare this goal, it can be inferred. Without the existence of this undeclared goal in the writer's mind, the book might have turned into a compilation work. If that did not happen it is because of the rational evidence he tried to provide in order to make his point.

Many European writers who deal with the same subject usually begin with Enlightenment philosophy, as they consider it to be the main source of revolutionary thought in modern times. Social theorists have two tendencies: leftists tend toward the tradition established by Marx's discussion of Hegel, who, like Immanuel Kant and others, was an admirer of the French Revolution, while the rest take a different approach based on classifications that are still being taught in sociology, including collective behavior and social movements, crowd dynamics, contagion theory, convergence theory, leadership and mobilization, theories of social change, and conflict theory.

Bishara moves away from both groups and sees that Aristotle's contribution to political thought cannot be overlooked, as it is the basis for the first Arab Muslim thought, as well as the pioneers of the Renaissance in Europe, and those who came after, especially since we still recognize Aristotle's view of revolutions up until today. This view, Bishara reminds us, divides revolutions into two types: "a type that leads to changing the existing constitution, so it shifts from a system of government to another system, and another type that changes rulers within the structural framework of the existing system." (p. 7) Despite the different times and political systems, social realities connected to the issues of identity and equality and justice have not changed. The motive for a revolution, as Bishara indicates (p. 8), is that of the masses demanding equality, which stems from a pre-existing presumption that all people should be treated equally, while the nobility and aristocracy revolt against equality because they like to feel that they are distinctive.

In fact, the idea of distinctiveness is also present in democratic revolutions, although it is not equivalent to the idea of distinctiveness held by the nobility and aristocrats. The former is crystallized in a national identity that is a product of "the nation's awareness of its sovereignty [...] through the rights of citizens" (p. 9).

The French Revolution, as well as the revolutions of 1820-1848 in Europe, contributed to the "development of a sense of nationality and the formulation of nationalism" (p. 9). Bishara sees that this will also apply to the impact of the current Arab revolutions because they "contribute to the formulation of the national identity that has not received sufficient legitimacy so far" (p. 10), and because of the pan-Arab-nationalistic feeling that is competing with it. This will not happen unless the revolutions succeed in "building democratic institutions" (p. 10). Does this mean the establishment of regional entities and the consolidation of the region's petty states on a new basis? The author does not try to answer this question because he does not raise it. And he does not raise it directly because it goes beyond the brief and concise framework of his book, and perhaps Bishara will return to it elsewhere, particularly since he suggests that he is considering this issue when he writes: "if democracies are established, this will not occur at the expense of Arab nationalism, but the concept will change into a cultural identity, empathy, and political and economic interests that complete the national identity" (p. 10).

## Discussion of Bishara's Opinion

The previous paragraph related to the expected spread of democracy and the bolstering of national identity needs to be discussed. Bishara does not provide an answer to the issue of regional entities and subsequent joining of the states above. The writer cannot ignore the possibility that the failure of democracy could also happen. The success of democracy in one country does not necessarily lead to its success in other countries. It is also not necessarily the case that the success of democracy leads to the promotion of a patriotic understanding of political and economic interests that are complementary to national identity. Democracy is well established in Britain and Norway, for example, but Britain did not agree to replace its currency, nor has it submitted to all European Union decisions, while Norway has refused to join the EU. Some EU member countries have not approved the draft European Constitution, and in some there are political parties that call for abandoning the Maastricht Treaty and the single currency, returning to the previous status quo, and they call themselves "sovereignists". In sum, democracy, because of the diversity of opinions and interests within and among countries, can hinder the building of unity but can also consolidate it and make it stronger. The United States, for example, is born from the war between the

North and South. There were conflicting interests between those who wanted to maintain the system of slavery, and those who sought to abolish slavery to build a union on the basis of freedom and equality for all, as affirmed by the constitution. The Soviet Union was also built by force and collapsed when perestroika (restructuring) and glasnost (openness) accompanied Western-style ideas of democracy. China was united by force and is still united. Thus, the issue of how democracy may have an effect on building the pan-Arab national project still needs study and scientific treatment. However, it is fair to say that this is not the subject of the book, so it does not have to be dealt with here.

## The Return to Classical Islamic Thought

When Bishara asks: "Is there a scientific definition of the concept of revolution?" (p. 12), his answer is no, because the word (i.e. revolution) has spread to a point where it is used to describe various phenomena. He links this spread and the difficulty of scientifically defining revolution to ancient and modern Arab and Islamic heritage, and to the European revolutionaries of the 19th century and German leftist methodology. Bishara reminds us that the word "revolution" was a term given to different movements, from the zinj (black slaves) and Qarmatian, to Omar al-Mukhtar, the Palestinians, the Algerians, Gamal Abdel Nasser, Abdul Karim Kassem, Spartacus, and Thomas Muntzer. In his opinion, "the closest word to the concept of contemporary revolution is al-khurooj, meaning to go out and ask for rights" (p.14), according to ancient Arab writers. The undeclared part of the author's agenda appears here in terms of his quest to link the current reality of the Arab Spring to the cultural and political heritage of the Arab nation, and to establish an Arab revolutionary theory from outside the ideological framework that guided the contemporary Arab thinkers, including nationalists, whether Nasserists or Baathists. It is clear that Bishara's main concern is scientific, not ideological, and intellectual, not political or factional, as he reviews a variety of influential classical Islamic personalities from Abu Dharr al-Ghafari, Al-Mawardi and Ibn Khaldun, to Ibn Taymiyya, Ibn Hanbal, Shafi'i, Ibn Mujahid al-Basri, and Ibn Hazm al-Dhaheri.

He connects all of these to the duality of going out (al-khurooj) and defeat (al-taghallub, or forceful domination), while acknowledging that this duality is not a theory of revolution (p. 14) even if the two concepts coincided for classical Muslim writers. Bishara hints as to how these two concepts developed in the works of these classical writers, where al-khurooj always meant revolt, while al-taghallub practically justified al-mubaya'a (allegiance), which gave legitimacy to the khurooj state. He also points out differences among these writers concerning khurooj and taghallub, noting that some justify submission because "a tyrant sultan is better than lasting sedition" (p. 18), while others are surprised at "how he who does not find sustenance in his house does not go to the people wielding his sword" (p. 15). This in fact summarizes the whole of the history of Islam.

In this context, Bishara invites us to distinguish "between the apparent and the hermeneutic Salafist positions" (p. 19), remarking that contemporary Salafists only adopt "part of the discourse of the founders of Islam such as Ibn Hanbal and Ibn Taymiyya, which includes the forbidding of khurooj (revolt) against the sultan" (p. 19). However, it is worth noting that these Salafists benefitted from "khurooj against the sultan" in Tunisia and Egypt, and they were then eager to grab power. If they were really preserving this particular part of the founders' rhetoric that is related to al-khurooj, then there is no doubt that this position is linked to the fact that they are in power since it cannot come from a group not in power. Of course, some Salafists, for example in Saudi Arabia, justify submission to the regime by stressing "the necessity of obeying the rulers". This is not necessarily the position of Salafists in other countries, as their presence in opposition would have no meaning if they avoided revolutionary discourse.

Bishara attributes the position of Ibn Taymiyya, who in general rejected revolt against dictators to his "realism" and belief that "Sunnis do not feel it is right to revolt against imams and fight them with the sword, even if they are unjust" (p. 21), because Ibn Taymiyya does not see that "an imam is the source of legitimacy, but applying Sharia is" (p. 22); therefore, it is more correct to say "fight those who do not follow Sharia, not the Imam". This is how the revolt of Muawiya against Ali ibn Abi Talib was justified by each one of them as it included a difference in interpretation of the Quran. Bishara clarifies how this position developed with the Wahhabis to become hostile to revolution. He concludes "Islamic jurisprudential thought justifies accepting an unjust Sultan and rejects khurooj, which is similar to armed revolution against the regime in our time" (p. 25).

## Revolution in the Modern Age

After Bishara tries to determine the Arab understanding of revolution, and expresses surprise at some intellectuals' suspicion about current Arab revolutions, he sets out to make a distinction between words that are sometimes used as synonyms, such as revolution, intifada (uprising), coup, and reform. In the context of comparing reform with revolution, Bishara recounts the history of thought leading to the debate that kept socialists such as Rosa Luxemburg, Eduard Bernstein, Karl Kautsky, and others occupied, and fueled the split in labor movements into communist and social democratic parties. In Bishara's opinion, comparing the two concepts is unjustified "except for the rivalry within Marxism" (p. 33) because, for him, revolution and reform go hand in hand, and a lack of revolution would lead to nihilism, anarchy, and a new tyranny.

It becomes clear that Bishara is offering a genuine analysis of the concept of revolution, not only through his quest to illuminate relevant classical Islamic texts, but also through his linking it to reform, while others have treated revolution and reform as two contradictory concepts. The author affirms by rational argument that "in any serious reform there are elements of revolution, and in any revolution that is not satisfied with destruction and chaos, and is engaged in construction, there are elements of reform" (p. 35). He compares the modern concept of revolutions based on "novelty and renewal" with the concept that ancient Greek philosophers had for it as a "repeated cycle of regime change" (p. 36). What also distinguishes modern revolution, in his opinion, is that it is a "secular issue even if it originally was religious" as it rejects "acknowledging that there are fixed grounds justifying the current regime" (p. 37) even if these grounds were based - as sometimes happens - on the interpretations of religious teachings.

## Problems Facing the Arab Revolutions

Bishara employs his broad philosophical knowledge and his knowledge of the history of thought to shed light on fundamental problems facing the Arab revolutions today. He makes clear how revolution and democracy do not necessarily coincide, something that can be forgotten when the struggle for power develops after a revolution. "A revolution for freedom does not always guarantee the building of a democracy" (p. 49), he writes, indicating that, in contrast, countries such as Canada and Australia did not need revolutions to achieve democracy. Indeed, how can one forget that the revolutions in Russia and China led to the establishment of bureaucratic systems of government ("dictatorships of the proletariat") that can be given any description except "democratic"? In Iran, after the overthrow of the shah in a popular revolution, in which all major parties and active forces from the right, left, and center participated, the country became a prisoner of a class of turbaned clerics who excluded anyone who disagreed with their views, gagged the opposition, and appointed themselves rulers in the name of safeguarding religion.

In spite of this, revolution in the modern age was linked to new ideas and innovation, and with what Bishara sees as the "emergence of the public or crowd" (p. 53). Its objective became "people's happiness" (p. 54), and the social dimension became the elimination of poverty, the emergence of the concept of citizenship, its rights and duties, and what is necessary from public and private freedoms. All of this was expressed within the boundaries of what is called the nation-state or the national state.

## Toward a Model Theory for the Arab Revolution

Bishara dedicates a chapter to clarifying what he means by a "revolutionary situation" and links it to a series of elements, some of which were mentioned by Lenin. At the same time, he offers a critique of the Russian revolutionary approach. These elements include: people's rejection of old lifestyles, their refusal to suffer intolerably, and the Arab's awareness of injustice's results. In the Arab situation in particular, though not yet a complete model, it seems to Bishara that secession within the ruling class and the army is necessary for revolutionaries to be able to seize power (p. 66). He also concludes from this analysis of the incomplete Arab model that there is no need for the existence of a leadership from a particular party or group (p. 67).

In my opinion, Bishara seeks to explore the "Arab revolutionary model," which is evident in that he makes many comparisons, and continues on saying that "the period between 1830 and 1848 [in Europe] is the period that is most similar to the current Arab period" (p. 69), where the spread of revolution coincides with the government's effort to thwart it. At times, here and throughout the text, he turns to historical analysis, while at others to social and philosophical analysis, using these as evidence to show the solid connections between the social sciences and humanities. He concludes with some thought-provoking results, such as the comment that the Arab world "was a body connecting the revolutions" (p. 75) in time and space, moving from the Free Officers' coup in Egypt in 1952, fairly called "revolution" (p. 76), to the revolution of July 14, 1958, against the monarchy in Iraq, to the revolutions of 2011 in the Arab world. All of this with reference to national revolutions in the 18th century in the US, Ireland, Belgium, the Netherlands, and France, and those in Eastern Europe, the Balkans, and Russia in the 20th century. His aim is to explore the truth about the revolutionary situation that has taken hold of the Arab world and made "a revolution in a small Arab country like Tunisia [flow] like an electric current crossing an Arab body that is weak, yet connects concerns, hopes, agendas, and ideas" (p. 79).

Additionally, he concludes that since political parties did not lead the Arab revolutions, it is essential to "have a plan and a program agreed upon by as broad a group of political powers as possible to control and direct the process of democratic transition" (p. 90). Bishara touches on the main problem of the post-revolutionary phase, and, like many other intellectuals and observers, he is aware of the possibility of a counter-revolution and the dominance of ideological issues over political action that would return matters to the starting line.

On the whole, this brief and concise study should be read in one sitting, if possible, with a pencil and highlighter for researchers interested in the subject of the revolution in the Arab world. Bishara's book seeks, through logical argument, historic and philosophical deduction, and comparative analysis to lay the basic foundations for what, in the future, could be an integrated project for a scientific theory (not ideology) on Arab revolution, removed from stereotypes, particularly ideological ones, that prevailed before the Arab Spring.[1]

---

[1] This article was translated by the ACRPS Translation and English Editing Department. http://english.dohainstitute.org/release/f0939182-df42-41a0-b38f-dfea907d5634

On Revolution and Revolutionary Potential- Author: Dr. Azmi Bishara- Publisher: Arab Center for Research and Policy Studies- Date and place of publication: Doha/Beirut, 2012- Number of pages: 104.

# ABOUT THE AUTHOR

Dr. Hichem al-Karoui is a Research fellow at the Arab Center for Research and Policy Studies, where he coordinates the work of the political Unit, and the US Think Tanks monitoring. Before joining the Center, he has long been active as a political journalist and researcher for various media organizations. Throughout his career, he has published dozens of articles and books (in Arabic, English and French) about politics in the Middle East, the USA, Europe, and international relations. His scholarly papers have been regularly disseminated through the Social Sciences Research Network. In 2009, he founded in Paris an online peer-reviewed scholarly journal: Middle East Studies Online Journal, to which several renowned scholars were associated as members of the international Editorial Board. While serving as Editor-in-Chief of the Middle East Studies Online Journal, he was also a member of the editorial board of the Maxwell Science journal "Current Research Journal of Social Sciences," an Adjunct Fellow of the Guild of Independent Scholars (Florida, USA), which publishes the "Journal of Alternative Perspectives in the Social Sciences," France's Editor for the World Security Network Foundation (WSN), and a columnist for different media outlets. His weekly column is published by The Gulf Today newspaper (UAE) every Sunday.

www.ingramcontent.com/pod-product-compliance
Lightning Source LLC
Chambersburg PA
CBHW082208290526
45794CB00009B/3465